Diagrammatic Immanence

Diagrammatic Immanence
Category Theory and Philosophy

Rocco Gangle

EDINBURGH
University Press

© Rocco Gangle, 2016

Edinburgh University Press Ltd
The Tun – Holyrood Road
12(2f) Jackson's Entry
Edinburgh EH8 8PJ

www.euppublishing.com

Typeset in11/13pt Adobe Sabon by
Servis Filmsetting Ltd, Stockport, Cheshire

A CIP record for this book is available from the British Library

ISBN 978 1 4744 0417 4 (hardback)
ISBN 978 1 4744 0418 1 (webready PDF)
ISBN 978 1 4744 0420 4 (epub)

The right of Rocco Gangle to be identified as the author of this work has been asserted in accordance with the Copyright, Designs and Patents Act 1988, and the Copyright and Related Rights Regulations 2003 (SI No. 2498).

Contents

Acknowledgements	vi
Introduction	1
1 Spinoza and Relational Immanence	20
2 Diagrams of Structure: Categories and Functors	70
3 Peirce and Semiotic Immanence	104
4 Diagrams of Variation: Functor Categories and Presheaves	139
5 Deleuze and Expressive Immanence	162
6 Diagrams of Difference: Adjunctions and Topoi	211
Conclusion	242
Bibliography	245
Index	255

Acknowledgements

For helping to shape the ideas in this book in manifold ways, I would like to thank Dan Barber, John Bova, Ellis Cooper, Creston Davis, Simon Duffy, Brian Glenney, Julius Greve, Tom Higgins, David Kamitsuka, Eleanor Kaufman, Michael Kilburn, François Laruelle, Paul Livingston, Lorenzo Magnani, Chris McDaniel, Helen Betsy Mesard, John Milbank, John Ó Maoilearca, Micah Murphy, Woosuk Park, Peter Ochs, Joshua Ramey, Anne-Françoise Schmid, Jason Smick, Anthony Paul Smith, Ken Surin, Tim Titus, Ahti Pietarinen, Lydia Voronina, Corey Walker, Gitte Wernaa, Dan Whistler, Willie Young and probably several names whose inadvertent omission I here promise to remedy with a stiff drink on me. Among many other things, these comrades have taught me the viability and vibrancy of shared intellectual exploration. I would like to express particular gratitude for the patience, brilliance and intrepidity of my mathematical collaborators at the Center for Diagrammatic and Computational Philosophy: Gianluca Caterina and Fernando Tohmé. Any mistakes or oversights in the text are wholly mine.

In the pachinko game of academic life under liberal capitalism, I have been fortunate to find graduate and professional work at a highly enjoyable series of institutions: University of Virginia, Oberlin College, University of California Merced and Endicott College. My gratitude to the professors, students and colleagues I have learned from at these schools is immense. I wish especially to thank Endicott's Department of Humanities and School of Arts and Sciences for multiple forms of research support related to this project including a spring 2014 sabbatical leave in conjunction with the Instituto de Investigaciones Económicas y Sociales del Sur at the Universidad Nacional del Sur, Argentina, studying functor categories, steak and Patagonian mountains. Funding from a 2010 Davis Foundation grant and a 2013 Whiting Foundation fellowship are here gratefully acknowledged as well. Thanks also are due to the scattered audience members who offered critical comments and useful suggestions in response to various talks linked to this project given at the following universities and conferences between 2008 and 2014: World Congress of Philosophy XXII (Seoul National University), Deleuze Studies (University of Cologne, University of Amsterdam and University of Lisbon), Model-Based Reasoning in Science and Technology (Universidade Estadual de Campinas and Sestri Levante), ConstructPeirce Workshop (Harvard University), Loyola University Maryland, Brown University, Haverford College, Santa Clara University, Muzeum Sztuki Łodz, Universidad Católica Argentina, Sociedad Argentina de Análisis Filosófico, Universidad Nacional del Sur, Universidad Nacional de Cuyo, and the Centre Culturel International de Cerisy-la-Salle. The editorial team at Edinburgh including Carol Macdonald, James Dale, Michelle Houston, Rebecca Mackenzie and Naomi Farmer have been marvellously helpful and efficient in bringing the book to press.

Finally, the profoundest thanks go to my wife Margaret and my son Quentin for bearing so graciously with a diagram book scrivener in the house.

Introduction

> Now, in its turn, consider also how the intelligible section should be cut.
>
> How?
>
> Like this: in one part of it a soul, using as images the things that were previously imitated, is compelled to investigate on the basis of hypotheses and makes its way not to a beginning but to an end; while in the other part it makes its way to a beginning that is free from hypotheses; starting out from hypothesis and without the images used in the other part, by means of forms themselves it makes its inquiry through them.
>
> Plato, Republic

> I could talk talk talk talk talk myself to death / but I believe I would only waste my breath / ooh show me . . .
>
> Roxy Music, 'Re-Make/Re-Model'

The present book develops an immanent ontology of relations based on the dynamics of formal diagrams. Elements of Spinoza's metaphysics of immanence, Peirce's semiotics and Deleuze's philosophy of difference are here integrated in an ontology of diagrammatic relations expressed formally in the framework of elementary category theory. The book has three broad goals: to outline an integrative approach to the problem of immanence in Spinoza, Peirce and Deleuze; to develop a model of ontology based on diagrammatic relations; and to introduce some of the most important constructions and basic techniques of category theory to a philosophically but not necessarily mathematically informed audience. The book thus brings together a philosophical concept (immanence), an experimental methodology (diagrams) and a contemporary field of mathematics (categories). Throughout the text the relations and overlaps across these areas are emphasised and the connections among them foregrounded. The three areas correlate roughly to three central theses:

- Immanent metaphysics entails relational ontology.
- Diagrams are the appropriate method for investigating immanence immanently.
- Category theory is the appropriate mathematics for modelling and investigating diagrams.

The book's overarching aim is to show the inner coherence of these three claims and to suggest something of why contemporary philosophy ought to care about them. The remainder of this introduction offers a synopsis of each thesis, some general remarks to place the overall argument in context, and an outline of the topics treated in each chapter.

IMMANENT METAPHYSICS ENTAILS RELATIONAL ONTOLOGY

To make sense of this initial claim, the terms 'metaphysics' and 'ontology' obviously need to be distinguished and clarified. 'Metaphysics' here is meant to refer to the philosophical study whose object is the most general structure of being, whatever that in fact is. Metaphysics aims to express how beings, whatever those in fact turn out to be, hang together or, to put it otherwise, how they stand among and with respect to one another. Regardless of what exists, it investigates reality's fundamental articulations. In this way, metaphysics often involves a division of being into various types of entities, for instance ideas and physical things (a dualist metaphysics) or God and the created world (a traditional theist metaphysics), but it tends more essentially to express a compact list of formal categories or Great Kinds in the style of Plato's *Sophist* whose conjugations delineate what is necessary, possible and impossible for particular beings. It thus tends to maintain close connections with logic, whether formally or informally.

'Ontology' on the other hand is understood to suggest the catalogue of what in fact exists, what Russell colourfully described as the 'ultimate furniture of the world'.[1] If there are badgers, that is an ontological matter. If badgers, like everything else, must come to be and pass away in time, such is an issue for metaphysics. The usages invoked here are probably closer in spirit to the way these terms are used in contemporary analytic philosophy than in post-Heideggerian continental thought, but in any case nothing much hangs on this choice of semantics. It is simply introduced in order to help make the term 'immanence' a bit more precise at the outset. It is assumed that some such distinction between the 'structure' and the 'content' of reality is necessary to get any foothold whatsoever when scaling certain philosophical inclines.

At any rate, in the senses just sketched metaphysics and ontology are obviously closely related concepts. Just how closely related is itself a metaphysical question. There would be little sense from a metaphysical standpoint to dualism, for instance, if there were no beings at all. However, even if nothing existed (the ontologically void position sometimes called 'nihilism' in contemporary analytic literature) not all metaphysical problems would necessarily be settled. *How* exactly 'nothing exists' – the structure of nothingness or emptiness – might very well remain a source of dispute, as in certain divergent lines of Mahayana Buddhism. Typically, metaphysical questions abstract from ontological ones at least provisionally, but often only then to use this very act of abstraction as a kind of leverage for transposing their own structure back onto beings, 'finding' it there where it has in fact merely been projected. This insight is at the heart of Kantian critique. It is also what brings Kant's transcendental method to within a hairsbreadth of immanence, were it not for the impassable limit separating thought from the thing-in-itself in Kant. For philosophies of immanence such limits can only be at best provisional and merely local.

'Immanence', roughly, names then any metaphysical position or method rejecting the notion that the ultimate structure of reality may be investigated independently of its real content in the way that Kant's, for example, does. Immanence disallows 'one-way' arrows from metaphysics to ontology, or from logical grammar to real semantics. Thus, to put it positively, immanence attributes a universally self-modelling structure or global plasticity to the fold of metaphysics and ontology, or of being and beings. Furthermore, it posits this ultimate chiasmus to hold without remainder, without 'exterior'. Immanence on these terms appears then as the type of metaphysical-ontological position that withholds the final pertinence of this very distinction. It is a metaphysical position because it involves a claim about how things ultimately hang together, but its claim of how things hang together is in part the claim that they do not hang together in any way that is illuminated finally by differentiating between what is and how what is is structured. The thesis above simply states that any such metaphysical view implies a generalised relationality at the level of ontology, an ontology of relations and not objects.

Arguably, something like an intuition of immanence impels and grounds the western philosophical tradition at its very inception. The earliest Ionian and Eleatic thinkers did not so much think universally for the first time as express a peculiarly new style or flavour of universality in thought. When Thales claimed all to be water or Anaximander the elements of the world to be condensations of the cloudy *apeiron* or Parmenides truth to be One, in each case a certain milieu was established or marked out for thinking the global real locally through itself, that is, for thinking it immanently. *Physis* for pre-Socratic philosophy was in general necessarily both object and method, and at the most basic level of explanation, the explaining and the explained were understood to coincide. It is convenient to take the more overtly 'materialist' figures here as exemplary, since this enables an especially vivid contrast with the next step in the familiar narrative.

The antagonist or dialectical complement of immanence is, of course, transcendence. As Socratic irony transformed into Platonic institution, a break with immanence followed naturally from the fundamental critique of materialism by ideality: ideas, concepts, the forms that are thought by thought – these just are not the kinds of things that physical things are or could be. Thus to think the unity of the All there must be at least a sufficiently real gap or crack in the All itself to separate ideas from material things. With the important exceptions of such liminal figures as Eriguena and Bruno, dualism via transcendence provided the canonical scheme of metaphysics through the middle ages up to the early modern period, until with the figure of Spinoza the metaphysics of immanence found its great modern articulation. Spinoza's more or less definitive account of immanent metaphysics in the *Ethics* still stands as the touchstone of the concept of immanence for the entire subsequent tradition. In particular, Spinozist radical immanence haunts subsequent philosophers in their various attempts to reconcile immanence with transcendence in multiple ways, sometimes directly, often through displacements into rejected mystical or spiritualist guises. This is evident for instance in both Kant and Hegel, the former under the shadow of Swedenborg and the latter the shadow of Boehme. In the twentieth century, Husserlian phenomenology marked a revival of the term 'immanence', ascribing it to the mutual enfolding of object and method in the investigation of conscious experience. Today, the term has become something of a rallying-cry for strains of philosophy like that of Deleuze and certain varieties of contemporary materialism and new realism.

At any rate, history and polemics are of little concern. It is not really the point of this book to argue for an immanent metaphysics or to mount a philosophical critique of transcendence. Instead, within the limits of the first thesis, it is simply a matter of proposing and defending what is claimed to be a necessary implication of any immanent metaphysics. If immanence is how reality is ultimately structured, then ontology is ineluctably constrained to relations. Things must be relations 'all the way down' (however far that is) without remainder. It is normally thought that there are things, or objects. It is also commonly understood that relations depend upon there being things that they relate. It is argued here that if immanence is correct metaphysically speaking, then this normal way of thinking is wrong on both counts, or rather both these 'truisms' must be elaborated and ultimately understood in ways contrary to their usual senses. They should finally be expressed solely as claims involving distinctions among kinds or degrees of relations themselves. 'Things' in the usual sense are ultimately no more than relations of some kind or another that hold or do not hold among other sorts of relations, and so on.

The arguments in support of this claim are primarily advanced in the discussion of Spinoza in Chapter 1, but Spinoza's philosophy is taken as emblematic in this regard for any consistent metaphysics of immanence. So it is not simply a claim about Spinoza's own thought, but about the ontological implications of the *kind* of metaphysics Spinoza proposes. If the argument is found convincing, some readers might therefore choose to take it as a premise for a *reductio* style argument against any metaphysics of immanence. Fair enough. In the present context, it provides the basis for posing a further question: if Spinozist metaphysics is in the relevant respects actually correct and things are thus ultimately relations, what would and should this entail methodologically for philosophy?

DIAGRAMS ARE THE APPROPRIATE METHOD FOR INVESTIGATING IMMANENCE IMMANENTLY

The central claim of the present work is that because it is possible both to represent and to instantiate an ontology of relations by means of diagrammatic notation, diagrams are particularly efficient tools for studying relations by means of relations themselves, that is to say, immanently. Under philosophical conditions of immanence, method and object must do more than merely conform to one another, they must partly overlap if not fully coincide. Because of their partial coincidence of representational power and relational instantiation, diagrams are especially suited to philosophical inquiry into the metaphysics of immanence.

Explaining fully what diagrams are and how they work will be tasks for the book as a whole. Nonetheless, at this stage diagrammatic method may be at least schematised by the following principles:

(1) Diagrams imply a partial blurring of the distinction between sense and notation, or between object and sign. In other words, diagrams are essentially iconic. They are what they mean. One effect of the seldom questioned linguistic dominance in philosophical method is that the peculiar and restricted form of semiotic relation that holds generally between words (or sentences) and things (or propositions, states of affairs and so forth) is often transferred uncritically to the relation between thought and what thought thinks. Diagrammatic thought is situated on a terrain wherein problems of linguistic signification and representation are relatively circumscribed from the outset. This is because diagrams are constituted always to some degree by a mode of representation (*Vorstellung*) that is *also* an 'immediate' non-linguistic presentation (*Darstellung*), for instance via sense perception or physical movement. If *Vorstellung* is the mark of the transcendent sign, *Darstellung* tends intrinsically towards a model of immanent signification, meaning not necessarily the simple identity of sign and thing, but their at least minimal overlap and ontological continuity. Diagrams thus represent systems of relations and at the same time instantiate (at least some of) those relations directly. In this way the 'content' of a diagram is already at least partly present directly and immediately in its 'form'. Its syntax is already an instance of its semantics.

(2) Diagrams are always realised within some already given system of relations that serves as an ambient environment for their inscription and selection. Diagrams are made or picked out from among pre-existing structures, which may be relatively abstract or more concrete depending on the case but which must at any rate exist as real systems of relations already instantiated in some differentiated field. It is not necessary to decide questions of materiality and ideality in this regard (if true ontology includes immaterialities, so be it) but every diagram must still be made or inscribed – and hence indexed – 'somewhere' in a pre-existing relational domain of some kind, whether among things, concepts, images or something else, using the structures and relations already to be found there. In a very general

sense, this implies a certain 'spatialisation' of diagrammatic thought, although the kinds of spaces in which diagrams may be inscribed are much more varied than is probably commonly considered. Diagrams in this enlarged sense are not necessarily two-dimensional drawn or written structures or even spatio-temporal objects. Nonetheless, sketches drawn on paper will serve as paradigmatic diagrams for present purposes. We are after all communicating via paper and ink (or perhaps with pixels on some electronic screen – you are obviously in a better position to know this than I am). In any case, the two-dimensionality and relative stasis of the current medium should not lead to a narrowing of conception. The more familiar kind of diagram is in fact only a special case of a much more general notion of diagram that it is the task of this work to develop, yet in order to clarify this more general notion we will make extensive use of the special case. The diagrams themselves are thus both explicatory instruments and illustrative examples. The very possibility of being both at once will prove to be one of the most powerful aspects of diagrammatic expression. Diagrams may be – and indeed are – constructed anywhere (everywhere), from anything (everything).

(3) Diagrams function according to a formal reversibility between stipulation and evaluation, or between abstraction and selection. A diagram highlights certain relations among a local system of relations by actualising new relations, precisely those that determine the diagram itself with respect to its user and its use. When certain subsystems of relations are abstracted from their immediate context, they naturally form a diagrammatic 'unit' that may be used to pick out other systems of its relevant type. Every stipulated part of a diagram becomes by that very token a tool of comparative evaluation. It is here that the self-modelling and plastic character of immanence positively infests the diagram and energises it. Obviously the dynamics of this process itself will need to be further specified and to some degree formalised. Such is the work especially of Chapters 3 and 4, the theoretical core of the book. Indeed in Chapter 4 we will formalise a rigorous theory of diagrammatic signs within the mathematics of category theory using the specific structure of presheaves.

The formal reversibility or quasi-invertibility that holds between abstracting structures and selecting parts of diagrams serves as the ground for conceiving 'conventionality' in the broad sense of common agreement on semiotic vehicles in a way consistent with the metaphysics of immanence. It is also the basis on the same terms for understanding processes of 'paideia' in the sense of the regimented communication of knowledge. In the terminology of Peirce that will be examined in Chapter 3, it has the general character of 'thirdness' or 'symbolicity'.

Diagrams are understood here as a general type of sign. To explain what diagrams are is to indicate how they signify. What specifies diagrammatic signs as contrasted, at least initially, to linguistic signs as usually understood – taking words as paradigmatic – is that typically the parts of diagrams are also diagrams *and* the signifying power of parts and whole arises naturally at least as much as conventionally from the evident relations that structure them. Rather than drawing a sharp line between linguistic and diagrammatic representation, however, it is more in the spirit of the view of diagrammatic immanence advocated here to conceive the former as a species of the latter, one in which the diagrammatic structure tends to be more abstract and less directly evident. In any case, a diagram *as such* will be conceived as a manifest system of relations that signifies something that also instantiates some relevant part of that same system of relations. In addition, the mode of signification itself must depend to some appropriate degree upon this homology of relations. In other words, the *how* of diagrammatic signification will lean heavily, in a load-bearing way so to speak, on the *what* of relational structure common to sign and significance.

Consider the sorted collection of generic diagram parts in Figure 0.1. In each case, to describe *what the thing is* is already to indicate *how it might signify* diagrammatically. These dots, arrows, lines and frames will serve as basic elements of the diagrammatic syntax that we will employ throughout the text.

0.1

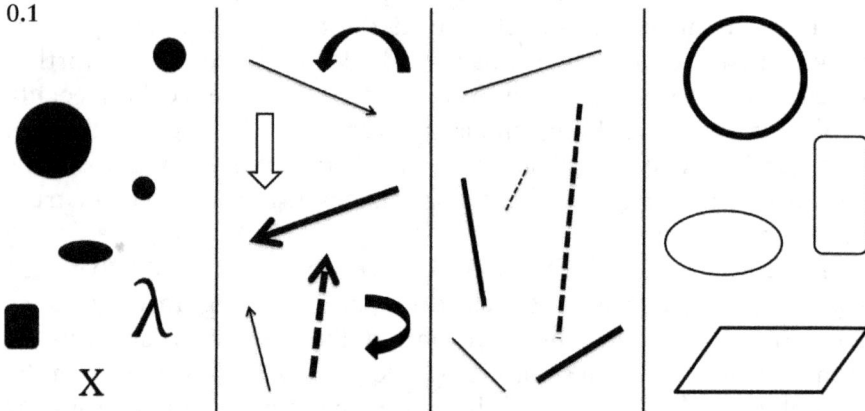

What is a dot? Dots are simple differences, lacking internal differentiation or evident structure, set off against a contrasting background. They are simple, but they are not points. They are extended and cover a continuous area in a homogeneous manner, like a stain (it is important to note that this description is already to some extent stipulative; it guides perception). What then will a dot 'mean'? Something, some thing. Anything that has the relevant structural similarity to a dot: indicable unity. Conversely, anything with such a structure may be treated diagrammatically as a 'dot' of this sort in its own right. Dots thus function naturally like variables in standard formal syntax, with the important difference that in general they are determined indexically ('this one here') and not via an axiomatic iterability (repeating a dot makes it different). From the diagrammatic point of view, then, formal variables like 'X' or the Greek letter lambda may be understood as aesthetically degenerate dots, dots that carry just a bit too much information, too much irrelevant structure for their intended purpose. Of course, this extra information is sometimes quite useful. In accordance with our diagrammatic method we will require that the meaning of the dot (its 'semantics' in a broad and rough sense) be instantiated *at least* in itself. The class of what it can represent must include at a minimum the dot itself as well as a dot *as such*, which is to say, by extension, all actual and conceivable dots.

What is an arrow? An arrow is a path drawn from somewhere or something to somewhere or something else. It possesses the unity of a line, and is thus a special sort of dot, one with two distinct 'ends'. In addition, the two ends of the line are ordered, that is, one comes first and the other comes next, the arrow's tail and its head. To establish the difference between the tail and the head of the arrow, one endpoint is specially marked, which is what makes an arrow an arrow and not just a line segment or a mere arc. What will an arrow mean? Besides signifying itself and other arrows, its naturally iconic semantics include any ordering or asymmetrical relating of two things, any path in a space, and any process or interval with a beginning and an end. Conversely, any of these latter structures may be treated diagrammatically as an arrow in its own right, under appropriate conditions.

What is a line? A line is an arrow minus the distinction of head and tail. It connects its endpoints by tracing a link through the space they share, and it separates neighbourhoods in a plane along its length. Some of its possible meanings may be surveyed by examining the many contexts where lines of various sorts are drawn.

Finally, what is a frame? A frame distinguishes an inside and an outside and gathers the contents of its interior. It is like a hollow dot that may perhaps be 'filled' with other things, other diagrams. A frame's meanings are at least as diverse as those of all possible territorial boundaries.

This is neither a formally defined nor an exhaustive collection of diagram parts. Diagrams may be composed of anything whatsoever, even ideal entities such as mathematical concepts. But in any case the quite limited diagrammatic toolbox indicated in Figure 0.1 remains capable of a great range of expression, in part because these particular tools may be reproduced and composed with one another in a great variety of topologically interesting ways. Structures of dots and arrows alone will be sufficient in their own way to organise the diagrammatic structure immanent to category-theoretical mathematics, although liberal supplements of lines and frames of various kinds will certainly ease the presentation and its deciphering significantly.

Category theory is the appropriate mathematics for modelling and investigating diagrams

If diagrams in general prove useful material for modelling and investigating relations in an immanent manner, how should the formal workings of diagrams themselves be modelled and investigated? The third thesis asserts that categories in the sense of the mathematics of category theory may serve as a rigorous and theoretically rich platform for treating diagrammatic relations as such. Mathematical categories may be understood roughly as systems of relations that organise objects of a given type, the characteristics of such objects being determined (from the perspective of the given category) solely in terms of their concomitant system of relations. There is thus a naturally 'pragmatic' epistemology intrinsic to categories: from the standpoint of category theory objects are investigated and known only via their interactions with other objects, not 'in themselves'. The space of possible maps from one object to another determines what can be known of those objects as such. Over the past several decades, category theory has proven extraordinarily successful in unifying diverse fields of mathematics and providing a less arbitrary and more productive foundation for mathematics than set theory. Because of its intrinsic orientation towards relations, it connects more readily and with fewer idealist assumptions than set theory to the real world and its component structures.

Of course category theory did not spring Athena-like from the head of Zeus as a fully-developed autonomous branch and potentially revolutionary foundation for mathematics. Rather, it emerged initially in a quiet, germ-like and natural way within the field of algebraic topology. In 1945, Samuel Eilenberg and Saunders Mac Lane published the long article 'General Theory of Natural Equivalences' which first introduced what would become the basic elements of category theory, including the mappings specific to categories, functors and natural transformations, in the context of homotopies. Later, with the explicit introduction of adjoint functors by Kan in the 1950s and then especially with the formulations of topoi by Grothendieck, Lawvere and Tierney, among others, category theory began to take on the character of an autonomous mathematical discipline involving its own internally formulated problems and research programmes. Since the turn of the millennium, category theory has advanced rapidly with the study of n-categories and with diverse ramifications throughout mathematics as well as in logic, computer science, physics and other sciences. It has strongly impacted the recent and highly promising development of homotopy type theory.

Category theory itself makes extensive use of diagrams as a rigorous formal notation for expressing statements and demonstrating proofs. With these categorical diagrams come new mathematical practices, in particular the notational *habitus* of 'diagram-chasing'. In the present book the aim is to elicit the emergence of category theory and its indigenous diagrammatic notation in a somewhat different fashion, beginning from within the Spinozist metaphysics of affective relations. What is most interesting from this perspective is how diagrammatic expression comes equipped with its own naturally ordered degrees of rigour and intuitive, explanatory power. It is the capacity of diagrams to tend smoothly towards their increasingly rigorous formulation and to deform when necessary into more practical and experimental tools that makes them especially important here. There is a pedagogical and communicative dimension to how diagrams work that is both distinct from and yet correlative to their efficiency as a mathematical formalism within the theory of categories.

What do diagrammatic methods derived from category theory have to offer philosophy? One background assumption of the present book is that the global practice of philosophy is enlivened by institutional and methodological pluralism. In philosophy as elsewhere, monocultural dynamics are often contrary to adaptability and tend to sterility. The introduction of new methods in philosophy not only might facilitate solving old problems, it may also help to bring into focus the often unseen presuppositions and limits built into more established and familiar methods. In philosophy, language (both oral and written) has achieved such dominance as the basic tool of thought that it is often assumed without question that philosophy is and always has been nothing more than a species of linguistic practice (perhaps in more recent times supplemented with some elementary logical tools). Yet the history of philosophy provides many examples of diverse non-linguistic philosophical practices, from the visualisation exercises and theurgic rituals of ancient philosophers, to the pictorial art of memory carried from antiquity through to the early modern period, or the alchemical experiments of the Renaissance.[2] As already suggested, one key theoretical problem to which the present book responds is that of the conflictual if not contradictory relation between the traditional linguistic-discursive form of philosophy on the one hand and the drive to metaphysical immanence and its formal expression on the other. Breaking out of language's panopticon in one way or another has been on the philosophical agenda for quite some time, but this aim has taken on a certain intellectual and increasingly institutional urgency in the wake of the somewhat narrow-minded 'linguistic turn' that established itself as the hegemonic form of Anglophone philosophy in the previous century and in many ways still holds sway. A resurgence of interest in speculative and formal metaphysics and a variety of broadly pragmatist programmes arriving from different quarters are healthy and enlivening signs on the contemporary philosophical scene. This book follows along both these currents and looks to their confluence. Category theory offers a versatile collection of formal tools for accomplishing this.

The presentation of the main text alternates between chapters focusing on philosophical concepts and chapters introducing formal methods in the mathematics of category theory enabling these concepts to be brought into the unity of a systematic theory. The argument thus proceeds in a zigzag fashion. Chapters devoted to the distinct conceptualisations of immanence in Spinoza, Peirce and Deleuze alternate with chapters introducing and developing the fundamental objects and operations of category theory. Conceptual motivations arise in each of the philosophical chapters for the specific formal instruments elaborated in the subsequent mathematical ones. Diagrams appear throughout but are especially prevalent in the chapters on categories. If the overall plan is successful, the zigzag presentation should function as a kind of zipper aligning and locking together the conceptual, methodological and mathematical notions at issue. Thus, the back-and-forth motion between odd and even numbered chapters ought to be understood as implying or inducing a virtual synthesis – the real object of the book – running parallel between its otherwise at least seemingly independent philosophical and mathematical trajectories. This synthesis itself is the concept of 'diagrammatic immanence'.

This seems to be the appropriate place to signal some background and collateral connections that for reasons of space and smoothness of presentation did not always find their way explicitly into the body of the text. They represent multiple open lines of research linked to the present proposal and together sketch out a certain theoretical milieu in which it is probably most fittingly situated. On the philosophical side, besides the main trio of Spinoza, Peirce and Deleuze, the theoretical background that has shaped the present work comes on the one hand from a mostly French cohort: Albert Lautman, Jean Cavaillès, Gilbert Simondon, Alain Badiou and Fernando Zalamea, and on the other from a group of more analytically oriented Anglophone philosophers: Timothy Williamson, Theodore Sider, Graham Priest, Robert Brandon and Stewart Shapiro.[3] On the more methodological side, the study and use of diagrams as a viable philosophical notation has long possessed a relatively minor and subterranean status in the fields of logic and the philosophy of logic. Nonetheless, the literature on diagrammatic logic and diagrammatic reasoning is far more extensive than may be outlined here in even a cursory way, and it is quickly growing. Several sources, however, stand out as especially relevant to the approach pursued here. I would like to mention John Mullarkey's *Post-Continental Philosophy*, the writings of Gilles Châtelet, the Peircean studies of Frederik Stjernfelt and the work of Franck Jedrzejewski.[4] Other central works in the literature on Peirce's diagrams in particular are indicated in the notes to Chapters 3 and 4. Finally, the mathematical literature on category theory is vast and fruitfully multiplying at an astonishing rate.[5] Besides the ocean of technical work in category theory itself and in various specialised branches of mathematics, logic and computer science, there is a nascent subliterature of category theory oriented especially to the employment of category theoretical methods in the physical sciences that is particularly relevant to the approach pursued here. Among others, the work of Ellis Cooper, Michael Epperson and Elias Zafiris, and David Spivak should be highlighted.[6] This work has deep and largely unexplored connections with a variety of contemporary proposals in metaphysics and philosophy of science, such as those of structural realism and scale-free systems analysis, in the work of Steven French and Mariam Thalos, as well as links to systems-theoretical work in the social sciences like that of Niklas Luhmann.[7]

It is important to be clear on two things that will *not* be found herein. First of all, there cannot be anything approaching full and comprehensive presentations of the philosophical systems articulated by Spinoza, Peirce and Deleuze respectively. I am treading among the footsteps of giants and must forfeit any claim to completeness when mapping the territory. By the same token, there is no attempt made here to forge some sort of global synthesis or unified narrative of the three thinkers. It is no claim of this book that these three philosophers are somehow 'saying the same thing' or are 'part of one story', only that they have something structural in common: immanence – which may yet become fully diagrammatic. It is impossible to give all the necessary introductory background on their respective systems: the reader is assumed to be somewhat philosophically informed. More importantly, the reader is asked to advance through the text in an active and abductive mode, forming and testing hypotheses, sketching and experimenting on diagrams, and sprinkling grains of salt when appropriate. Despite the above formulation of 'theses', I am not especially concerned to elicit anyone's philosophical conviction in particular philosophical views or textual interpretations, but rather to advocate for a novel approach to some important traditional questions and to enable the construction of new and possibly more interesting problems via diagrammatic techniques and category-theoretic mathematics. It is more a matter here of forging useful philosophical tools than of trying to win academic disputes.

Secondly, this is not and should not be a mathematics textbook. The presentation of category theory in Chapters 2, 4 and 6 is selective (which is to say, fragmented and incomplete); accessible (that is, oriented towards intuitive insight rather than formal proof); and tendentious (namely, looking to philosophical and not primarily mathematical or scientific application). Curious mathematicians who might find material of interest here should keep in mind that the book is written not for them but explicitly for the intelligent *non*-mathematician. That said, I have made every effort to balance clarity and rigour within the rather severe restrictions inherent to the project as a whole. Readers with little or no mathematical training yet in possession of a basic philosophical fluency in conceptual operations of abstraction, generalisation, hypostasisation and logical inference should be capable of tracking the progressively determined mathematical constructions from the most basic (order-structures and functions) to the fairly sophisticated (adjoint functors, presheaf categories and topoi) without the need for external supplementation or undue hair-pulling. In this respect, from a purely mathematical standpoint the even numbered chapters may be seen as an unusual and truly introductory hybrid approach – partly intuitive and partly formal – to the otherwise thoroughly abstract realm of mathematical categories. If the latter only come to be understood at best in their broad conceptual outlines, that will count as an unmitigated success from the present standpoint.[8]

A brief note on terminology: I bow to standard usage and treat the adjective form of category as 'categorical'. This has nothing to do with the more familiar philosophical and logical notions of, for example, 'categorical' statements, syllogisms or imperatives. I cannot, however, bear the lexical monstrosity of 'toposes' and instead call topoi 'topoi'. Generally in the text when traditional variables are used, categorical objects (dots) are represented by capital letters (X, Y, Z), categorical arrows by italicised lower case letters (f, g, h), categories themselves by boldface capitals (**C, D**) and functors by italicised capitals (F, G). Any deviation from these protocols should be quite clear from the context.

The chapter by chapter organisation is as follows. Chapter 1 elaborates a series of themes in Spinoza's *Ethics* flowing from its central assertion of a metaphysics of immanence: the rhetoric and ethics involved in the geometrical method of presentation, the doctrine of relational individuation, the epistemological consequences of Spinoza's affective understanding of language, and finally the consolidation of these issues in Spinoza's concept of the 'third kind of knowledge'. What emerges from this sequence is a unified approach to interpreting Spinoza's immanent metaphysics through the concept of diagrammatic relations. For Spinoza, individuals are determined by regularities of relations among the parts that compose them, yet at the same time Spinoza's ontology of the affects entails that individuals are determined essentially by what they can do and what can be done to or with them. Conceiving such relations as diagrammatically structured is to understand them as existing concretely and as being structured nonetheless according to the possible ways they may affect and be affected by others. Such a diagrammatic interpretation of

Spinoza presents an ontologically univocal and yet essentially relational and pragmatic conception of entities.

Chapter 2 shifts to more purely methodological terrain. How, if the general relational immanence proposed by Spinoza's *Ethics* is in fact true, should cognitive projects of all sorts, including philosophy, be most intelligently and effectively pursued? This chapter introduces the basics of category theory in view of the broader proposal that this branch of mathematics has key philosophical significance, especially for conceptualising immanence. In effect, the analysis of Spinoza in Chapter 1 in terms of diagrammatic relations is translated here into the basic conceptual and formal framework of categories. The presentation proceeds through several intuitive mathematical structures – directed graphs, partial orders and functions – as a way to lead smoothly into the fundamental concepts of categories and functors.

Chapter 3 turns back from mathematics to philosophy and examines Peirce's semiotic conception of triadic relations, a conception which is at once metaphysical, ethical and epistemological. Most importantly, Peirce's semiotics enables a continuity to be thought between forms of practice and types of signs. In contrast to the dyadic Saussurean sign, from Peirce's point of view signs are patterns of practical relations themselves and are thus correctly modelled by triadic and not dyadic relations. In this way, a general ontological framework of pragmatic relations as signs works to support and helps to clarify Spinoza's doctrine of relational individuation. The shared framework is one in which relations (both 'internal', that is, those constitutive of individuals, and 'external', namely those through which individuals affect one another) take both logical and ontological priority over the terms they relate. The core division of Peirce's semiotics into three kinds of sign – icon, index and symbol – becomes in this light a means for treating immanent ontological relations among entities as essentially variable forms of signification. On the basis of Peirce's semiotics, a constructive theory of diagrams is then outlined coordinating three phases of selection, experimentation and evaluation.

Chapter 4 continues the methodological line begun in Chapter 2 and extends the technology of diagrammatic and categorical mappings from arrows within categories and functors between categories to natural transformations between functors. In both Spinoza and Peirce, the problems of representation and signification under conditions of immanence appeared as especially salient. The category-theoretical framework continued in this chapter begins to address these strictly philosophical problems from a purely formal standpoint in which the difference between 'internal' and 'external' categorical determinations serves as a basis for reconceiving the internal and external relations of entities understood as diagrammatically structured. The key insight is a continuation and extension of that begun in Chapter 2, namely that within the framework of category theory categories themselves may appear as objects with well-defined systems of relations to one another via functors. Such systems of relational objects and meta-relations among them can constitute categories in their own right. This formal 'flattening' of meta-systems and meta-relations back onto the systems and relations they relate is in this chapter lifted to the level of functors themselves: whereas functors in category theory are essentially mappings between categories, natural transformations are structure-preserving mappings between functors (mappings between mappings). Taken together, they form categories of functors, or functor categories. With this notion in hand and after introducing the important categorical concept of presheaves, it then becomes possible to define presheaf categories as a species of functor category. These are then used to construct a categorical theory of diagrammatic signs based on presheaves. This categorical theory is closely linked to the earlier presentation of diagrams in terms of Peirce's semiotics, and a concise example of how the theory works is provided drawn from Peirce's logical notation of Existential Graphs.

Chapter 5 introduces the problematic of creative difference into the concept of diagrammatic immanence, linking the insights of Deleuzian philosophy to the issues previously raised by Spinoza and Peirce. This chapter shows in particular how Deleuze's reading of Spinoza connects up with the central theses of *Difference and Repetition* and *The Logic of Sense* in such a way that the dominance of the cognitive ego is displaced in favour of a diagrammatic conception of mobile and collective sign-systems oriented towards relational construction. In particular, this applies to the actors and traditions within philosophy itself. The sense of philosophy (according to the Deleuzian conception of sense as expressive virtuality) must be mapped directly onto the immanence it proclaims, thus raising a series of questions concerning the role of the 'Non-' or Other in Deleuze's thought with respect to which philosophy itself learns to become.

Chapter 6 continues the line of formalisation developed through Chapters 2 and 4. It examines two higher-order categorical concepts with deep connections to logic: adjunctions and topoi, and links these to the important and far-ranging logical difference between Boolean and Heyting algebras. Taken together, these formal constructions provide the subtle and delicate necessary tools for further immanent philosophical investigation of the world of diagrammatic signs.

Notes

1. Bertrand Russell, *Introduction to Mathematical Philosophy*, p. 146.
2. For some examples of such practices, see Pierre Hadot, *Philosophy as a Way of Life* and Frances Yates, *The Art of Memory*. These two texts, both of which examine past philosophical practices far removed from the philosophical mainstream today, should be understood as constantly present in the ensuing proposal as a kind of subterranean historical reference.
3. For representative works, see Albert Lautman, *Mathematics, Ideas, and the Physical Real*; Jean Cavaillès, 'On Logic and the Theory of Science'; Gilbert Simondon, *L'individuation à la lumière des notions de forme et d'information*; Alain Badiou, *Being and Event* and *Logics of Worlds*; Fernando Zalamea, *Synthetic Philosophy of Contemporary Mathematics*; Timothy Williamson, *Modal Logic as Metaphysics*; Theodore Sider, *Writing the Book of the World*; Graham Priest, *Beyond the Limits of Thought*; Robert Brandom, *Between Saying and Doing*; and Stewart Shapiro, *Philosophy of Mathematics*.
4. John Mullarkey, *Post-Continental Philosophy*, especially ch. 5; Gilles Châtelet, *Figuring Space: Philosophy, Mathematics and Physics* and 'Interlacing the Singularity, the Diagram and the Metaphor'; Frederik Stjernfelt, *Diagrammatology* and *Natural Propositions*; and Franck Jedrzejewski, *Ontologie des Catégories*.
5. The best beginner's introduction to category theory is William Lawvere and Stephen Schanuel, *Conceptual Mathematics*. Saunders Mac Lane, *Categories for the Working Mathematician* is a standard reference in the field. Highly recommended for readers with some basic mathematical training is Steve Awodey, *Category Theory*. My own admittedly informal 'diagrams-only' approach is greatly indebted to Peter Freyd's quite technical and still largely underappreciated work. See Peter Freyd and Andrej Scedrov, *Categories, Allegories*.
6. Ellis Cooper, *Mathematical Mechanics*; Michael Epperson and Elias Zafiris, *Foundations of Relational Realism*; and David Spivak, *Category Theory for the Sciences*.
7. See Steven French, *The Structure of the World*; Mariam Thalos, *Without Hierarchy*; Niklas Luhmann, *Social Systems*.
8. In particular, I have prescinded from tedious set-theoretical concerns with size and thus with the largely artificial distinction between concrete

and abstract categories. These issues, while certainly important mathematically, are philosophically irrelevant and even misleading at an introductory level and for present purposes. In general, highly technical issues and exceptions are passed over in silence. Diderot dreamt of strangling the world's last king with the intestines of the last clergy. With somewhat less violence we may nonetheless similarly invite both lazy hand-waving thinkers and nit-picky pedants to gather together in an adjacent, sound-proofed room, where they will no doubt rage quite justly at one another.

CHAPTER 1

Spinoza and Relational Immanence

> The more we understand singular things, the more we understand God.
>
> Spinoza, *Ethics* Vp24

A distinctive feature of Spinoza's thought is that it rejects any explanatory mechanisms grounded in mystery or *de jure* unknowability, in particular any explanatory criteria of experience and knowledge that would rely on 'objects' external to the mind. While Spinoza concedes that 'a true idea must agree with its object', he understands philosophical explanation to be grounded properly not in truth but in *adequacy*: 'By adequate idea I understand an idea which, insofar as it is considered in itself, without relation to an object, has all the properties, *or* intrinsic denominations of a true idea.'[1] From a Spinozist point of view, then, empiricism in anything like the Lockean style is a philosophical non-starter. For Spinoza, it will never be sufficient to rest any explanation of experience, knowledge or power on the sheer fact that it is given. No doubt one always begins with what is given, but on Spinoza's terms philosophy fails to think adequately if the given functions for it as an answer and not solely as a relative starting-point. Thought itself is a transitive activity and a continuous process, and so beginnings are as such exterior to thought. Because for a philosophy of immanence nothing can be absolutely exterior to thought, such thinking cannot countenance absolute beginnings. Among other reasons this is why the undivided term 'God, or Nature' in Spinoza must be understood not as a foundation or ultimate principle but rather as an incontrovertible milieu: real immanence.

If certainly no Lockean empiricist, Spinoza does seem to be grouped readily among the early modern 'rationalists'. And sure enough, Spinoza shares with Descartes and Leibniz a resolute willingness to blur if not entirely efface the distinction of logic – and mathematics – from metaphysics. For reason as such, conceptual and formal relations, not the experiential contents of the senses, are eminently knowable. Hence metaphysics as the rational science of reality's ultimate structure is feasible. Yet unlike Descartes and Leibniz, Spinoza makes no important contributions to mathematics and indeed demonstrates no exceptional aptitude in that arena. Perhaps this is because in Spinoza the deductive character of mathematics is immediately ontologised. There is no separable context in Spinoza's metaphysics for positing merely abstract entities like forms or numbers that would serve as the proper regional domain of deductive structure. For Spinoza rational deductive structure simply and immediately is what is. Metaphysics directly implicates ontology, without remainder.

Moreover, in both Descartes and Leibniz space is reserved for the decisive mystery of the will. In Descartes – Augustinian and Pelagian by turns – the human will's arbitrary power raises human beings almost to godlike status (it is the only thing infinite in us, other than the idea of God). And in Leibniz the will accounts for the single divine choice of which among the merely possible worlds to actualise in fact. Yet Spinoza rejects both human and divine will as philosophically explanatory. Among at least these three, then, it is only Spinoza who articulates a genuinely thoroughgoing rationalism, that is, a deductive determinism excluding any real power attributable to the will. In this respect, Spinoza appears to be aligned with the strict necessitarian materialism of such seventeenth-century thinkers as Hobbes and Gassendi, although the Spinozist God remains equally irreducible to causal mechanics. Mechanical causation, while certainly exhibiting necessity, still remains a form of exterior determination and does not attain the more radical necessity of immanence. In any case, as compared with Descartes and Leibniz it is Spinoza alone among the 'rationalists' who has the courage to equate the belief in an arbitrary power of wilful decision with the objective stupidity of a rock that once thrown thinks it has chosen so. For Spinoza only a mind that has failed to think things through adequately would identify true liberty with mere individual choice.

In opposition to such voluntarist conceptions of human action, Spinoza rejects any conception of mind that holds will and intellect separate, thus allowing for discontinuity between *what* is understood and *whether and how* one affirms or denies its truth. In contrast to the Cartesian and Sceptic-Academic distinction of perception from judgement, for instance, Spinoza asserts in Part Two of the *Ethics* that '[i]n the mind there is no volition, *or* affirmation and negation, except that which the idea involves insofar as it is an idea'.[2] One major difference between Spinoza and Descartes is found then in the conception of the self implied by this unity of will and intellect. By identifying will and intellect Spinoza rejects the Cartesian egoic conception in which the self or subject is able to stand removed from the objects of its regard and to judge or know them in relative freedom. In Spinoza's conception, human beings are not sites of subjective transcendence but rather immanent parts of nature. In his preface to Part Three, Spinoza writes:

> Most of those who have written about the affects, and men's way of living, seem to treat, not of natural things, which follow the common laws of Nature, but of things which are outside Nature. Indeed they seem to conceive man in Nature as a dominion within a dominion [*imperium in imperio*]. For they believe that man disturbs, rather than follows, the order of Nature, that he has absolute power over his actions, and that he is determined only by himself.[3]

The geometrical order of the *Ethics*, to which we will return, serves in this way as a metaphor for Spinoza's theory of mind.[4] The mind in its everyday functioning is like an ambiguous demonstration cut off in part from the axioms and theorems that support it. Reasonable thinking and reasonable life, on the contrary, are like coherent demonstrations, explicit truths, consistent integrations of principles, contexts and consequences.

On this basis Spinoza's deep mistrust of natural language becomes intelligible. He dismisses what he calls the 'first kind of knowledge', or 'knowledge through signs', because he understands such signs to be merely arbitrary connections between certain sounds or combinations of letters and pseudo-concepts or 'picture-thoughts' in the imagination. Words for Spinoza are little more than historical sedimentations of the same human puffery that asserts the will's power to choose. The very conventionality of natural language damns it philosophically. Like Wittgenstein two and a half centuries later, Spinoza will think with maximum caution in face of 'the bewitchment of our intelligence by means of language'.[5] And at least like the Wittgenstein of the *Tractatus*, Spinoza aims to remedy the inevitable falsifications and inadequacies of natural language with a formal presentation and a formal understanding. For Spinoza such formally adequate modes of thinking are embodied directly in the 'geometrical method' of the *Ethics*.

Gone with dependence on human words in order to think is any need among canons of philosophical explanation for external 'reasons to be' in Spinoza. The single, absolutely infinite network of immanent causation replaces the traditional reliance on (and shuttling between) efficient and final causality. Unlike every theologised or crypto-theologised demand for causal sequences to end their chain in divine creative *fiat* or spontaneous eventful upsurge, Spinoza's philosophy takes existence plainly to be the default of essence.[6] The irony is that only such a thoroughgoing rationalism opens thought to immersion in a rose-like Real that is *absolutely* 'without why'.[7]

Thus we come to the core of Spinoza's immanent metaphysics. For Spinoza Nature (or God, since they are the same thing and words do not matter) is not only infinite, but *absolutely* infinite: 'By God I understand a being absolutely infinite, that is, a substance consisting of an infinity of attributes, of which each one expresses an eternal and infinite essence.'[8] It follows that all negations and limits within being can only be local and selective. The import of Spinoza's all-too-misunderstood remark *omnis determinatio est negatio* is not at all the reality and ubiquity of negation but rather the ultimate unreality of any final or absolute determination.[9] There are no absolute cuts between one thing and the next in Spinoza's metaphysics, only more or less attenuated relations corresponding to variable degrees of commonality. Such relations (the affects and common natures) are themselves *constitutive* of higher-order entities, in such manner that the boundary between *relatum* and *relatio* is always at best localised and relatively unstable. To put it in more Spinozist terminology, the clear conceptual and systematic distinction between modes of substance on the one hand and the affects and common natures that structure these on the other does not in fact differentiate two separate real types of being but rather provides complementary perspectives on infinite substantial expression itself. What is, is expressed as structure. Ontology is just local metaphysics.

To develop the reading just sketched, this chapter begins by reviewing the overall structure of the *Ethics* and examining the role of unity and relations within it. It then turns to the geometrical order of the text and shows how this method of presentation raises unique interpretive issues for treating the *Ethics* as an ethics, that is, as a guide to praxis. These same issues arise in a transposed form in the problem of modal individuation and are partly resolved there. When the Spinozist account of individuation is in turn applied to language, a thoroughly affective theory of linguistic representation comes to light, indicating how the powers inherent to language express only a limited region of the potentials of thought. Finally, this sequence concludes by considering the role of the third kind of knowledge, traditionally one of Spinoza's most contentious notions, in light of the preceding analyses, and proposing a pragmatic and implicitly diagrammatic interpretation of this singular conception of thought's power.

UNITY AND RELATIONS IN SPINOZA'S *ETHICS*

It will be helpful first to review the main outlines of Spinoza's text. As indicated by its full Latin title – *Ethica Ordine Geometrico demonstrata, et In quinque Partes distincta* – Spinoza's *Ethics* is articulated in five main segments, or parts.[10] Two interpretive tasks follow from this division: (1) following the transitions and developments from one part to the next; and (2) understanding the five-part series as a whole in the unity of its sense.

Part One – 'Of God [*De DEO*]'[11] – presents the most general features of Spinoza's metaphysics: the unity of substance, the infinite attributes, and the modifications, or modes of those attributes. These three terms – substance, attribute and mode – become the basic metaphysical framework for Spinoza's ensuing discussions. In a concentrated series of propositions and demonstrations Spinoza quickly establishes the existence and unity of a single substance – God, or Nature – in which all things exist.[12] From the essence of this single substance necessarily 'follow infinitely many things in infinitely many modes [. . .]'.[13] Spinoza argues at length that all things are as they are through the necessary consequences of the divine nature – the primary emphasis throughout is on causal order and necessity: 'Things could have been produced by God in no other way, and in no other order than they have been produced.'[14]

The passage from Part One to Part Two, 'Of the Nature and Origin of the Mind [*De Natura & Origine MENTIS*]', marks a specification within this all-encompassing field of a domain with particular relevance for human beings. Among the infinite attributes of the one substance, Spinoza examines the two of which human beings consist as singular modes – thought and extension. Spinoza begins Part Two with God's power of thinking and concludes as in Part One with an affirmation of necessity as the identity of will and intellect.[15] Yet in distinction from Part One, Spinoza here emphasises 'how much knowledge of this doctrine is to our advantage in life'.[16]

The hinge that both separates and links Part Two with Part Three is a shift from the more general and static discussion of ideas and bodies in Part Two towards a consideration of their interactive affects, their ways of affecting and being affected by one another.[17] Part Three is entitled 'The Origin and Nature of the Affects [*De Origine & Natura AFFECTUUM*]', that is, the relational actions and passions of bodies (and their corresponding ideas). Here Spinoza outlines the dynamics of the affects and specifies a number of increasingly complex and differentiated human affects arising from the 'primary' trio of desire, joy and sadness and including such familiar emotions as love, hate, devotion, hope and fear, gladness, remorse, pity and gratitude.[18]

In passing from Part Three to Part Four the dominant note of Spinoza's text shifts from description to prescription. The theme of Part Four is 'Of Human Bondage, *or* the Powers of the Affects [*De SERVITUTE Humana, seu de AFFECTUUM VIRIBUS*].' Thus the main subject of Part Three, the affects, continues, but here in relation to the 'desire to form an idea of man, as a model of human nature which we may look to' in order to understand the negative consequences of the affects' powers over us.[19]

Ethical prescription also motivates Part Five, 'Of the Power of the Intellect, *or* on Human Freedom [*De POTENTIA INTELLECTUS, seu de LIBERTATE Humana*].' The respective titles of the two final parts thus signal how the movement from Part Four to Part Five is expressed through a pair of coordinated transitions: an analytic shift from affective to intellective power and an emancipatory movement from bondage to freedom. In Part Five the theme of God's unity from Part One returns in the form of the 'idea of God' to which singular ideas are necessarily referred in the 'intellectual love of God'.[20] In this there appears a key to understanding not just the series of steps from one part to the next but the immanent unity of the series itself.

Throughout the text, Spinoza's immanent metaphysics (developed most fully, it should be noted, in a book entitled *Ethica*) emphasises unity, particularly the unity of God and Nature in Part One and the unity of body and mind (the identity of extended and thinking modes, in Spinoza's terminology) in Part Two. The very form of these 'unities' raises particular problems for interpreting Spinoza's thought. The terms in which Spinoza presents them are not unique to Spinoza, of course, but are in each case inherited from tradition, whether theological or philosophical, ancient or contemporary. His novel account of immanence is thus cobbled from diversely given materials, and the account itself consists primarily in how these materials themselves are conceptually transformed by being syntactically rearranged.[21] This occurs at each of the three primary levels of

Spinoza's theoretical apparatus – substance, attribute and modes – and the problem of formal unity and relational difference manifests itself differently at each level.

At the level of substance, as we have seen, Spinoza affirms the unity of a single substance. Spinoza inherits the question of unity at this level especially from medieval Jewish and Muslim theologians, for whom God's unity is a primary subject for thought and the relationship between God and the created universe is an important and contentious theme.[22] In treating this traditional theme, Spinoza breaks with traditional interpretations of God's transcendence by identifying the terms God and Nature together in the concept of one universal *substance*, which he defines as 'what is in itself and is conceived through itself, that is, that whose concept does not require the concept of another thing, from which it must be formed'.[23] This single substance, itself alone 'absolutely infinite' and from which 'must follow infinitely many things in infinitely many modes', may be designated equally well in Spinoza's view as *Deus* or *Natura*, God or Nature.[24] This substance is one, or unity in an ultimate, almost Parmenidean sense.

At the level of the attributes, the problem of unity appears primarily as the relation or identity of the two attributes in which human being is involved, those of thought and extension.[25] Like the unity of God and Nature, the question of the essence of the relationship here is also a problem Spinoza inherits from tradition. In this case, however, it is the newly established Cartesian tradition that Spinoza inherits and whose disjunct terms he sets in parallel order. More broadly still, the problem appears at this level in the distinctions among all the attributes in their infinite diversity, since for Spinoza there are an infinite number of attributes, not only those of thought and extension. As the relation between this level and the preceding one, the problem of unity appears also with regard to the metaphysical distinction between substance and attributes themselves.[26] The attributes are many, yet the unity they share and express is the unity of substance.

Finally, the problem of unity comes into play equally at the level of individual modes (singular bodies and the ideas, or minds, of those bodies).[27] This is expressed first of all in Spinoza's identification of ideas and bodies. In contrast to the Cartesian distinction of thinking and extended substances (minds and bodies), Spinoza identifies ideas and bodies as expressions of one and the same mode of substance under distinct attributes. Here too the unity of and relation between the levels of substance and modes becomes an issue. The modes are individuated unities, yet they are plural and relational in essence. Still, they are modes *of* one substance. But in what sense?

This problem of formal unity arises for substance, attributes and modes in distinct ways, yet extending across and linking these three levels of Spinoza's theoretical framework is the question of *ethical practice*. Spinoza's metaphysics implies and expresses an ethics. Spinoza's *Ethics* is in fact an ethics in precisely the sense that its primary bearing is upon how one lives and acts. To this extent the philosophical problem of unity is expressed primarily as a problem of *practical relation*, first of all as the signifying relation between Spinoza's text and the possible contexts of its reading or use. It is clear especially in the contrast between Parts Three and Four on the one hand and Part Five on the other that *reason* is Spinoza's answer to the question of how one should live if one is to be free. Reason is itself the passage from the bondage of passion to the freedom of action, from the external power of the affects to the power of human freedom. Reduced to its most basic formulation, Spinoza's answer appears much like the answer given by the ancient Stoics: one's life should be lived in accordance with reason. From an ethical perspective, rationality is only secondarily a means of knowledge. Primarily, reason is a mode of conduct. In other words, reason itself for Spinoza is a form of practical relation. As essentially practical, reason enacts and produces the unity of part with part and of part with whole, and in this way reason expresses unity not because it subsumes a diversity of themes under a common theoretical form, but because it involves a relational way of being that is one of *agreement* (*convenire*).[28]

At stake is the distinction and relation internal to any ethical text between its theoretical meaning and its practical programme. On the one hand, there are the various logical and conceptual relations that constitute the systematic structure of the *Ethics*. On the other hand, there are the various relations of bodies, ideas and whatever else there may be that constitute the actual world itself (regardless of whether one accepts the premises and conclusions of Spinoza's metaphysics). Readers of the *Ethics* are inevitably caught up in these concrete worldly relations in myriad ways, and any interpretive strategy that would take the *Ethics* as a practical guide for action is faced with the task of outlining possible relations of agreement between the internal system of the *Ethics* and the wider and more complex world of human activity to which that text's meaning is addressed. The problem expressed here is, more generally, that of *signification* for ethics: how does one indicate, model or describe modes of practical relation in a way that facilitates effective translation into unforeseen contexts? In particular, how does one accommodate a discourse of ethical prescription within the framework of a necessitarian and thoroughly rationalist metaphysics? If there is a mystery in Spinoza, it is not the mystery of the cosmic or trans-cosmic All. It is the mystery of the mystery: how can there be (the illusion of) separation, mutilation or fragmentation of beings at all? Without a gap or crack between what is and what ought to be, why should there be an *Ethics* in the first place? What is a primer in immanence *for*?

The problem of practical relation as it appears in Spinoza's *Ethics* may be clarified by way of an analogy drawn from the mathematics of Spinoza's own day. Descartes' *Geometry*, published in the generation just prior to Spinoza's intellectual maturity, first established modern analytic geometry as the mapping of algebraic relations between real numbers onto geometrical relations between lines and figures in a Euclidean plane.[29] In Descartes' text, '*l'unité*' serves a central terminological and methodological role. 'Unity' represents the arbitrary choice of a fixed geometrical magnitude, 'one line', as Descartes writes, 'which I shall call unity [*que je nommeray l'unité*] in order to relate it as closely as possible to numbers'.[30] Once chosen, this unique magnitude (corresponding to the quantity 1) stands in fixed proportion to all other possible finite magnitudes in a Euclidean space. Since relations between the parts of geometrical figures may at every point be expressed or measured by the construction of lines, that is, magnitudes, it becomes possible on this basis to express geometrical relationships in terms of relations of numbers. This transformation of geometrical form into numerical proportion thus enables the rigorous, isomorphic translation of geometry into algebra. Establishing the conditions of possibility for such translation constitutes one side of Descartes' methodology; the other consists in using the established relation to then solve specific problems.[31]

How does Descartes' method work? To make Cartesian analytic geometry feasible, one must first designate an arbitrarily long, finite, continuous line segment as corresponding to the discrete quantity 'one' (or unity). It then becomes possible to express infinitely many (Euclidean) geometrical relations as corresponding uniquely to definite mathematical (numerical/algebraic) relations and vice versa. Thus Descartes' method institutes and enables a far-reaching and systematic correspondence – algebra to geometry – by first establishing a single, minimal correlation, the number one to the length of a chosen line segment.[32] The large-scale correspondence of algebraic and geometric relations does not proceed tautologically of itself (no point, no line is in itself a number), but is rather constituted hypothetically by the choice of a determinate 'unity'. To call such a choice hypothetical is not to question its validity (which can be demonstrated clearly to anyone who examines its results or effects), but only to emphasise its original contingency. It is to recognise that while its logical modality is not itself that of necessity, precisely *this particular kind of choice* does necessarily make a large-scale, rigorously demonstrable one-to-one correspondence of algebraic and geometrical relations possible. While in a certain sense it does not matter *which* definite magnitude is chosen as 'unity', the very possibility of analytic geometry as a mathematical science depends on the choice of *some such* definite magnitude. We may thus distinguish the relative necessity *that* a singular magnitude be chosen (for the definite purpose of establishing a correlation of algebra and geometry) from the relative indifference of *what* magnitude is in fact actually chosen.

The form of discursive presentation in Spinoza's *Ethics* may be understood as analogous to the relation-forming function of 'unity' in Descartes' *Geometry*. In reading the *Ethics*, practice is the mode of interpretation that translates text to context. Yet in relating the ideas expressed in the axiomatic system of the *Ethics* to the complex fields of worldly experience, a 'unity' has to be established bringing these systems of different kind into relation. A common term needs to be posited to make them commensurate. The discursive form of the *Ethics* offers itself as a *model* for this common term, but it is only interpretive practice itself that is able to play the role concretely.

According to the theoretical framework of Spinoza's *Ethics*, the very relation between the two orders – the textual and the worldly – must be understood from within the perspective of an immanent metaphysics. So what 'unity' would suffice to relate text and context? In Part One of the *Ethics* Spinoza shows how certain traditional arguments against attributing corporeality to God proceed 'from the fact that they suppose an infinite quantity to be measurable and composed of finite parts'.[33] In line with Spinoza's implied position here, any finite unity would thereby be insufficient to make the absolute infinity of a single substance proportional to any finite part of itself. Required instead would be an infinitely developmental form of relation, a relational process or method able to test and correct itself without limit rather than a static identity relating text and application according to a uniform model. Rather than answering the question who or what provides the unity of practice in Spinoza's *Ethics*, we must instead ask *how the unity functions* according to these criteria. The unity bridging text and context, theory and practice for Spinoza must itself be relational in an at least potentially infinite manner.

Descartes' analytic geometry enabled the rigorous translation of algebraic and geometric relations on the basis of a posited 'unity' of linear magnitude. For Descartes' method the positing of the choice is necessary but the particular choice made remains indifferent. Yet if we follow the line of thought from the analogy above, we must note that the reader of Spinoza's *Ethics* already finds him or herself immersed in a field of cultural, social, political and linguistic particularity, engaged in specific projects and constituted as an individual personality involved in concrete relations. The 'unity' relating text and context is already at least partially given in principle as the set of habitual practices in which any reader of the *Ethics* is already engaged. Yet in its general applicability, the *Ethics* cannot speak to its readers in their concrete singularity but must offer whatever ideas and practices it enfolds in a single, unified way to a general audience.[34] Whatever relation the *Ethics* means to establish between text and context must be expressed in the work's own communicative form. The text of the *Ethics* anticipates and addresses this necessity by casting its themes and arguments according to a particular form of abstraction: the geometrical method, a practical diagram of purely conceptual relations.

Demonstrating Geometrical Order: Spinoza's Diagrammatic Method

The *Ethics* presents itself to its readers in geometrical order, an order at once programmatic and hermeneutic. To a significant extent it is this presentational form of definitions and axioms, propositions and demonstrations borrowed from Euclid's *Elements* that unifies the five main parts of the *Ethics* and the passages from one part to the next.[35] Interpreting the *Ethics* accurately requires following and understanding the various series of progressive demonstrations with diligence and care. Indeed, the *Ethics*' geometrical order appears both to indicate and to typify the kind of thinking which Spinoza understands to possess 'the power of ordering and connecting the affections of the body according to the order of the intellect', the very power of reason.[36]

The geometrical order has two sides. On the one hand it serves as a genre of philosophical presentation, a way of communicating ideas and their logical relations.[37] In this respect the geometrical order or method may be distinguished from other forms of philosophical presentation, such as those developed in the ancient and medieval schools and those in general use today: dialogues, lectures, essays, articles, dissertations, all the various genres of philosophical saying.[38] One way the geometrical order is unusual among these other alternatives is in its degree of apparent depersonalisation. In distinction from the *pro* and *contra* method of Scholastic disputation, for example, which presumes distinctly opinionated individuals or at least points of view, a Euclidean proof does not weigh two sides of an argument, but rather arrives at demonstration through purely ideal constructions whose possibility and validity remain independent in principle of any particular mind. Such constructions are enabled by formal deductive steps taken from clearly defined terms, posited axioms and the set of theorems already proven at any given stage, a set of constructive resources that continues to grow as new theorems become available. Since the original definitions and axioms are not themselves derived logically, but are simply posited as such, the only internal criteria available for such systems are derivability and consistency.[39] What motivates Spinoza to cast his *Ethics* in this self-contained and impersonal manner?

The answer appears by way of indicating the second side of the geometrical order – not the order of presentation itself but the order of intelligible relations that the presentation is meant to manifest in and for its readers. In both Spinoza and Euclid the fixing of terms and axiomatic rules for constructing theorems appears to eliminate the role of the author as an independent mind, one individual communicating to others. The truths expressed in the propositions are – assuming the demonstration is valid – straightforward logical relations independent of the form of their expression and not in themselves subject to dispute. Surely someone had to write the text before us which we ascribe to Euclid, yet once its demonstrations are correctly understood, the very form of the text effaces any authoritative value we might ascribe to that singular name.[40] More generally, the status of authority in Euclidean proof takes an interesting shape: on the one hand no claim to authority is made in the conventional sense – at no point does Euclid refer to any external legitimating authority (history, scripture, common sense) and in this respect the validity of the theorems is to be found nowhere outside of the demonstrations themselves. Yet on the other hand, this very freedom from external authority is enacted in the imperative mood, not the indicative – Euclid's reader becomes convinced of the truth of the theorems by 'letting' the demonstrations prove themselves. The actual geometrical demonstrations are inseparable in this way from series of commands to construct diagrams of relations either in some material substrate such as ink on paper or in the pure imagination: 'Draw a line perpendicular to AB at C', 'Let there be a circle of radius R', 'Extend AB to infinity'.

Thus to follow Euclid's reasoning is to see and thereby directly to understand the necessity of his conclusions by taking the same series of constructive and deductive steps in the order given programmatically by the text. One attains adequate ideas by following determinate instructions and then perceiving the incontrovertible results. Spinoza's text is meant to suggest by its very form that a philosophical ethics may be organised in the same fashion. Spinoza refers to geometrical demonstrations as the 'eyes of the mind, by which it sees and observes things [*mentis . . . oculi, quibus res videt, observatque*]'.[41] By this, Spinoza suggests that diagrammatic demonstrations in the Euclidean sense do not merely lead to an insight, but are that very insight itself. To make this quite clear, consider a common geometrical property, for instance the equality of the sum of the angles of any triangle and that of two right angles. Even to question the possibility of such an equality one must first have conceived the idea of a triangle as such. Yet in adequately conceiving the idea of a triangle one must also have implicitly conceived the necessary logical concomitants of that idea (three vertices, three sides, a bounded figure and so on), these properties being involved necessarily in the concept of any triangle. Included among these many properties is the special property that the sum of the triangle's three angles is necessarily equal to the sum of two right angles. How does one make this necessity explicit? Constructing a diagram in accordance with the demonstration made in Book I, Proposition 32 of Euclid's *Elements* should be sufficient to convince any interested reader.[42] In general, diagrammatic demonstrations of this kind make such implicit yet necessary consequences both vivid and clear, and a valid demonstration of this sort is thus a constructive act of the mind that is in the very process of its activity an understanding and affirmation of the truth it discloses.

For Spinoza, this way of proceeding moves contrary to the 'picture-thinking' of representation since the mind's power to affirm or deny the object of its thought cannot be detached from the intrinsically dynamic form of that thought itself, the active evolution of its necessary properties. Spinoza writes, 'We must investigate, I say, whether there is any other affirmation or negation in the mind except that which the idea involves, insofar as it is an idea [. . .] *so that our thought does not fall into pictures.*'[43] And elsewhere, 'For to have a true idea means nothing other than knowing a thing perfectly, *or* in the best way. And of course no one can doubt this unless he thinks *that an idea is something mute, like a picture on a tablet*, and not a mode of thinking, namely, the very [act of] understanding.'[44]

Spinoza's interpreters have disagreed over how seriously to take the *Ethics*' geometrical order as an essential component of its meaning. These readers may be sorted roughly into two camps: those for whom the geometrical order is primarily a formal trapping for philosophical views that could just as well be translated into other idioms without loss; and those for whom the geometrical form of argumentation is inseparable from the *Ethics*' own distinctive philosophical content. The former camp includes figures such as Wolfson who claims in a classic study of Spinoza that one could reconstruct the whole of the *Ethics* by simply cutting up and rearranging the texts of various classical, medieval and early modern thinkers whom Spinoza drew on as sources, with the majority of these fragments coming from but three thinkers: Aristotle, Maimonides and Descartes.[45] More recently Curley follows Wolfson in seeing the geometric treatment of Spinoza's thought as at least partly obscuring the actual historical origins of Spinoza's ideas, in particular his contentious dialogue with his immediate, early modern predecessors, especially Descartes and Hobbes, 'a dialogue the geometric presentation served to conceal, and was, perhaps, partly designed to conceal'.[46]

The second camp includes thinkers such as Gueroult who take the geometrical presentation of the *Ethics* to be essential to Spinoza's thought, not just in form but equally in content.[47] Indeed, for this camp the form or structure of Spinoza's presentation constitutes the very meaning it is meant to convey. Thus in reading Spinoza's text Gueroult himself redoubles Spinoza's method through his own commentary, laying out in a structural manner the paths of deduction as they develop from proposition to proposition. For Gueroult the demonstrations themselves function as genetic ideas, replicating the processes of origination and development intrinsic to their specific objects: God, or substance in Part One, and the Mind, or power of thinking in Part Two.[48] Some philosophers strongly influenced by Marx such as Althusser and Negri – who rightly aim to link Spinoza's metaphysics explicitly with his separate analyses of society and collective power in the *Theologico-Political Treatise* and the unfinished *Political Treatise* – tend also to take this view since the impersonal, scientific rigour of geometrical proof promises to function as a kind of fulcrum for overcoming ideological misconceptions and developing emancipatory forms of thought.[49] For Negri, despite dismissing it at one point as 'fatuous' and 'the price that Spinoza paid to his epoch', the geometrical method nonetheless constitutes 'the methodologically constructed possibility of arranging the totality in propositions without shattering its intrinsic wholeness'.[50] The *Ethics*' geometrical order according to Negri becomes at once a representation and a repetition of the constructive pluralist ontology it describes: 'The causal and productive geometric method is neither unilateral nor unilinear; it corresponds to the versatility that the univocality of being produces.'[51]

What distinguishes the two camps is primarily how the *Ethics* is understood in relation to earlier philosophical and theological traditions. Wolfson and Curley tend to see continuity (albeit dissembled by the form of the text itself) where Althusser and Negri (and to a lesser extent, Gueroult) see rupture or 'anomaly'. What is at stake in the dispute is thus largely a matter of questioning the power of formal abstraction relative to thought's historical production and reception.[52] If the geometrical or demonstrative method is truly no more than a secondary and unnecessary appendage – an extrinsic form – then we as readers remain free to disregard it and to penetrate beyond it to Spinoza's own historically conditioned philosophical views, the real content of the text. But if the demonstrative method is intrinsic to the actual sense of the *Ethics* as a way of thinking at least partially independent of historical and linguistic context, then not only must we attend carefully to its mode of presentation and follow its method in following Spinoza's thought, we must also call into question the presumption that such a work of philosophy functions in the first place to represent and defend philosophical 'views' at all.[53]

In general, as one emphasises the geometrical presentation of the *Ethics*, one necessarily emphasises the practical component of reading the text in a corresponding way. One moves from a disputational or dialogical model of philosophy to one closer to the formal deductive systems arising well after Spinoza, like those in twentieth-century logic which are at heart mathematical. At its limit, such a view would deny that Spinoza's text has any relevant linguistic or referential content at all but is instead simply a set of formal operations and the relations they constitute. If the formal deductive method were to be entirely abstracted from its concrete instantiation in the *Ethics* as that text has come down to us, then nothing would warrant linking the method to any of the specific discursive contents of the *Ethics* at all. Spinoza's thought would become an attempt merely to indicate a pure method saying nothing, a deductive programme devoid of linguistic sense, a pure geometrical order without figure or form.[54] Rather than a set of philosophical judgements subject to discussion and debate, the *Ethics* on this reading would be something like a complex formal algorithm, expressible most nearly as a formal language. We will see how Hvidtfelt Nielsen develops such an approach to the *Ethics* in some detail below.

It should be clear in any case that the *Ethics* as Spinoza wrote it cannot simply be reduced to its geometrical presentation in this fashion. Critics of a strictly geometrical, demonstrative or deductive reading of the *Ethics* are quick to point out that Spinoza's demonstrations do not match the deductive rigour their geometric form would suggest.[55] If Spinoza meant his formal demonstrations to serve as the core method for following his thought, why would he have handled them so freely? There is in addition the undeniable importance of those parts of the text that in no way function within the deductive system proper. Each of Parts Three, Four and Five of the *Ethics* begins with a preface not contained in the text's network of explicit axioms, propositions and demonstrations but pertaining in essential ways to the philosophical meaning of Spinoza's thought. There is also the summarising *Appendix* to Part Four, in which Spinoza presents the conclusions drawn in the previous demonstrations in a more discursive fashion so that they may be 'seen at a glance'. There is as well Spinoza's own admission that the *Ethics* pertains neither to 'medicine' nor to 'logic', both of which need to be developed as supplements to his work.[56] More importantly, Spinoza's frequent and often lengthy 'scholia' – commentaries and digressions from the strictly deductive framework – contain many of his finest insights and most important philosophical claims. To read the *Ethics* merely as a formal deductive system would imply disregarding these sections of the text, and a strictly formalist reading would be forced to ignore them entirely. Outside the geometrically demonstrative framework, they would thus be outside the *Ethics* 'proper'. This implies that there is more in the hermeneutical dimension of Spinoza's text than the merely programmatic dimension of geometrical proof would suggest.

Clearly, a purely formalist reading of the *Ethics* is untenable. But so too is a reading that would ignore the logic of geometrical order entirely and that would reduce its power of formal abstraction entirely to historical and contingent factors. Both sides must be held together despite their tension; the *Ethics* is both a culturally and historically embedded text addressed to situated readers and a formal structure in part irreducible to history. The geometrical order disengages from the person and time of Spinoza, but in order to understand this order in relation to its possible applications in practice, we must look at the concrete context in which Spinoza originally composed his *Ethics*, as well as the relevant features of any context in which it might be applied.

Scholars such as Israel have shown in detail the historical importance of Spinoza for the development of modern European conceptions of reason and freedom.[57] Yet the ideas of Spinoza circulated primarily through second-hand accounts of his theoretical claims, not through first-hand trials of his ethical and practical prescriptions – although it was the ethical consequences that were thought to follow from Spinoza's ideas that especially worried his critics.[58] Even in contemporary scholarship, to the extent that the practical orientation of the *Ethics* is recognised explicitly, Spinoza's geometrical method is often conflated directly with his concept of reason. It remains generally accepted that Spinoza's philosophy at least tends in the direction of the identification of philosophical and mathematical reasoning associated with later Enlightenment rationalists such as Wolff.[59]

Yet recall our earlier reference to Descartes' *Geometry* and the analogy we drew there to the interpretive problem of Spinoza's *Ethics*. The analytic geometry developed by Descartes holds a central place in the development of modern mathematics primarily because of its emphasis on *relation*. This concept remains fundamental both to the objects and the procedures of mathematics. As a popular historian of mathematics puts it:

> We see [analytic geometry] not as a geographic scheme of location or an exercise in blending algebra and geometry or a painless path to Euclidean and more advanced geometries, but as a means of expressing relationships (*relations*, in mathematical terminology) of all kinds and making important deductions about them. This point of view makes analytic geometry the very core of mathematics, since many mathematical subjects – for example, trigonometry,

calculus, 'complex analysis', probability, mathematical statistics, and even one essential part of logic – are theories of general or special relations.[60]

In other words, analytic geometry – the initial frame for Newton's and Leibniz's subsequent development of the calculus – may be seen as the 'very core' of modern mathematics precisely to the extent that it formalises and enacts a logic of relations.

Yet the category of relation is by no means limited to the realm of formal mathematics. Relations may certainly be abstract, merely possible and thoroughly ideal but they are also discernable everywhere as concrete, actual and inescapably real. They respect no fixed limit between the conceptual and the real, and they require a rethinking of the easy identification of what is real with what is seemingly most concrete. In fact, relations are situated within an immanent conceptual 'space' *sui generis* varying continuously across infinite degrees of concreteness and abstraction, singularity and generality. Where are the 'things' such relations relate?

INDIVIDUATION

The philosophy of Spinoza takes the indivisible unity of the whole of nature as its starting-point, its primary hypothesis.[61] This emphasis on unity brings to the point of identity the terms tradition had kept absolutely distinct: God and creation, or nature. The oneness of this single substance is identified in Part One of the *Ethics* with absolute infinity.[62] Consider a spectrum of conceptual determination stretching from pure singularity to perfect generality. Where along the spectrum would this singular concept – the infinite idea of God, or nature – itself fall? At one of the poles? Which pole – the singular or the general? Nature, it seems, would be both singular and general – at both poles at once, embracing the entire spectrum.

In light of the comprehensive unity of nature, how are we to understand the unity of some particular finite thing – a grandfather's tuba, for instance, or some tarantula on a California backroad? What makes such a thing *one* thing, *it itself*? A subject-predicate structure and model of language leads traditionally to an understanding of individual things as distinct substances – *hypostases* – to which qualities and events may be attributed. Yet Spinoza holds that only one substance truly exists – Nature, or God. What we normally consider to be individual things are understood to be *modes*, or affections of this single substance.[63] What is the unity of such a mode? The problem arises at all levels of our hypothetical spectrum. At each stage or degree from the purely singular to the perfectly general we may pose the question of unity anew: what is the unity of the kind or species 'plant' or the concept of a 'living thing' or indeed a 'thing' as such? How would Spinoza understand the individual differences and stratifications within our imagined spectrum? In the unity and continuity of God, or Nature, where and how is discreteness manifest?

The problem of individuation took on new importance in early modern philosophy due to the emergence of a mechanistic conception of bodies and the Cartesian distinction of thinking and extended substances. The philosophical successors to Descartes, Spinoza among them, inherited this problem and addressed it each on his own terms.[64] This problem has engaged Spinoza's commentators as well on a variety of levels – metaphysical,[65] epistemological[66] and political.[67] One concern common to these various strata lies in asking how what constitutes the unity of an individual thing (whether a body, an idea or an essence in general) should be formulated in relation to Spinoza's distinctive conception of the unity of nature as a whole.

Spinoza claims that all individuals 'though in different degrees, are nevertheless animate', but qualifies this claim by interpreting the 'different degrees' of animation as different degrees of power determined by varying capacities to act and perceive.[68] Bodies are animated to a greater or lesser degree as they are capable of doing or experiencing more or fewer things:

> [I]n proportion as a body is more capable than others of doing many things at once, or being acted on in many ways at once, so its mind is more capable than others of perceiving many things at once. And in proportion as the actions of a body depend more on itself alone, and as other bodies concur with it less in acting, so its mind is more capable of understanding distinctly.[69]

On this view a table, for example, does have a soul – its mind or 'idea' – but a table's soul is capable of very few kinds of internally determined action. What a table does is in fact almost entirely exhausted by what is done to it.

What all the various degrees of animation share is how they constitute distinct individuality through the relative motions and affects of their component parts. Spinoza defines an individual as a composite of bodies which 'communicate their motions to each other in a certain fixed manner'. The complete definition is as follows:

> When a number of bodies, whether of the same or of different size, are so constrained by other bodies that they lie upon one another, or if they so move, whether with the same degree or different degrees of speed, that they communicate their motions to each other in a certain fixed manner, we shall say that those bodies are united with one another and that they all together compose one body or individual, which is distinguished from the others by this union of bodies.[70]

The relations of movement and rest among the component parts of this whole, taken together, constitute the essence or 'nature' of the individual in question. The 'manner' of this communication of motions is thus a fundamental component of the individual as such. *How* a body's various parts communicate their motions is a crucial aspect of *what* that thing is, its nature and unity.

The unity of a composite body is thus defined by Spinoza in terms of differential relations that compose it as a singular whole: 'Bodies are distinguished from one another by reason of motion and rest, speed and slowness, and not by reason of substance.'[71] This explains why they are *modes* of one substance and not independent substances themselves. Under the attribute of extension, such modal components are typically manifest as relative trajectories of bodies in space that may or may not affect one another in a variety of ways.

Affective relations are thus a sort of multi-scale ontological glue; in binding modes to one another, they constitute the modes themselves as local systems or parcels of variable relations that affect other such systems in similarly variable yet also partly regular and determinate ways. This progressive 'scaling-up' of individuating relations has no finite limit: 'if we proceed in this way to infinity, we shall easily conceive that the whole of nature is one individual, whose parts, that is, all bodies, vary in infinite ways, without any change of the whole individual'.[72] This is the 'infinite mediate mode' which Spinoza elsewhere calls 'the face of the whole universe'.

To summarise, Spinoza's theory of individuation in the *Ethics* has four essential characteristics. Together, these provide the necessary framework for understanding individual modes as affective diagrams:

(1) Modes are relatively stable systems of relations among component parts. These systems themselves become stable internally when certain of their relations take on a canonical or determinative status with respect to others. Such determining relations are typically 'local equilibria' within some space of possible states.[73]

(2) A duality of determination and indetermination is constitutive of modes as such. No mode can be fully determinate because all of a mode's constituent relations are characterised by variable affordances with at least some degree of elasticity. On the other hand no mode can be fully indeterminate because it would then be independent of all relation and hence a substance, not a mode.

(3) Every mode exists by virtue of being relationally situated vis-à-vis its local environment in an immediately affective way. Existent modes are *actual,* and the relations in which they are embedded at any particular moment are immediately responsible for the increase or decrease of those modes' powers to affect and be affected by other modes. Two consequences follow:

A. Each mode consists of a duality of internal (system) and external (environment) relations.
B. Each mode involves a duality of active (determining) and passive (determined) affects.

(4) Processes of modal individuation are never absolutely discrete, but are always finally determined through the ultimate continuity of nature as a unique substance. Modes are local inflections of a universal relational field, not separate 'things'.[74]

Take note of Figure 1.1. The diagram on the left is meant to suggest in an intuitive way the dynamics of modal consistency. Its arrows represent affective relations, and its dots represent modes individuated at some level of organisation 'lower' than that pictured. Such a distinction of levels or scales is essential to Spinoza's conception

1.1

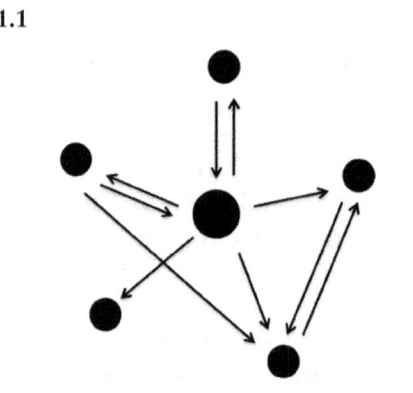
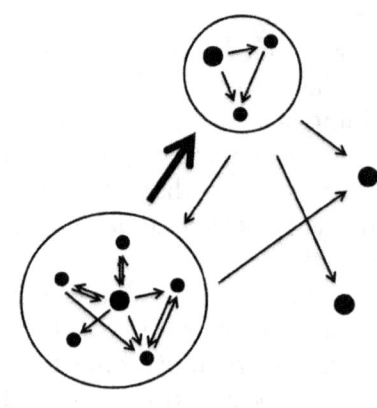

of individuation and its structural dependence on the doctrine of affects.[75] The diagram on the right shows how the mode individuated by the relatively stable affective relations pictured on the left becomes capable by that very process of individuation of entering into higher-order affective relations with other modes. To put it more exactly, it is only in respect to such higher-order relations that the process of individuation at the lower level can even be registered or identified.[76]

Individuation is thus always a matter of degree, never a binary criterion for membership in some special metaphysical kind, 'entities', distinguishable from properties or relations. The question 'how many individuals are there?' is meaningless for Spinoza, or, taken strictly, the answer is simply *one*: God-or-Nature. Anywhere we locate a set of bodies moving together with any degree of regularity – that is, practically anywhere we look or can imagine looking, short of absolute chaos – we are able to identify an individual in Spinoza's sense. The problem of individuation is thus primarily a matter of identifying the continuous 'selective' processes by which sets of relative motions attain relative consistency.

How does a set of component parts *attain* the consistency of a relatively fixed set of motions? How do individuals *become* individuals in any determinate sense? The question of what constitutes an entity can only be answered by indicating the process or event that consolidates or renders consistent a given set of relations of movement into a single, integrated whole *for something else* which they affect and by which they are affected. An individual is such that its component motions are united *for* something other than itself according to some specific way of affecting the latter. In contrast to the dyadic subject-predicate structure of representational judgement, the affective structure in Spinozist individuation involves essentially three term relations: X affects Y in manner Z. Affects are thus intrinsically potentialities or powers.[77] They range in their very essence across a spectrum of possible instances or expressions. See Figure 1.2. The arrow highlighted on the right in Figure 1.1 above is here elaborated as a range of possible relations to a variety of different individuals varying within conditions or affordances intrinsic to the affective relation (the arrow) itself.

In the human sphere, this is the point at which the Spinozist conception of individuation intersects with the phenomenological. In perception and lived experience objects are individuated *for us*. The place where this experience of individuation becomes itself public and communicable is language.[78]

1.2

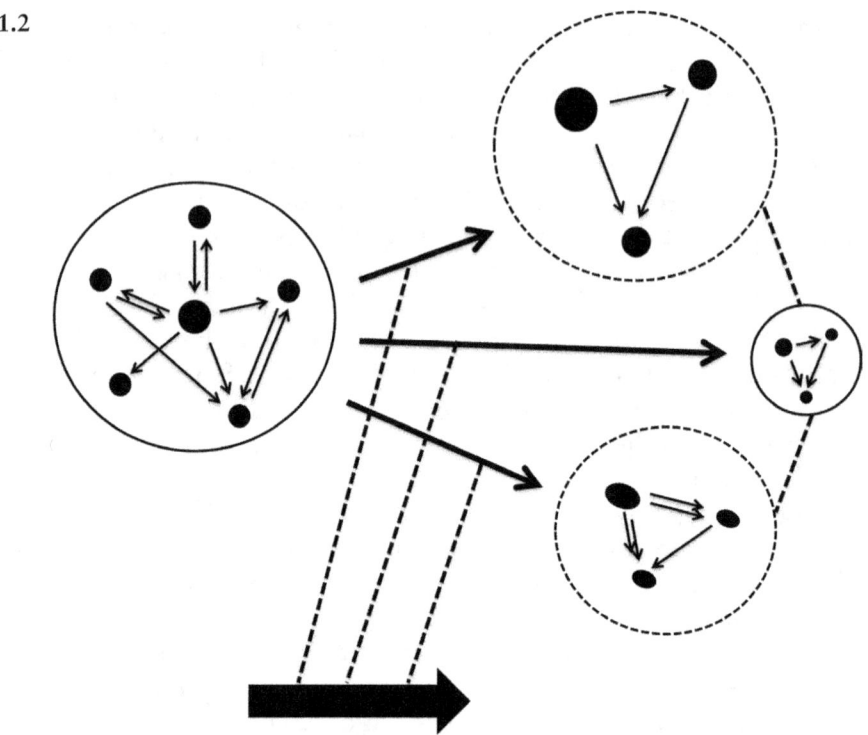

LANGUAGE, AFFECT AND FORM

Unlike the image of thought guided by linguistic representation, a conception of thought like that of Spinoza that thoroughly saturates thinking within the immanence of relationality does not require a constitutive break between the vehicle and the object of thought. On the Spinozist view, language itself is directly relational, as are all forms of experience, perception and knowledge. Yet such worldly relations obviously possess a status distinct from the pure relations investigated by mathematics. In particular, the relations expressed in and through human language are *meaningful* and thus subject to interpretation in a different sense than, say, a theorem of geometry. The context for practical application of the *Ethics* must be understood to include these sorts of meaningful relations as well. One challenge for Spinoza in attempting to link geometrically ordered relations of adequate knowledge to practical or ethical relations in the world is to find a criterion and method by which this linkage itself might be conceived and understood adequately.

Rather than presuming a more or less properly functioning technology of language and text with which to generate and perform philosophy with artfully chosen words, for Spinozist thought it is necessary to work instead at each step of cognition within an immanent framework that is at once both singular and universal and that would thus bypass from the very beginning any necessary reliance on a presupposed mediating level of linguistic or conceptual generality. It is here that Spinoza's relational account of individuation comes to the fore as an explanatory account of language as such. On Spinoza's terms, it is only on the basis of an account of modal individuation as universal, multi-scale, affective relationality that language and linguistic representation may themselves be understood, rather than the reverse.

The problem of language from this point of view is just one slice of the more general question of how individual modes and their affects are able to reside somehow 'between' the singular and the universal. At or very near the pole of singularity along our previously discussed spectrum we encounter some particular, individual thing – a sprig of mint, say, or rather *this* sprig of mint. Simply by identifying such a particular thing *as* belonging to some definite kind, however – as *mint*, in this case – we find we have already moved along our spectrum some minimal degree in the direction of the opposite pole, that of generality. As we are then enveloped or led back in thought to more general kinds (herb→plant→living thing→thing) we approach the pole of maximum generality, where we would expect to find the most general forms of being, or categories.[79]

It is a commonplace that human beings are distinguished from the rest of nature by their collective participation in language: anthropology – the *logos* of 'humankind', or *anthropos* – states a pleonasm. Not only is language the medium of communication *about* all sorts of things, it is also the primary domain in which human individuals are recognised as such; it is in and through participation in language that human beings speak *to* and *for* one another. In the terms of our discussion of individuation we might say that the affect of linguistic communication individuates both human nature as well as the natures of singular human beings. This is not to say that language exhausts or even originates essential humanity, only that language is one very important thing humans do through which we are what we are. In this way we pass from the communication of the motions of the composite parts of bodies and natures in general to the singular problem of communication in the sense of *human language*.

Language is the point where the question of individuation may be asked of 'universals', or general ideas as they arise in contexts of human communication, giving rise to debates that have traditionally been framed in terms of nominalism and realism. Spinoza appears at first sight to be clearly a nominalist. If any two moving bodies can be described by a ratio of motions (for example, the ratio of the vectors corresponding to their velocity and direction) and are thereby considered to be 'communicating' their movements, then any pair of moving bodies chosen at random would constitute an individual. Such individuals and the general types by which they are called would be mere names. Similar cases would hold for any number of bodies, and as a result all possible sets of relations of movements of actual bodies would have to be considered individuals. If communication is thus understood as merely abstract, quantitative relation (*ratio* in the mere sense of a mathematical ratio), then individuation loses any qualitative aspect and becomes simply an arbitrary assemblage of parts. In fact, however, Spinoza has provided a guard against this thoroughly nominalist conception through his doctrine of the affects. The question of whether two or more bodies are truly communicating their movements must be displaced onto the question of whether and how they *actually affect* one another. To genuine affects would then correspond genuine individuals. More importantly, different kinds of communication of movement would thus correspond to discrete and distinguishable affects. Thus the manner in which two or more bodies affect one another corresponds to the *way* they communicate their movements and therefore determines what sort of individual those bodies compose. The reality of distinguishable affects implies and envelops the reality of any structures that might conceptualise those affects or name them. The affects thus absorb and 'immanentise' any transcendent conception of *logos* as an a priori linguistic condition of thought.

Language would in this way be understood in terms of the kinds of affects it makes possible and the affective relations it sustains. We have seen how Spinoza's 'parallel postulate' claims that '[t]he order and connection of ideas is the same as the order and connection of things'.[80] This identification of ideal and material orders makes the problem of linguistic meaning an especially thorny one. The difficulty may be illustrated through the following example: a woman reads. This act of reading constitutes a complex, embodied event. It is a matter of bodies in motion, communicating affects in a variety of ways. She sits at a café on a busy street. She sips her coffee. In one hand she holds a large, blue book. Her eyes scan the page, a rhythmic iteration from left to right in conjunction with a slower movement from top to bottom. The words – differentiated as patterns of black ink on a white page – evoke a series of sounds and images that combine and retroactively charge one another to produce the unity of a complex sense, a meaning *for* or *before* her.

How, on Spinoza's terms, are we to understand the woman's experience of this text's *meaning*? The seeming implication of *Ethics* IIp7 is that if meaning occurs in thought and is thus a complex of ideas, a sufficient description of this event of meaning will necessarily be parallel to a corresponding description of a complex of physical events. Meaning would be reduced to a set of related physical events, or rather identified with those events according to the parallel postulate. Yet our everyday experience of meaning mitigates against this. It is not just that the description is not detailed enough (that we must, for example, go all the way to a description of photons reflecting off the fibres of the page, individual neural firings in the woman's brain, and so on). Rather, what we mean (and experience) in the term 'meaning' would seem to be in principle irreducible to any such description.

Philosophers coming from perspectives as different as Althusser and Nielsen have seen this aspect of Spinoza's thought as a positive opportunity for eliminating or at least minimising the domain of meaning and advancing a consistent philosophical materialism.[81] The elimination of meaning in this way would accompany the elimination of the egoic subject as the ground of thinking. The domain of meaning would be effectively evacuated because the unity of a subject for whom meaning would, precisely, *mean* will have been exchanged for the standpoint of radical immanence. Thought, then, would no longer be the privileged domain of a subject, but rather the unity of an infinite attribute the order and connection of whose parts would be strictly parallel to that of the world of things. In our example, the woman would no longer be thinkable as a 'kingdom within a kingdom'. She would be, rather, a local inflection in a continuous field of material (ideal) relations. Does such a conception entail the annihilation of meaning?

It is important to remember that the relations constituting the field are not themselves objects of possible representation, but are instead actual affects. In Spinoza's thought, the affective mingling of bodies (and the realm of ideas conceived as strictly parallel to this mingling) dissipates every illusion of thought as a mirroring of subject and representation. And it does seem as though the very generality and communicability of meaning would mitigate against any reduction of meaning to absolutely singular affective events. Yet perhaps the problem with our exemplary image of the woman reading is that by its very nature as example it has already fallen under the generalised illusion of representational thought, of presuming that the meaning of a text *and* the representation of that meaning must both somehow be thought-pictures. Surely *something* is present to the woman's mind as the object of her intentional regard, but any implicit theoretical model that already places conditions on what sort of 'something' that object might be tends to beg the question of how thought *actually relates* to what it thinks. In the end, the doctrine of the affects does not preclude representation, but merely circumscribes it and displaces its auto-foundational role in theorising thinking.

In particular, the dynamic character of the affects precludes any neutral, or strictly representational model of textual interpretation. Because ideas for Spinoza are always affective, and the interpretation of a text – like everything else – involves the movement and ordering of ideas, interpretation is itself necessarily affective through and through. Among other things, then, one cannot adequately grasp the meaning of Spinoza's own text without simultaneously recognising the implications of one's very act of interpretation within the meaning thus generated. This self-reflective exigency is something the *Ethics* shares with any text that either implies or explicitly develops a more or less comprehensive theory of meaning or interpretation.[82] Yet the singular strategy of the *Ethics* involves leading any work of interpretation – in particular, the act of reading – back to a dynamic interplay of affects that renders them increasingly rational.

Spinoza ultimately reduces all affects to the three 'primitive' affects of desire, joy and sadness. Because of the universality of the affects, no interpretive method or procedure can be abstracted from the interplay and movement of affective dynamics. Not even a single step in any interpretative process is exempt from this reduction to the affects. Thus a Spinozist mode of reading opens the possibility at every stage to ask the question: What affects are being mobilised at this point in the reading? For Spinoza, the answer will always necessarily be plotted along the three dimensions of desire, joy and sadness and the multitude of affects generated through combinations and interactions of these. These are not rational foundations, but component vectors of a real space of relational becoming. Rationality, for Spinoza, consists of gradients of increasingly active relationality along pathways through this affective space (transitions from passive to active affects). Such gradients of affective power *explain* linguistic reason, or *logos*, as a special case rather than requiring explanation in terms of the latter.

Consider the demand for logical consistency. Apparent contradictions in meaning between two parts or phases of a single text (or often separate texts by a single author) are cause for displeasure, even a kind of righteous indignation in careful readers. Indeed, much contemporary philosophical work consists in demanding consistency from canonical and authoritative texts, and policing those texts for logical inconsistencies. This highly ritualised process of assertion and critique takes place against the background of a presupposition that is usually taken for granted to the point of becoming practically invisible – the presupposition that consistency is somehow philosophically *required*, that a self-contradictory text ought necessarily in this respect to be devalued. But why without begging the question should we demand consistency of an argument or text at all?

A Spinozist analysis of reading calls such presuppositions into question and renders them potentially explainable on the basis of investigating the actual affects deployed in any singular case or across some discernable class of cases. In Spinoza's view any interpretive criterion that actually functions in any specific context however broad or narrow, even one as apparently basic as simple logical consistency, must be understood through its singular affective connections always traceable back to those of desire, joy and sadness. Thus texts and the varied processes of reading are taken out of a strictly representational framework and brought back to the individually and collectively affective contexts within which they circulate. Meanings no longer serve as representational contents, but are rather active strivings and dynamic passages *for* individuals (which are just relatively local collectivities) and collectivities (which are just relatively regional individuals). Therefore, to return to the example, the criterion of logical consistency is inseparable from – indeed for Spinoza, strictly identical to – the ensemble of affects it engenders: the pleasure of seeing ideas cohere, the conviction aroused in a listener, the smugness of a pat argument, the interpretive frustration in the face of manifest contradiction, and a potentially infinite list of others.

It would be mistaken, however, to see this turn to the affects as something like a mere psychologisation of logic or a cheap reduction of logical criteria to mere feeling. The affective interpretation of logical consistency, for example, does not *reduce* consistency to affect but rather understands logical consistency in terms of its intrinsic relation to possible ways of affecting and being affected by texts, arguments and so forth in practical ways across multiple situations. Whatever logical principle of validity is contained in the demand for consistency, for the *unity* of thoughtful expression, that principle itself is manifest only in and through the specific affective relations it engenders for individuals and collectivities, from private readers of Spinoza's *Ethics*, say, to communities as general as those of 'rational language-users'.

It must be remembered that for Spinoza affects always correspond to transitions in some particular essence's power to act. For Spinoza, all bodies, and especially bodies as affectively complex as human beings, are in constant flux, becoming more powerful and active in certain respects while being inhibited and weakened in others. Thus language itself must be understood as a dynamic field of real relations both empowering and enfeebling human beings in countless ways across innumerable contexts.[83] On the basis of such an understanding, the sense of *philosophical language* in particular becomes transformed. How philosophy is communicated must be integrated into both the idea of what philosophy is and the sense of what it says.

How, on this basis, should we interpret the *Ethics* itself and the affects it mobilises? What happens when we examine Spinoza's own text from the standpoint of language and individuation just given? Following Spinoza's own methods, the distinction between natural language and logical form comes to the fore, a dimension of Spinoza's thought in which rhetoric and logic are problematically and interestingly entwined. In the present context, conceiving of language in terms of affective, signifying relations between individuals who are themselves essentially, or naturally relational helps us to understand Spinoza's writings themselves as linguistic texts that nevertheless work practically to reorient language towards its intrinsically formal dimension.

It is helpful here to turn to the interpretation of Spinoza advanced in Nielsen's detailed study, *Interpreting Spinoza's Arguments*.[84] According to Nielsen, Spinoza's geometrical order of presentation and his affective-materialist conception of language work together to transform natural language use itself into the *mimesis* of a formal language. Nielsen's reading of linguistic practice in the *Ethics* finds in the text's logical form a kind of ethical prototype that anticipates the formal systems of logic developed by later analytic philosophers. Notable is Nielsen's reduction of this logic to *practice*. Nielsen understands Spinoza's use of the geometrical method as an attempt to produce within an inherited Scholastic Latin vocabulary something akin to the formal deductive systems that were only to emerge much later in the early twentieth century and that have become ever more sophisticated up to our current day. For Nielsen, Spinoza's aim in producing a deductive system was to pass from the ambiguities inherent within conventional language to the unqualified, formal certainties of logic. Thus, Nielsen's abstraction of a formal method from the *Ethics* provides a thoroughgoing critique of the linguistic form of the *Ethics* itself. In Nielsen's view, '[Spinoza's] usage was meant to help readers escape being trammeled by their ordinary verbal meanings (affects), and so to enable them to undertake the attempt at thinking along the same deductive lines as Spinoza thought he had been following in his writing.'[85]

Yet Nielsen emphasises that Spinoza is not only producing a formal logic, but intends by means of this logic to be able to reach scientific truths about the actual world. Formal truth and referential truth must thus somehow coincide, despite Spinoza's distinction between true and adequate ideas. Nielsen writes:

> Spinoza had to solve two problems. Besides discarding ordinary usage, he also had to provide referents for his theory of mind. He tried to solve the first problem by turning his Latin into a predecessor of a formal system. The second problem he believed would disappear the moment one would realize (and utilize) the concurrence of logic and science. Whenever usage is logical it will, simply by its being so, enable users to speak (and think) of real existing physical events.[86]

This coincidence of logical form and epistemological reference is supposed to be guaranteed both by the parallel postulate and by the doctrine of the common notions. Thus, Nielsen sees Spinoza as presenting a form of logical realism – logical and natural truths straightforwardly coincide. To think according to the formal demands of logic is necessarily to come to correct conclusions about actual states of affairs.

For Nielsen, formal logic empowers its users to critique and modify their linguistic practices, particularly the ways they relate linguistic utterances to specific meanings. Nielsen views Spinoza's overall method as a self-reflective process through which the pre-critical use of meanings becomes thoroughly sceptical. Thus students of formal logic would 'conceive of verbal meanings, not as objects to be understood, but as transitions in our mental dispositions'.[87]

To make sense of this, Nielsen shows how Spinoza's *Ethics* deals with language on two distinct levels. It provides, first and foremost, a unique theory of mind in which linguistic meanings must be construed according to Spinoza's doctrine of ideas. Nielsen calls this the 'essential part' of Spinoza's notion of language, distinguishing from this a conception of linguistic usage or practice that he calls a 'minor part'.[88] These two levels of meaning and usage interact at the heart of the argumentative structure of the text of the *Ethics* itself. Nielsen thus reads the *Ethics* as an endlessly self-deconstructing text.[89]

> On the basis of the theory of meaning and that of usage, a theory of verbal meaning may be constructed according to which natural language meanings come out as initerable and affective events. Applying this result to *Ethica* itself, a text of a, once, very natural language, would make what *Ethica* might mean an ever changing subject inaccessible to reason (cognition).[90]

In other words, by taking the *Ethics* to be a kind of formal, interpretive operation that converts natural language meanings into unrepeatable, affective events and by then treating the text of the *Ethics* itself as the object of this same operation, the 'meaning' of the *Ethics* dissolves into a series of discontinuous and self-contradictory happenings. The *Ethics* thus becomes a complex version of the 'liar's paradox' in which an inhabitant of Crete exclaims that all Cretans are liars, although at a practical rather than theoretical level.

If this were the last word in interpreting the *Ethics*, then we would be left with a thoroughgoing scepticism with respect to its practical sense. Yet Nielsen does not use this as an argument against the cogency of Spinoza's argument. Instead, he sees this paradox – and Spinoza's own recognition of it – as the root cause of Spinoza's use of the geometrical method of demonstration as the form of his reasoning. Because Spinoza was aware of the inevitable ambiguities of natural language and was striving for the kind of knowledge represented by mathematics and exact physical science, Nielsen argues, he embedded his natural language assertions in a complex and self-critical logical structure that undoes natural language meaning at every step. In this way even while the natural language 'sense' of the text negates itself, the *Ethics*'s logical form remains intact and indeed positively and progressively infiltrates the cognitive practices of its careful readers somewhat as sketched in Figure 1.3. Nielsen writes,

1.3

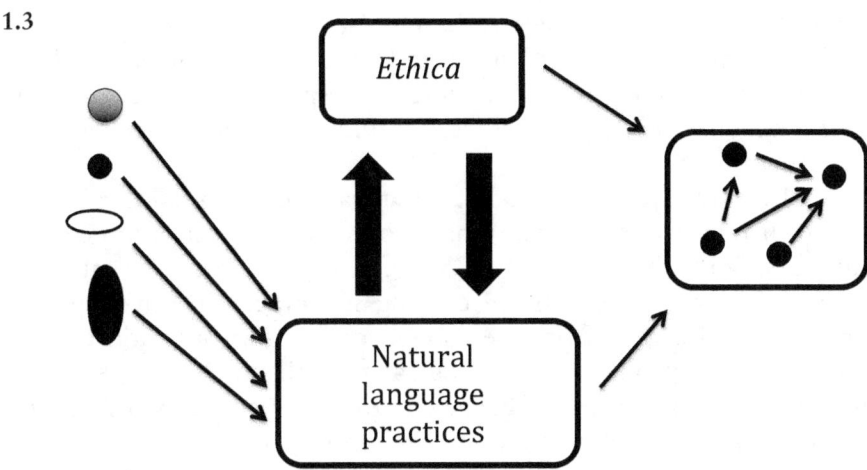

> In my opinion, Spinoza clearly realized this implication of applying the theory of *Ethica* to *Ethica* itself as a text of natural language. He was aware of the self-defying nature of his theory, but believed that he could counteract it by installing in the Latin of his text the semblance of a logical structure.[91]

The logical structure Nielsen refers to is not simply the axiomatic-deductive system that Spinoza borrows from Euclid. It is, more importantly, the self-referential logic that allows the *Ethics* to refer to its own natural language practices at the same time that it undermines them. Nielsen goes on to remark that '[Spinoza's] idea was brilliant, but [. . .] the logic of the time was not ripe for his design.'[92]

According to Nielsen a proper reading of Spinoza's *Ethics* from the standpoint of its own theory of meaning is directed teleologically towards overcoming meaning as such. In Nielsen's view, only the well-formed and logically precise statements of science are capable of being used in a rational (and repeatable) way without attributing meanings to those statements:

> If the acts of ordinary verbal meaning are inherently initerable – as I believe they are – then obviously we cannot make them iterable without thereby changing them into something which cannot be verbal meaning anymore. But what we can do is use our acts of verbal meaning as gradual preparations for one day dispensing with verbal meanings altogether.[93]

In Nielsen's view, Spinoza was motivated by the desire to produce a formal system along the lines of contemporary second-order symbolic logic, and while the *Ethics* itself is not adequate to that desire, we as later readers benefiting from the developments in logic over the past three and a half centuries (especially the last hundred years) may be able to reconstruct an *Ethics* closer in fact to Spinoza's own intentions.

Nielsen's analysis reveals the practical mechanism in Spinoza's text (self-reflective scepticism) that produces the effect of impersonal discourse and impels both logical formalisation and a negation of ordinary language use. In evacuating meaning, Nielsen's Spinoza abstracts philosophy from the context of interpersonal address and response. The problem is that logical formalism – while generated initially out of a natural language context – appears capable of transcending that context to the point of annulling it.

Nielsen's study reveals something interesting and important about the mixture of natural language meaning and formal structure in the *Ethics*. His analysis shows that a basic incongruity holds between the two domains, and more importantly it traces how this incongruity is demonstrated or performed in the text itself by referring the text's meaning in part to the logical structure that frames it and by taking the text's logical structure as operative on the natural language meanings that it frames. Yet Nielsen never conceives Spinoza's project in terms of its own concrete initerability, in particular its momentous contributions to transformations in the actual cultural and historical field within which Spinoza himself worked.

Whether or not Nielsen's reading is ultimately successful, we must stress the limits within which his reading moves. Nielsen's bias is that of the formal logician for whom logical rigour is a basic criterion and goal. As a frame for his entire analysis Nielsen explicitly limits himself to the second kind of knowledge, claiming 'We want no truck with infinity, nor any other merely abstract entities; neither could we afford one, lest we jeopardize the whole idea of our investigation.'[94] To repeat, the 'whole idea' of Nielsen's investigation is to find in Spinoza's *Ethics* a mode of practical understanding that would escape the equivocal senses of everyday language. In short, Nielsen brackets the infinite at the same time and with the same gesture by which he brackets the singularly concrete (the 'initerable'). Both are a function of the ambiguities of natural language meanings. What Nielsen demonstrates with extraordinary rigour in his study (and the detail of his analysis can scarcely be indicated here) is that a formalist reading of the practical logic (language as use) inherent in the *Ethics* can be both consistent with Spinoza's text and highly relevant to current debates concerning the rigorous use of symbol systems in scientific practice when restricted to this domain. Yet to limit oneself to what Spinoza calls the second kind of knowledge (adequate but merely general ideas) is to limit oneself to only part of the *Ethics*. Spinoza's text also refers to and makes use of the third kind of knowledge, and it is precisely here that a wedge may already be inserted into the apparently formal and logical closure of Spinoza's text.

Spinoza's third kind of knowledge

In early 1678, less than a year after Spinoza's death, a coterie of his friends published and distributed his *Opera Posthuma* with the *Ethics* included, the author's identity indicated only by the initials 'B. D. S.'.[95] With this act, the *Ethics*, the culminating product of decades of Spinoza's solitary thinking, intensive study and dialogue with others – the three primary foci of his intellectual life – passed beyond the limits of his own immediate world and became part of a larger cultural and intellectual heritage.[96] Today Spinoza is read and discussed in dozens of languages throughout the world. In the passage from the personal, individual and regionally limited to the public, historical and globally connected we may recognise a familiar figure of the modern notion of reason. Seen in light of the subsequent developments of philosophy, Spinoza's work may appear as a constitutive factor in the turn to such a view of modern reason. Is this image of reason valid? Is it applicable to Spinoza's *Ethics*?

As we have already seen, the ethical consequences of Spinoza's thought appear first of all as a problem implicated in the very form of Spinoza's discourse. The way Spinoza's text presents itself to be read implies certain specific interpretive practices. This is evident particularly in the system of axioms, definitions and theorems that constitute the *Ethics*' 'geometrical order'. The form of the *Ethics* implies an ethics of interpretation.

The interpretive practices entailed by the *Ethics*' discursive form are closely linked to Spinoza's notion of reason, 'the power of the intellect'.[97] For Spinoza, reason entails freedom. Part Five of the *Ethics*, according to Spinoza's preface, 'concerns the means, *or* way leading to freedom', a path he outlines in an exposition of the intellect's power over the affects and an examination of 'what kind of dominion it has for restraining and moderating them'.[98] It is important that this dominion of the intellect over the affects is by no means absolute.[99] The practice of reason takes place always in a shifting context of affective life and contingent events. While reason may develop general principles of conduct on the basis of experience and inference, the practical application of reasonable principles remains contingent upon the specifics of individual cases.[100] This is clear from Spinoza's discussion of maxims from later in Part Five:

> The best thing, then, that we can do, so long as we do not have perfect knowledge of our affects, is to conceive a correct principle of living, *or sure maxims of life* [*certa vitae dogmata*], to commit them to memory, and to apply them constantly to the particular cases frequently encountered in life. In this way our imagination will be extensively affected by them, and we shall always have them ready.[101]

The role of Spinoza's *Ethics* as a whole may be understood as that of a complex maxim of this type, and the problems involved in its interpretation and application need to be understood accordingly. The use of general maxims in handling particular cases recalls the Aristotelian problem of *phronesis*.[102] As Aristotle recognises, the philosophical investigation of ethics 'does not aim at theoretical knowledge' since ethics is by nature oriented towards something other than knowing a subject matter. Ethics is a matter of practical self-transformation: 'we are inquiring not in order to know what virtue is, but in order to become good'.[103] In this regard, any discursive presentation of ethics is confronted with a kind of paradox: what is said is typically general; what is done is always singular. Aristotle recognises the difficulty of providing a theoretical account of particular practices, 'for they do not fall under any art or precept but the agents themselves must in each case consider what is appropriate to the occasion, as happens also in the art of medicine or of navigation'.[104] Even a philosophy that posits or produces theoretical certainties still finds itself irremediably unsure in confronting the contingencies of practice.

The *Ethics* must be applied, and the means of application are themselves part of the subject matter of ethics as a mode of philosophy. How are we to conceive of a mode of relation comprehending both the specific interpretive difficulties of Spinoza's text and the problem of practical application in general? By examining the problem of language and signification under the aegis of Spinoza's immanent and relational ontology, we have been led naturally to a broadly pragmatic conception of signs and meaning. Epistemology in Spinoza is integrated into ontology, and knowledge is always a matter of power and processes of individuation. Conversely, for Spinoza, ontology is essentially epistemic. What *is*, precisely in the degree and amplitude of its being, *knows*.

In Part Two of the *Ethics*, Spinoza distinguishes three kinds of human cognition, or knowledge (*cognitio*).[105] What differentiates the three kinds is the manner in which they are formed or received by the mind. The first kind of knowledge arises either (1) 'from singular things which have been represented to us through the senses in a way which is mutilated, confused, and without order for the intellect', which Spinoza calls 'knowledge from random experience'; or (2) 'from signs, for example, from the fact that, having heard or read certain words, we recollect things, and form certain ideas of them, like those through which we imagine the things'.[106] Either of these sources leads to potentially faulty judgements which Spinoza designates with two names, *opinion* and *imagination*. The second kind of knowledge, in contrast to the first, arises 'from the fact that we have common notions and adequate ideas of the properties of things'.[107] This Spinoza calls *reason*. Finally, the third kind of knowledge 'proceeds from an adequate idea of the formal essence of certain attributes of God to the adequate knowledge of the essence of things'.[108] Spinoza's name for this highest sense of knowledge is *intuitive knowledge*.[109]

The basic sense of Spinoza's first and second kinds of knowledge is clear enough. To know that Ulaan Bataar is the capital of Mongolia because the atlas says so and to act on that knowledge – say, to buy an airline ticket with the intention of travelling there – is to follow the first kind of knowledge. To understand gravity by investigating the common properties of falling bodies or to comprehend a general theorem of geometry is to know according to the second kind of knowledge. The sense of the third kind of knowledge is less clear.[110] When do we as knowers 'proceed from an adequate idea of the formal essence of certain attributes of God to the adequate knowledge of the essence of things', and in what sense would this knowledge be *intuitive*? Despite its initial appearance in Part Two, the third kind of knowledge plays no explicit role in the *Ethics* until it reappears in Part Five. There, in the context of Spinoza's discussion of active freedom, immortality and the 'intellectual love of God', the third kind of knowledge appears in the following affirmation: 'The greatest striving of the mind, and its greatest virtue is understanding things by the third kind of knowledge.'[111] In other words, the third kind of knowledge would constitute a maximum for the mind's desire and its power. The sense of this maximum is then explicated as a relation between the unique essences of singular things and the singular *idea Dei*. In any case, it is clear that the difference between the second and the third kinds of knowledge is relevant to Spinoza's discussion primarily (if not solely) in Part Five where Spinoza provides his image of human freedom and offers his view on human immortality. Evaluation of the third kind of knowledge usually goes hand in hand with how these issues are interpreted and understood.

In Part Five of the *Ethics*, after having clarified the famous third kind of knowledge which manifests 'the greatest striving of the mind, and its greatest virtue',[112] Spinoza shows that in so far as this third kind of knowledge provides knowledge of singular things, rather than rational generalities, it provides especially powerful ways of affecting the mind. In proposition 36, we read:

> The mind's intellectual love of God is the very love of God by which God loves himself, not insofar as he is infinite, but insofar as he can be explained by the human mind's essence, considered under a species of eternity [*sub specie aeternitatis*]; that is, the mind's intellectual love of God is part of the infinite love by which God loves himself.[113]

The point to stress is that Spinoza makes a distinction here between God's self-love *as infinite* and God's self-love 'insofar as he can be explained by the human mind's essence'. Only the latter is accessible to and realisable by the finite intellect. The finite intellect participates in God's own self-love by means of the third kind of knowledge – the 'intellectual love of God [*amor intellectualis Dei*]'. This form of knowledge knows singular things *sub specie aeternitatis,* that is, it knows them not as possible or merely represented, but as actually and singularly existing and therefore, by means of God's essence as the necessary cause of all that exists, as necessary in God. Spinoza makes this clear in the demonstration of proposition 30. There he writes:

> Eternity is the very essence of God insofar as this involves necessary existence (by ID8). To conceive things under a species of eternity, therefore, is to conceive things insofar as they are conceived through God's essence, as real beings, *or* insofar as through God's essence they involve existence.

'Knowledge through singular things' would seem to suggest a discrete subject knowing discrete, particular objects, but by using the context of Part Two of the *Ethics* to refigure here the apparent meanings of Part Five, this phrase comes to stand for an immediate and active knowledge through the affects by which one has been individualised. *Scientia intuitiva* is not the intellectual cognition of an intelligible object, but rather the affection of active and communicative relations with other individuals. The third kind of knowledge is the very act of becoming a (relative) individual in and through certain kinds of relations. The passage into modes of relationality 'conceived through God's essence' constitutes the third kind of knowledge.

Spinoza makes clear that knowledge of the third kind – intuition through singular things – is to be cultivated by the wise person even above knowledge of the second kind, or reason (which is itself universally true and indubitable). General reason – due to its necessity and thus its power to resist transitory affections – can provide the source for relatively strong affects.[114] Yet the third kind of knowledge is even more powerful and therefore more excellent. Spinoza shows 'how much the knowledge of singular things I have called intuitive, *or* knowledge of the third kind (see IIP40S2), can accomplish, and how much more powerful it is than the universal knowledge I called knowledge of the second kind'.[115] In a remarkable moment of textual self-reflection, Spinoza uses his own treatise as an example:

> For although I have shown generally in Part I that all things (and consequently the human mind also) depend on God both for their essence and their existence, nevertheless, that demonstration, though legitimate and put beyond all chance of doubt, still does not affect our mind as much as when this is inferred from the very essence of any singular thing which we say depends on God.[116]

In other words, knowledge of generality cannot affect us as powerfully as knowledge through singularity. Importantly, such singularity must be instantiated directly in concrete relations. It can only be indirectly mediated by the representational powers of language that always generate the appearance of separating what words are from what they do. For similar reasons, singularity cannot be formalised adequately in any system of merely general relations. There is no illustrative example of such a singularity outside of a determinate function in a determinate context that is knowable only from within that context – in this case, Spinoza's own treatise. This would apply first of all to the interpretation of the *Ethics* itself. It has the structure of an immanent sign. Despite Spinoza's own disparaging remarks about using signs, the third kind of knowledge involves semiotic functioning.[117]

Although the knowledge gained in Part One of the *Ethics* concerning the nature of God is beyond doubt, it remains only knowledge of the second kind and its affective power for particular human beings is relatively limited. Any reader of the *Ethics* – or community of readers – will understand the text primarily as signifying a set of interrelated claims. After having passed through the analyses of the affects in Part Two, however, and having come to understand the bondage of inadequate ideas and the liberatory and active power of adequate ideas in Parts Four and Five, the readers of the *Ethics* have – it can be hoped – begun to relate the general truths of Part One to their present circumstances. They will have internalised the truth of Part One in so far as it pertains to the activities of their own essence. In the case of a community, this essence involves particularly the ways and means they communicate. The affective power of *this* knowledge will be significantly stronger than knowledge of the second kind because its associative resonance for a particular mode is so much greater. It puts the *Ethics* in a role of correction, not origin.

By explicitly including the third kind of knowledge as a component of the *Ethics*, Spinoza challenges from within the seemingly totalising logic of a book (or a method) that would say (or do) *everything*. With the recognition of the third kind of knowledge, Spinoza acknowledges the limits of his own text. Or, if one prefers, the text calls itself into question by indicating an even more powerful potential. Only by entering into contingent relations with the ideas and practices of separate individuals is the *Ethics* capable of engendering the third kind of knowledge. By holding room for a level of knowledge (and experience) that is neither in conflict with the general truths of the second kind of knowledge nor reducible to them, Spinoza's text remains communicatively open. Rather than simply reiterating a universal logic, it also holds itself accountable to unforeseeable communication with other discourses.

Garrett interprets the third kind of knowledge in terms of Spinoza's geometrical method and the inferentialism it implies.[118] The Euclidean method of geometrical proof constantly uses inferences that may be drawn from the construction of geometrical figures. A circle, for example, may be defined as the set of points in a plane equidistant from a given point. Yet this description – more precisely, this construction – necessarily implies other properties that may not be immediately apparent (such as the property that given any two straight, intersecting line-segments the endpoints of which are on the circle and which do not pass through the circle's centre, the line-segments will not bisect one another).[119] Some of these properties may be counter-intuitive and surprising. Only by carefully following the steps of the relevant proof does the entailment of the property by the original construction become apparent. One of the pleasures of geometry is coming to understand how numerous and complex are the properties implied by even the simplest geometrical forms. In an analogous fashion, Garrett reads Spinoza as saying that 'the transition toward the third kind of knowledge is the recognition of how our minds are eternal in and through what follows from them'.[120] For Garrett, the structure of the *Ethics* itself is irregular, with 'certain crucial ideas' having greater weight and value than others, particularly the 'idea of God' [*idea Dei*].[121] These salient ideas are rich with implications and entailments. In them are consolidated and condensed (Spinoza uses the verb *involvere*) many other ideas and the various series of consequences following from them. For Garrett the third kind of knowledge would consist in an intuition of the implicit consequences of our ideas, consequences that may not be apparent immediately. The third kind of knowledge would involve comprehending in a practical manner how effects are generated out of causes in the form of entailments made explicit through relational constructions – diagrams – and how, in particular, such consequences are entailed by the ideas that compose our own minds. To think according to the third kind of knowledge would be to enact and to understand the singular effects of our ideas and simultaneously to understand ourselves through the diagrammatic effects our ideas and actions imply.

Read on the basis of the third kind of knowledge, the *Ethics* is thus transformed from a representational and explanatory system, a theoretical model of everything that is, to a pragmatic tool, a corrective instrument of thought and practice. Here the therapeutic dimension of Spinoza's text comes to the fore. Singular forms of thought and practice may *use* the *Ethics* (or rather, the forms of thought it entails) to clarify and correct themselves relationally. The geometrical method of presentation indicates a clear direction for expounding philosophy in a practical and immanently relational mode, but in Spinoza's own text it is perhaps not yet a methodological tool fully adequate to its purpose. Spinoza's is a diagrammatic metaphysics that still at least partly seeks its most effective expression.

Notes

1. Benedict Spinoza, *Ethics* Ia6, IId4. Spinoza clarifies: 'I say intrinsic to exclude what is extrinsic, namely, the agreement of the idea with its object', E IId4, exp. All citations from the *Ethics* – hereafter abbreviated 'E' – are from Edwin Curley's translation, with the standard form of reference to Spinoza's text by part number in Roman numerals, 'a', 'd', 'p' and so on to represent 'axiom', 'definition', 'proposition' and then final number.
2. E IIp49. Ultimately for Spinoza '[t]he will and intellect are one and the same'. E IIp49c. Michael Della Rocca has analysed this proposition in detail, particularly with respect to the divergences it implies from Descartes' thinking, in 'The Power of an Idea: Spinoza's Critique of Pure Will'.
3. E III, preface.
4. Yirmiyahu Yovel writes of the geometrical order as a 'metaphor' in this sense. See *Spinoza and Other Heretics*, vol. I, pp. 139–40.
5. Ludwig Wittgenstein, *Philosophical Investigations*, part I #109, p. 47.
6. Although the theme of essence and existence is an especially subtle one in Spinoza, I take the discussion in E Ip11 to be definitive: 'a thing necessarily exists if there is no reason or cause which prevents it from existing'. Essentially, Spinoza reduces existential modality to the binary necessary/impossible and reserves *essence* as an incommensurable category irreducible to the possible, like Deleuze's later concept of the *virtual*. A clear and relatively thorough analysis of the relevant conceptual issues is provided in Valtteri Viljanen, *Spinoza's Geometry of Power*.
7. This reading is thus contrary to Michael Della Rocca's emphasis on the Principle of Sufficient Reason in his *Spinoza*. A careful study of the problem of freedom and necessity in Spinoza appears in Henri Atlan, *Sparks of Randomness*, especially vol. 1, ch. 2 and vol. 2, chs 4 and 6.
8. E Id6.
9. The phrase '*omnis determinatio est negatio*' is in fact a misquote by G. W. F. Hegel taken from Spinoza's letter to Jelles (letter 50 in the *Complete Works*) that Hegel uses to critique Spinoza in his *Lectures on the History of Philosophy*, vol. 3, p. 267.
10. The best general introductions to Spinoza's metaphysics in English are Harry Wolfson, *The Philosophy of Spinoza*, 2 vols (published together); Stuart Hampshire, *Spinoza and Spinozism*; Edwin Curley, *Behind the Geometrical Method*; Jonathan Bennett, *A Study of Spinoza's Ethics*; and Michael Della Rocca, *Spinoza*.
11. I have preserved the idiosyncratic capitalisation from the Latin contents page. The standard scholarly edition of the *Ethics* in Latin is that of Gebhardt. I have used the Gebhardt edition as it appears alongside

the French translation of Pautrat in *Ethique* (Paris: Seuil). References to Spinoza's Latin throughout the following are drawn from this edition. I have preserved the ampersands but not the dropped s's from the Gebhardt typography.
12. E Ip1–p15.
13. E Ip16.
14. E Ip33.
15. E IIp48.
16. E IIp49s(iv).
17. In this way the discussion of common notions in Part Two (E IIp37–p39) functions as a kind of prolepsis of Part Three and the succeeding parts.
18. See E IIIp11s and the summary of definitions of the affects at the end of Part Three.
19. E IV preface.
20. E Vp14–p36. We will examine the intellectual love of God, or 'third kind of knowledge', at the close of the present chapter.
21. Zourabichvili refers to this as Spinoza's 'strategy of the chimera'. Spinoza's rhetorical strategy in this regard is analysed more fully in Rocco Gangle, 'Theology of the Chimera', in Smith and Whistler, eds, *After the Postsecular and the Postmodern*.
22. See, for instance, Maimonides, *The Guide for the Perplexed*. The Platonic and Aristotelian influences on Jewish philosophy, going back at least to the Hellenistic period with thinkers such as Philo of Alexandria, represent the confluence of the Greek philosophical and Hebraic revelatory traditions. This concern with Greek philosophy was reintroduced into Jewish thought through contact with Muslim intellectual culture in the eleventh and twelfth centuries. See Ze'ev Levy, *Baruch or Benedict*, especially ch. 1.
23. E Id3. See the discussion of the sources and sense of this definition in Wolfson, *The Philosophy of Spinoza*, vol. 1, pp. 61–78.
24. E Ip10s, Ip14c1, Ip16.
25. Within each attribute, the exact same necessary causal order is manifest. See E IIp7: 'The order and connection of ideas is the same as the order and connection of things.'
26. In Part I *substance* is defined (E Id3) as 'what is in itself and is conceived through itself, that is, that whose concept does not require the concept of another thing, from which it must be formed', while *attribute* is understood (E Id4) as 'what the intellect perceives of a substance, as constituting its essence'. There are thus infinitely many attributes (including thought and extension), but all of them express one and the same substance (E Ip11).
27. E IIp7s: '[A] mode of extension and the idea of that mode are one and the same thing, but expressed in two ways.' The human mind is thus

nothing other than the idea (under the attribute of thought) of the human body (under the attribute of extension) in E IIp11, and furthermore 'The mind does not know itself, except insofar as it perceives the ideas of the affections of the body' (E IIp23). See also E IIp13.
28. The common notions are the primary source of such agreement. The term 'agreement' itself appears in a variety of contexts in Spinoza's five-part discussion of how to live, such as in his claim that 'All bodies agree in certain things [*Omnia corpora in quibusdam conveniunt*]' (E IIp13s Lemma2). See also IIp23.
29. *La Géometrie* initially appeared in 1637 as the third appendix to Descartes' *Discours de la Méthode pour bien conduire sa raison et chercher la vérité dans les sciences*. It is available in English translation with the French original *en regard* as *The Geometry of Rene Descartes*, trans. Smith and Latham.
30. *The Geometry of Rene Descartes*, p. 2.
31. It would be misleading to characterise Descartes' 'invention' of analytic geometry as completely without precedent. Interpreting geometrical magnitudes as numbers occurs as early as Book VII of Euclid's *Elements* (Def. 1 of that Book defines *unit* as 'that by virtue of which each of the things that exist is called one'). Further contributions to what would become the Cartesian line of thought are to be found from the third-century bce geometer Apollonius of Perga to Nicole Oresme (fourteenth century ce) and Francois Viète (late sixteenth century). See the discussion in Edna E. Kramer, *The Nature and Growth of Modern Mathematics*, pp. 134–66.
32. Consider, in an analogous fashion, how the planar coordinate system which has become associated with Descartes' name functions through the assignment of an arbitrary point of 'origin' and the fixing of perpendicular axes orienting the entire plane in definite relation to this origin. In a more metaphorical analogy, the role of *l'unité* in the *Geometry* might be compared (and contrasted) with the role of the *cogito* in Descartes' general philosophical/scientific method.
33. E Ip15s.
34. The publishing world into which the *Ethics* entered was in many respects a new and rapidly evolving one. See Jonathan Israel, *Radical Enlightenment*, chs 5–7. The appearance of the *Ethics* in this context should be read in light of the emergence of a European and specifically Dutch 'public sphere' in the 1600s. For an analysis of these and later developments especially in Germany, England and France, see Jürgen Habermas, *The Structural Transformation of the Public Sphere*.
35. Although each part begins with a new set of definitions and axioms, the results of previous parts are preserved and instrumentalised in the demonstrations of propositions in succeeding parts. The form itself of proposition and demonstration remains common to all five

parts. Within the *Ethics* the geometrical order functions according to Spinoza's own understanding of a 'common notion' as 'equally in the part and in the whole'. See E IIp37–p39.
36. E Vp10.
37. While the *Ethics* is perhaps the best-known example of this form, Spinoza's text is not unique in this regard. See the discussion in Wolfson, *The Philosophy of Spinoza*, vol. 1, pp. 40–7, and ch. 2 generally.
38. Any distinction between *ordo* and *more* is irrelevant to our purposes here.
39. Indeed Steinberg has argued that Spinoza's use of the geometrical order reflects more generally a 'nonlinear' and 'holistic' conception of knowledge-justification for philosophy. Such a reading emphasises the complex, inner coherence of the constructed system of theorematic consequences rather than their relations of founded dependence upon the initial axioms and definitions. Diane Steinberg, 'Method and the Structure of Knowledge in Spinoza'.
40. In this light Hampshire interprets Spinoza's use of geometrical order in terms of a 'rationalist' desire common to many of Spinoza's contemporaries, including Bacon, Descartes and Leibniz. In Spinoza this desire extends to the very form of his treatise: '[Spinoza] wished to be entirely effaced as individual and author, being no more than the mouthpiece of pure Reason', Hampshire, *Spinoza and Spinozism*, p. 32, cited in Steinberg, 'Method and the Structure of Knowledge in Spinoza', p. 152.
41. E Vp23s. Deleuze shows how Spinoza's notion of demonstration follows from his conception of the difference between nominal (or abstract) and real (or genetic) definitions, *Spinoza: Practical Philosophy*, pp. 61–2.
42. For a detailed study of how diagrams function in Euclid, see Reviel Netz, *The Shaping of Deduction in Greek Mathematics*. A related, more formal analysis of such diagrammatic reasoning from a broadly Kantian perspective is found in Jesse Norman, *After Euclid*.
43. E IIp48s.
44. E IIp43s, emphasis added.
45. Wolfson, *The Philosophy of Spinoza*, vol. 1, pp. 3–4.
46. Curley, *Behind the Geometrical Method*, p. xi.
47. Martial Gueroult, *Spinoza*, 2 vols. See also Pautrat's preface to the French translation of the *Ethics*, Seuil.
48. See especially Gueroult, *Spinoza*, vol. 2: *L'Âme*, ch. 16. For a discussion of the structuralist approach of Gueroult see Deleuze's review of the first volume of Gueroult's work on Spinoza, 'Spinoza et la methode generale de M. Gueroult', in *L'île Déserte et Autre Textes*, pp. 202–16.

49. Althusser gives an account of his own discovery of Spinoza: 'I discovered in [Spinoza] first an astonishing contradiction: this man who reasons *more geometrico* through definitions, axioms, theorems, corollaries, lemmas, and deductions – therefore, in the most 'dogmatic' way in the world – was in fact an incomparable liberator of the mind', 'The Only Materialist Tradition, Part I: Spinoza', in Montag and Stolze, eds, *The New Spinoza*, p. 4.
50. Antonio Negri, *The Savage Anomaly*, pp. 177 and 47. These remarks show clearly that for Negri it is less the geometrical order of presentation than the geometrical form of thought that remains essential.
51. Ibid., p. 47.
52. Derrida's complex reading of Husserl's *On the Origins of Geometry* raises similar questions in the context of phenomenology and the mathematical sciences.
53. Bernard Pautrat goes so far as to claim that any accessory notes or commentary on Spinoza's text would be extraneous, just as one does not annotate a mathematical proof: '[O]n n'annote pas un traité de mathématique, on le lit, on tente de le comprendre, on l'assimile [. . .].' 'Avertissement' to *Ethique*, pp. 9–10.
54. Compare the notion of logical form in Wittgenstein's *Tractatus Logico-Philosophicus* in which a tautological system of relations undergirds the unity of an infinite collection of worldly 'atomic facts'.
55. Bennett, for instance, asks, 'How could someone as supremely able as Spinoza have been satisfied with demonstrations so many of which are invalid and unrescuable?' *A Study of Spinoza's* Ethics, p. 27. This is not simply a rhetorical question but raises the important issue of the relation between the logical form of Spinoza's arguments and their implicit motivations.
56. E V preface.
57. Israel, *Radical Enlightenment*.
58. Ibid., part III. The *TTP* was much more widely read than the *Ethics* until after Kant.
59. See Volkmar Poppo's negative reaction to eighteenth-century Wolffians in his *Spinozismus Detectus* discussed in Israel, *Radical Enlightenment*, pp. 542–3.
60. Kramer, *The Nature and Growth of Modern Mathematics*, pp. 136–7.
61. Strictly speaking, the unity of the whole of nature is deduced in the *Ethics*, not hypothesised. This is the function of the first fifteen propositions of Part One (E Ip1–p15). Yet this series of deductions itself follows from the set of definitions and axioms with which Spinoza begins. These axioms and definitions are themselves the conditional framework for Spinoza's subsequent claims. Taken together, they serve as a collective hypothesis: begin here, if you would, and see what follows.

62. E Ip8.
63. See E Id5 and Ip15. Bennett's interpretive solution of this basic problem in Spinoza through his 'field metaphysic' is an initial point of reference in what follows. Bennett shows how modes for Spinoza are best conceived as adverbial properties, regional ways of being. See *A Study of Spinoza's* Ethics, pp. 92–6.
64. See the discussion in Thomas M. Lennon, 'The Problem of Individuation among the Cartesians', in Barber and Gracia, eds, *Individuation and Identity in Early Modern Philosophy*, pp. 13–39.
65. Don Garrett's overview of the question brings together the views of several other scholars, including Curley, Bennett, Lachterman, Gueroult and Matheron. 'Spinoza's Theory of Metaphysical Individuation', in Barber and Gracia, eds, *Individuation and Identity in Early Modern Philosophy*, pp. 73–101.
66. Della Rocca addresses the individuation of ideas in light of concerns with knowledge and representation by coordinating two problems: (1) in what sense does a mind have an idea of some particular thing?; and (2) how is the identity of mind and body conceived with respect to the causal independence of the attributes of thought and extension? Michael Della Rocca, *Representation and the Mind-Body Problem in Spinoza*, esp. ch. 2, pp. 29–38. See also Robert Brandom, 'Adequacy and the Individuation of Ideas in Spinoza's *Ethics*', ch. 4 of *Tales of the Mighty Dead*, pp. 121–42.
67. Alexandre Matheron, *Individu et communauté chez Spinoza*; and Negri, *The Savage Anomaly*.
68. E IIp13s.
69. E IIp13s.
70. E IIp13a2", definition of individual. This 'physical digression' in Spinoza's *Ethics* is analysed more fully in Rocco Gangle, 'Theology of the Chimera: Spinoza, Immanence, Practice', in Smith and Whistler, eds, *After the Postsecular and the Postmodern*.
71. E IIp13L1.
72. E IIp13L7s.
73. These local equilibria are typically 'metastable' in the sense developed by Simondon. See the discussion of this concept in Levi Bryant, *Difference and Givenness*, pp. 217–19.
74. This is in accord with Bennett's interpretation of extended substance in Spinoza as what he calls 'the field metaphysic' in *A Study of Spinoza's Ethics*, p. 92 and more generally, ch. 4. For a related systems-theory account of individuation in contemporary science, see Sunny Auyang, *Foundations of Complex-System Theories*, ch. 3 and *How is Quantum Field Theory Possible*, chs 19–20.
75. This need not imply that the levels or scales of individuating organisation are absolute (since the only non-relative scale is that of God itself,

which is 'absolutely infinite'). For a proposal of how to reorient thinking both metaphysically and scientifically in a 'scale-free' manner, see Thalos, *Without Hierarchy*.
76. The question of whether it may be consistently posited that such relations go 'all the way down' without depending upon foundational atoms of one sort or another may be at least partially addressed mathematically in terms of the consistency of non-wellfounded models of set theory. It is a standard expedient in certain mathematical arenas to simply define the 'content' of any node in some system of relations *as* the set of its relations in the system. This fractal-like structure does not necessarily lead to any paradoxes or inconsistencies. For details, see Jon Barwise and Lawrence Moss, *Vicious Circles*, parts 2 and 3.
77. This need not imply that only potentiality is real. Affects are not *merely* potentials; they also directly and immediately affect and are affected by other modes. See David S. Oderberg, 'No Potency Without Actuality', for an interesting analysis of this problem in terms of directed graphs.
78. While Spinoza in the *Ethics* is generally dismissive of language as a dependable mode of access to adequate ideas, equating natural linguistic practice with the 'knowledge through signs' of the imagination, his sensitivity to the formal structures of language is evident in the detail and sophistication of his *Hebrew Grammar*, in *Complete Works*.
79. The Greek *kategorein* meant originally to accuse in the public gathering-place, the *agora*. The term has always retained some of this public and communicable connotation. In Aristotle, for instance, the categories are conceived as modes of discourse; in Kant, as universal structures of experience.
80. E IIp7.
81. Consider Althusser's notion of history as a 'process without subject'. See 'The Only Materialist Tradition, Part I: Spinoza', in Montag and Stolze, eds, *The New Spinoza*.
82. A theory of the disciplinary specificity of philosophy based on a similar conception of self-reference is proffered in Thomas-Fogiel, *The Death of Philosophy: Reference and Self-Reference in Contemporary Thought*.
83. To speak in Saussure's terms, *parole* here takes precedence over *langue*. Yet *parole* must be understood in this context primarily as affective rather than as representational or propositional. The problem of language's *force* comes to the fore. See François Laruelle, *Machines textuelles*, for a rich account of this theoretical problem.
84. K. Hvidtfelt Nielsen, *Interpreting Spinoza's Arguments – Toward a Formal Theory of Consistent Language Scepticism Imitating* Ethica.
85. Ibid., p. 158, with 'escaping' in the original corrected here to 'escape'.

86. Ibid.
87. Ibid., p. 6. Following a parallel line of thought, Aaron Garrett has related *meaning* to *method* as the core sense of Spinoza's philosophy. Garrett summarises his position in terms of a threefold thesis, claiming 'that [1] Spinoza's philosophy is a kind of self-clarificatory therapy for those capable of self-clarification; that [2] this self-clarification arises not just from reflection but also from other sorts of knowing; and finally that [3] the choice of the method by which to establish appropriate knowledge and the vehicle or means by which to present it, as a consequence, is absolutely central'. Aaron V. Garrett, *Meaning in Spinoza's Method*; the citation is from p. 7 (bracketed numbers added).
88. Nielsen, *Interpreting Spinoza's Arguments*, p. 28.
89. Indeed, Nielsen draws explicit parallels between Spinoza's rhetoric and Derrida's method of deconstruction, but these are left largely undeveloped.
90. Ibid., p. 28.
91. Ibid.
92. Ibid. One recent innovation in logic that Nielsen marshals in his updating of Spinoza is Saul Kripke's theoretical and notational introduction of the formal analysis of 'possible worlds'. In accord with the reduction of metaphysical issues to questions of linguistic usage that characterises the 'linguistic turn' in Anglo-American philosophy, possible worlds ought to be considered merely 'stipulations which we may make when trying to describe the use of certain utterances'. Ibid., p. 78.
93. Ibid., pp. 76–7, with 'using' in the original corrected to 'use'.
94. Ibid., p. 141.
95. For details of the initial publishing of the *Ethics*, see Israel, *Radical Enlightenment*, pp. 285–94.
96. For a recent narrative of Spinoza's life and works in the context of both his Jewish heritage and the developments of seventeenth-century Dutch economics and politics see Steven Nadler, *Spinoza: A Life*. For a concise synopsis of the major streams of the critical reception of Spinoza's work from the early modern period to the present, see Pierre-Francois Moreau, 'Spinoza's Reception and Influence', in Don Garrett, ed., *The Cambridge Companion to Spinoza*.
97. Title of E V.
98. E V preface.
99. Spinoza emphasises that it is not possible to overcome the affects through mere willpower. Instead, 'much practice and application are required to restrain and moderate them'. E V preface.
100. In this may be seen one major difference between Spinoza and Hegel. For Spinoza the practice of philosophy is related foremost to the

individual, not to the historical movement of reason as trans-individual Spirit. This does not imply that Spinoza is insensitive to the role of reasonable practice at the level of history and politics, but it does mean that the locus of philosophy in such large-scale developments is first of all a matter of individual thought and action. For a study of some of the apparent similarities and real differences between Spinoza and Hegel, see Pierre Macherey, 'The Problem of the Attributes' in Montag and Stolze, eds, *The New Spinoza*. For studies of Spinoza's thought linking his philosophical methods to the rise of political liberalism, see Stephen B. Smith, *Spinoza's Book of Life: Freedom and Redemption in the* Ethics.
101. E Vp10s.
102. See Wolfson, *The Philosophy of Spinoza*, especially vol. 2, pp. 233–40 and 251–60.
103. *Nicomachean Ethics* 1103b. In McKeon, ed., *The Basic Works of Aristotle*, p. 953.
104. Ibid., 1104a, p. 953.
105. E IIp40s2. It is important to note that Spinoza uses the term cognition [*cognitio*] to refer not only to knowledge in the conventional sense (as justified true belief) but more generally as the act of thinking. Despite this, the Latin *cognitio* and its genitive form *cognitionis* are generally translated in English as 'knowledge'.
106. E IIp40s2.
107. E IIp40s2.
108. E IIp40s2.
109. Scholars have debated the importance of what Spinoza calls the third kind of knowledge for Spinoza's thought more generally. Reception of Spinoza's third kind of knowledge has ranged from Bennett's frank dismissal contending 'that Spinoza is talking nonsense and that there is no reason for us to put up with it' to Gueroult's painstaking analysis culminating in the identification of the active power of the third kind of knowledge and the genetic method of geometrical demonstration of the *Ethics* itself, both of which express 'truth in action [*le vrai en action*]'. Bennett, *A Study of Spinoza's* Ethics, p. 85; Gueroult, *Spinoza*, vol. 2: *L'Âme*, p. 477. Between these two extremes it is also worth noting Negri's balanced but mostly critical comments in chapter 7 of *The Savage Anomaly* asserting that the sequence of propositions Vp25–p27 concerning the third kind of knowledge constitute 'a reemergence that deals with desire and hope more than it deals with the progress of the system'. For Negri, this is a drawback. For the reading considered here, it may instead be a (self-critical) strength. Wilson's lucid analysis of the issues at stake concludes that the third kind of knowledge leaves its interpreters with 'a riddle': 'What is it, exactly, to come to perceive the "inmost essences" of singular things

as they follow from the necessity of the divine nature?' Margaret D. Wilson, 'Spinoza's Theory of Knowledge', in Garrett, ed., *The Cambridge Companion to Spinoza*, ch. 3.
110. The mathematical example (based on numerical proportions) that Spinoza subsequently provides to clarify his meaning is only marginally helpful. In many respects it raises more questions than it answers. See the final paragraph of E IIp40s2.
111. E Vp25.
112. E Vp25.
113. E Vp36.
114. E Vp6, Vp7.
115. E Vp36s.
116. E Vp36s, emphasis added.
117. The apparent contradiction is resolved by distinguishing between dyadic and triadic models of signification (to be described in Chapter 3). When Spinoza disparages signs, it is in a dyadic sense. The third kind of knowledge is semiotic in the triadic sense.
118. Garrett, *Meaning in Spinoza's Method*.
119. This property is demonstrated in Euclid, *Elements*, Book 3, Proposition 4.
120. Garrett, *Meaning in Spinoza's Method*, p. 211.
121. Ibid. It is worth noting in this regard what Spinoza says in E IIp8 regarding the relationship between the ideas of singular modes and the infinite idea of God, namely that due to the relationship's very uniqueness one cannot provide an alternate example that would illuminate it: 'If anyone wishes me to explain this further by an example, I will, of course, not be able to give one which adequately explains what I speak of here, since it is unique' (E IIp8s). Nevertheless, Spinoza does go on to provide an example, a geometrical example that must therefore be understood analogically.

CHAPTER 2

Diagrams of Structure: Categories and Functors

Let us presume as a working hypothesis that the views expressed in Spinoza's *Ethics* are in broad strokes metaphysically and ontologically correct. We thus presume that what really exist are relational structures of infinite variety and that these structures everywhere enter in turn into higher-order relations with one another and so on without limit. We and all the things around us are both immersed within relations of these kinds and thoroughly saturated by them. At any particular scale of investigation, then, we may take relatively stable linkages of more or less determinate local relations to constitute 'things' or 'objects' in a quite general sense, and we may expect to find a variety of relations linking such scare-quoted objects to one another depending upon which we decide to select. Furthermore such relations frequently come packaged together in internally differentiated systems of some common type: chemical, linguistic, military-strategic, stellar-galactic and so forth. Our aim is to develop a workable method for plunging philosophically into this immanent relational sea.

We proceed accordingly at two distinct levels. At an initial level, we will develop an informal diagrammatic notation for representing and analysing arbitrary systems of relations, with objects represented by dots and relations of the relevant type by arrows between dots. At a secondary, reflective level, we will treat the same notation in a more regimented way in order to introduce category theoretical mathematics. At both levels, we will be using systems of partly determined and partly undetermined relations (a variety of dot-and-arrow diagrams) to represent and investigate systems of partly determined and partly undetermined relations (worldly phenomena and mathematical categories). To some extent these representations and patterns of investigation will be reversible, that is, the represented will by virtue of the very form of representation at work serve as a potential representing medium in its own right. It will be a diagram too. The fact that the same notation serves as object, method and mathematical formalism provides the primary link here to Spinoza's philosophy of immanence. The key idea throughout is that an act of abstraction or formalisation may be at once effected and represented by the construction of a diagram and that the abstractive act itself is thus accomplished in each instance as a new object that thereby becomes subject to further critical investigation and direct experimentation.

DIRECTED GRAPHS

We begin with a very basic and flexible diagrammatic structure: directed graphs, which we will simply call graphs. Graph theory is a highly interesting area of mathematical study in its own right, but here it will serve as little more than an elementary notational convenience. All that matters for present purposes is the following: Diagrammatically we may represent graphs as systems of dots and of arrows connecting those dots, the relative positions of the dots being irrelevant, as well as the lengths and curvatures (if any) of the arrows. The only unwavering rule for such diagrams is that each arrow in them must go from one dot to one dot. In other words, every arrow will be associated with a unique dot at its 'tail' called its *source* and one at its 'head' called its *target*. In specifying a graph, then, necessary and sufficient information consists in how many distinct dots and how many distinct arrows there are in the system and which dots are connected by which arrows and in which 'direction'. Note that this leaves open various degrees of freedom along which different types and instances of graphs may be determined: there may be dots in the system without any arrows attached to them; there may be arrows that go from a given dot 'back' to that same dot; there may be multiple arrows going from one dot to another. The only structures that are excluded are those involving 'free-floating' arrows, that is, arrows without a single determinate dot at its tail and one at its head (these may in fact be the same dot). As an example of a graph, see the diagram in Figure 2.1 on the upper left.[1]

We now introduce a convention that will serve as one of our most fundamental tools as we progress through the levels of category theory: selection. We will think of graphs as inscribed on discrete 'sheets', like sheets of paper, one graph per sheet. This will provide us with a natural way to represent more than one graph simultaneously by juxtaposing their two-dimensional 'sheets' in a common three-dimensional space, either stacking them in some ordered way or allowing them, as it were, to float freely. We may then introduce

2.1

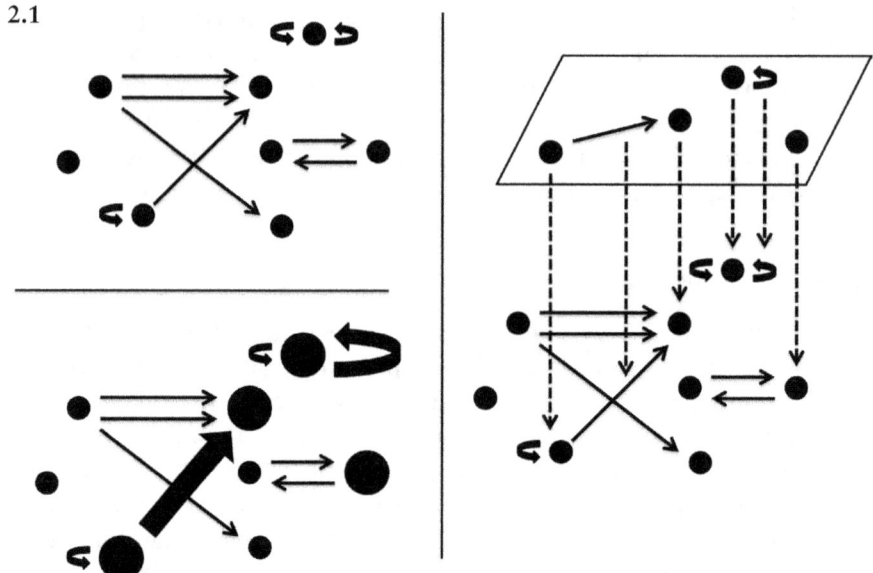

arrows going from one sheet to another in order to represent various relations between the graphs inscribed on those sheets. In particular, we may use this convention to represent the selection of some arbitrary part of a given graph that is itself a graph.

Take the graph diagrammed on the upper left in Figure 2.1 and compare it to the graph immediately below it and to the more complex diagram on the right. These two latter diagrams represent the selection of a part of the original graph in two essentially equivalent but notationally distinct ways. The first way, placed below the line, highlights the selected part by thickening its arrows and slightly enlarging its dots. The second way, presented to the right, treats the selected part as a distinct graph on a separate sheet. A single mapping – represented by dashed arrows – associates each dot and arrow in the graph on the upper sheet with a corresponding element in the larger graph below it. It thus demonstrates directly how the smaller graph is 'included' within the larger. This may serve as a general method for representing parts of any graph that are themselves graphs. In effect, a part or subgraph of some arbitrary graph G may be treated as a mapping from a graph representing the relevant part (call it P) into G. Each element of P (that is, any of the dots and arrows out of which it is made) is carried by the mapping to a corresponding element of G that it selects or designates. In order to preserve the basic 'shape' of P in G, all the dots with arrows attached to

Diagrams of Structure: Categories and Functors

them in P must remain 'glued' to those arrows in their role as source or target across the mapping into G. For such a selection, it is also often convenient to stipulate that distinct dots (and arrows) in P may not 'collapse' into identical dots (or arrows) in G. We will return frequently to these crucial notions of 'gluing' and 'collapse'.

It is possible to restate the earlier characterisation of graphs (the description of their essential properties) in terms of ranges of possible selections. For any graph G, we may select any dot (or any collection of dots). For any dot selected, implicitly selected as well are all the arrows going into and all the arrows coming from that dot. Both these – possibly empty – collections of arrows are uniquely determined by the graph as a whole. Conversely, we may select any arrow in the graph, and by selecting that arrow we are compelled to determine the dots at its tail and its head in the very same 'gesture'. In this case, there is always exactly one of each. In other words, the selection of some arrow in a graph at the same time necessarily comprises two additional selections within it, those of a unique source-dot and a unique target-dot (which may, again, be identical) for that arrow. Graph-arrows, in this sense, carry more definite information than the dots they connect and order – this notion of hierarchies of nested information will also be a recurrent theme in what follows.

We will now use this general graph-notation to specify two paths in the direction of a full characterisation of categories.

First way in: via partial orders

Consider a room full of people enjoying themselves at a cocktail party. A dense cloud of abstract properties and relations floats among them, a swarm of tangled intelligible connections visible only to gods and perhaps philosophers. By imagining these abstract connections as fine threads of various types attached to the party-goers and labelled with small tags, the party itself becomes vividly transformed into a partly virtual space saturated with interconnected webs of diagrammatic lines. First of all, each person appears 'attached' by one end to a huge collection of loose threads with tags identifying that person's various one-place or monadic properties ('__is a man', '__is a woman', '__works downtown', '__is miserable', '__smiles beautifully'). In addition – and this is what in fact makes the scene a party rather than an autistic congeries or mere set – the very 'fabric' of the common space inhabited by these individuals as they drink, talk and move about is structured and restructured by a constantly shifting web of dyadic, triadic and higher-order relations, threads (sometimes split into two or more branches) linking the partygoers to one another. These threads are labelled by the predicative connections according to which the partygoers actually relate to one another: '__sees__', '__notices__seeing__', '__brings__a drink', '__tells__a story about__and__'.

Included in this sea of threads and tags among the gathered bodies are such systematic properties as basic spatial orientation ('__is to the north of__'), communicative networks ('__is talking to__and__') and predicates of comparison ('__is taller than__'). Such relational types may be described as 'systematic' to the extent that each one taken in its aggregate (that is, as the collection of all the relations of its given kind), forms a naturally unified, interrelated web of meta-relations. In many cases, these meta-relational systems involve intrinsic logical structures such as implication, negation, compossibility and incompossibility. For instance, if a certain woman is to the north of a certain man and that man is directly east of a second woman, then the second woman must be more or less southwest of the first (given certain reasonable assumptions, such as the party not being spread out across an entire hemisphere!). Such meta-relations are the diagrammatic schemata for where and how conceptual and physical systems interact.

While there is obviously much to investigate in this partly concrete, partly imagined space, it is important to note that its construction began with a single, severely restricted act of selection: we attended only to the people at the party and imagined the threads and tags only with respect to them. A very different 'space' of threads and tags would have appeared had we selected all the party's constituent molecules instead, or its sound-waves, or just the hors d'oeuvres.

Given, however, our initial selection of partygoers as the relevant 'elements' to which the thread-ends were attached, we were thereby assured at the cocktail party that every such element was associated with certain definite common properties: for instance, each person present was necessarily linked unambiguously with a single, definite age. This property is of course just one of the innumerable predicate 'tags' attached to the person at issue, but we may be certain in any particular case that this tag must be there, uniquely determined for each individual (our background knowledge of what makes people people is the source of our assurance). We now select via a further act of abstraction the 'simplified' space containing and thus concerning nothing but the initial collection of partygoers on the one hand (irrespective of their determinate spatial orientations, current conversations, specific degrees of intoxication and so on) and the tag of exact age (in years, say) associated with each of these individuals on the other. Picture this newly abstracted 'cross-section' of the party as a collection of dots labelled by numbers. It is then quite straightforward on the basis of this much-reduced field of information to induce a new well-structured system of relations from it. One simply tracks in a global way the comparative relation 'is as old or older than'. We will assume that no two distinct partygoers have been born at the very same instant. Thus for any two distinct partygoers, one is necessarily older than the other, even if only by a day or a moment (see criterion 4 below). Each partygoer will be precisely 'as old' as himself or herself alone. Any instance of the interpersonal relation 'is as old or older than' at the party may then be pictured as an arrow going from one dot to another in the reduced system in the naturally evident way. See Figure 2.2.

The graph representing this system on the upper right exhibits a variety of properties, or to conceive it otherwise, satisfies a number of different criteria. We will examine several of these and provide a justification of each one demonstrating that the property or criterion in question is not just a contingent aspect of the particular graph pictured here, but is rather a necessary feature of any such graph representing any relevantly similar situation:

2.2

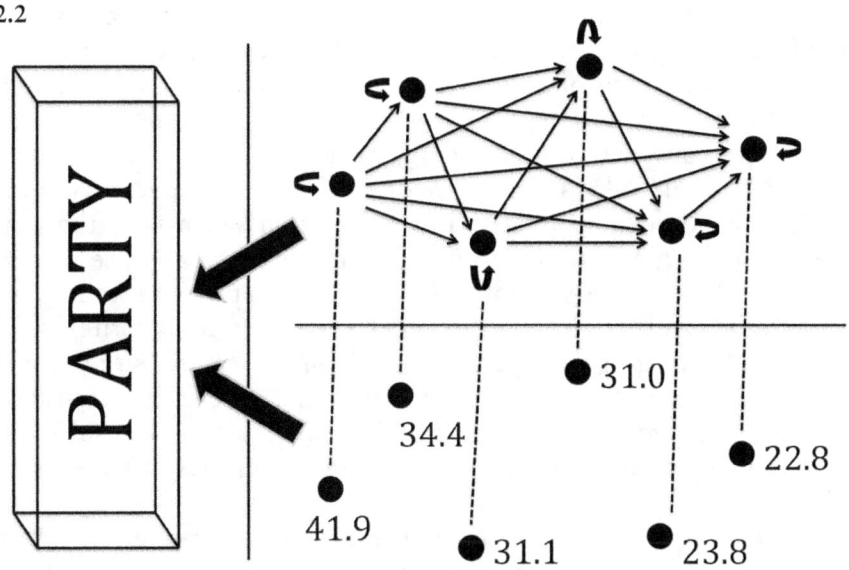

(1) There is at most one arrow going from any dot to any other.

Justification: We understand the relation at issue to be a simple yes-or-no matter, so there would be no sense in the present context to two or more distinct arrows between the same two dots. Any such arrows would merely 'repeat the same meaning'. To put it another way, there are no relevant differences in degree or type of the relation 'is as old or older than' that would need to be distinguished by different arrows.

(2) An arrow goes from each dot to itself: $X \to X$.

Justification: Every person is necessarily 'as old or older' than himself or herself.

(3) Every 'head-to-tail path' of one arrow followed by another implies the existence of a third arrow that 'composes' them: If $X \to Y$ and $Y \to Z$, then $X \to Z$.

Justification: Being 'as old or older' is the kind of relation that 'translates' from one pair of dots to the next in the sense that whenever one partygoer is as old or older than some second partygoer, and that second partygoer is as old or older than some third, the first is necessarily as old or older than the third. Such 'transitivity' is guaranteed in this case by the presumptively linear nature of time.

(4) The graph contains no 'loops' or 'cycles' of more than one arrow: If $X \to Y$ and $Y \to X$, then $X = Y$.

Justification: Two or more distinct partygoers cannot all be 'as old or older than' one another since we have assumed that no two were born simultaneously. Any 'cycle' of arrows would imply that this relation held among all pairs of dots in the cycle, because of criterion 3.

Note that in addition, this system also happens to satisfy the supplementary criterion:

(5) Given any two dots X and Y, either $X \to Y$ or $Y \to X$.

Justification: There are no pairs of partygoers unordered by age.

Considered in a general manner, criterion (1) means that the arrows of the graph may be taken in an unequivocal sense to represent a relation (in set-theoretical terms, the set of arrows may be taken to be a subset of the set of ordered pairs of dots). Criteria (2), (3) and (4) are graph-properties called *reflexivity*, *transitivity*, and *anti-symmetry*, respectively. Any relation that is reflexive, transitive and anti-symmetric in this way satisfies the necessary and sufficient conditions of a *partial order*. If in addition a partial order satisfies criterion (5) it is a *total order*.

Because it satisfies the above criteria, the order-relation represented here by the arrows really defines a system of general relations

Diagrams of Structure: Categories and Functors 77

and not merely a particular dyadic property. We happened to make use of the property 'is as old or older than', but in this particular case we might just as well have used the property 'has been able legally to drink alcohol for as long or longer than' or 'has travelled around the sun as many times or more than' or any of a host of other determinations. In other words, the order-relation pictured by the arrows in the graph in fact generalises *all* the properties that are, with respect to the given context, 'equivalent' in a still somewhat ambiguous sense. While we used a single, determinate property to generate or discover the order-relation, the order-relation itself as both represented and instantiated by the arrows in the graph is in an important sense *more abstract* and hence *more general* than that particular property. The order as such is thus a kind of meta-property that may be satisfied or instantiated by a wide variety of different and more or less determinate relational properties. These properties themselves need not necessarily be linked explicitly to one another. For example, if it happens to be the case at our party that all the partygoers present admire only themselves and all their juniors, then the identical order-structure characterises the independently defined relation 'admires' at this particular celebration.

It is worth noting too that although this general order-relation or structure abstracts away from all other properties of the individuals concerned, so that each individual is treated as 'no more than' a simple dot, there are certain special individuals who nonetheless become describable or locatable solely through intrinsic properties determined by no more than their particular 'position' in the derived system of arrows. We know, for instance, that the *oldest* partygoer will be represented by the unique dot characterised by the property that an arrow goes from it to every dot. By the same token, the *youngest* partygoer will be represented by the only dot in the diagram such that an arrow goes from every dot to it. Importantly, if all the arrows were to be reversed (with sources exchanged everywhere for targets), the resulting diagram would represent the logically 'dual' property 'is as young or younger than' which would nonetheless provide exactly the same overall information as the original diagram and would possess the very same extremities (albeit inverted). This notion of 'duality' is another deep structural property to which we will return.

For the sake of illustrating certain key diagrammatic concepts, we have followed a somewhat wayward path. In fact, the two-step 'constructive' approach taken above by first abstracting the collection of individual partygoers with their respective ages and then inducing the order-relation on this collection via a global act of comparison was strictly redundant. Given the original party with its cloud of relations, we might have proceeded more directly by simply 'selecting' the dyadic predicate '__is as old or older than__' from among the innumerable predicates readily available. Then in just one step of simple inspection (recall that the 'space' of properties and relations was presumed visible to deities and philosophers) we would have immediately obtained exactly the same result: the abstraction of a determinate partial order defined over the set of partygoers. The wayward path and the immediate selection coincide in this case because of certain relationships 'built in' as it were to the concepts of time and age at issue. It should thus start to become evident how layers of abstraction and patterns of determination are in fact subject to a variety of non-arbitrary, that is, 'natural' relations and metarelations. In general, such layers and slices of structured situations and the relations that inevitably emerge among them produce an effect of higher-order relations that nonetheless, strangely, become expressible within the same diagrammatic framework of object-like dots and relation-like arrows.

In the example given, since the particular order of age also happens to be total, it is a rather special or restricted example. All the dots 'line up' in their respective order (total orders are also sometimes called *linear orders*).[2] What happens if we relax this restriction? In other words, what kinds of partial orders are conceivable that do not 'line up' in a way that can be mapped in a 'structure-preserving way' onto a continuous line? By allowing some pairs of dots to have no arrows connecting them in either direction, we then find ourselves free to vary the single, connected line of arrows in a total order by letting it 'spread out' like a road that forks and also 'break apart' into unconnected (independently ordered) sections. A simple way to describe this increase in freedom is to say that criterion 5 above is annulled or relaxed. Figure 2.3 shows increasingly free partial orders in this sense among the upper diagrams as they proceed from left to right.

In subsequent diagrams of partial orders, for ease of readability the identity arrows that go from each dot to itself (criterion 2) will often be suppressed. They should be understood to be present but not pictured. In addition, since the transitivity of arrows is assured for all partial orders (criterion 3), we will also assume that any paths of arrows joined head to tail in partial order diagrams will always imply

Diagrams of Structure: Categories and Functors 79

2.3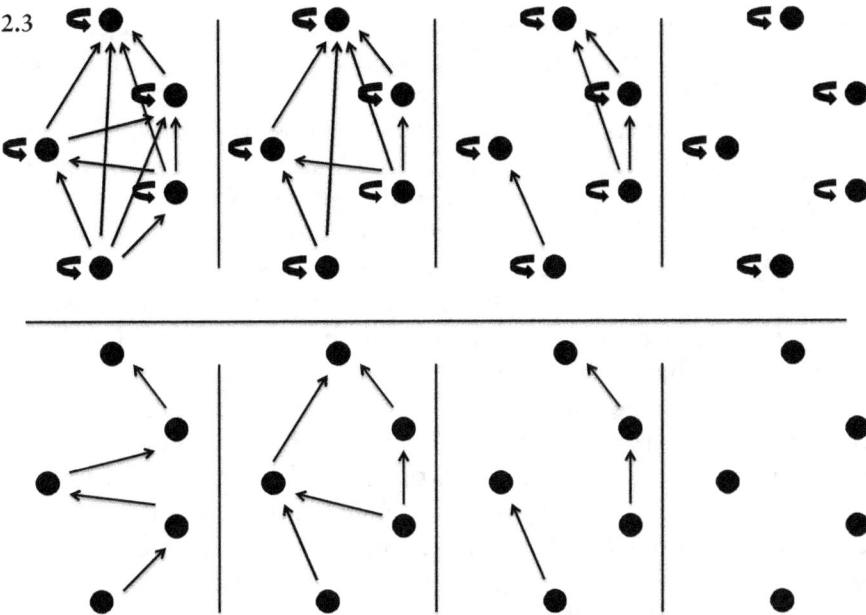

the existence of the transitive arrows that connect such paths without having to make the latter explicit. The graphs below the line in Figure 2.3 are thus meant to represent exactly the same partial orders as those above the line, although with the arrows implied by criteria 2 and 3 unmarked and merely implicit. The reader should check above and below in each case to understand the pattern. For simplicity of presentation, except when noted otherwise we will use this pair of conventions regularly in the diagrams that follow.

In general, partial orders are very useful mathematical constructions, and they are practically ubiquitous. Any time we confront an object or a system that is composed of parts (or of levels, degrees or ordered types) and whose parts are composed of sub-parts and so on, to whatever arbitrary 'depth' of parthood, we may define a partial order on the parts themselves, so long as the criteria above are satisfied.

To take one quite general class of partial orders, consider any ordinary physical object, say, the 1957 Chevrolet Bel Air Convertible in your neighbour's driveway. With a word or a gesture you may designate the car itself as a single entity (a dot). You might also point to any of its various component parts, for instance its classic V8 engine. Of course, its parts are generally also composed of parts, and it seems reasonable to assume that all the parts of the parts of the Chevy are also parts of the Chevy. Thus the collection of all the parts of the Chevy (whatever these are in fact taken to be) form a partial order under the relation 'is a part of' (if we accept for simplicity's sake that everything counts as 'a part of' itself). A 'flow' of arrows naturally emerges from this relation passing from smallest parts through larger parts up to the largest *terminal* part, the whole car.

Indeed, this will be true not only for the Chevy and *all* its parts taken together, but also for any particular selection of its parts we may choose, for example the arbitrary collection: engine, spark plugs, tyres, front tyres, rear tyres, dashboard. In effect, all that we require is (1) that each element of the collection be 'a part of' itself; (2) that it be decidable for any two elements of the collection whether or not one is 'a part of' the other; and (3) that parthood function in the expected way so that parts of parts of X are also parts of X (transitivity) and any two distinct elements cannot both be parts of one another (anti-symmetry). Notice that any such collection for any object is in principle nothing other than some selection of a 'fragment' of the partial order defined over *all* the parts of that object. If the selection is meant to pick out not only the relevant parts but also the order-relation that structures them, the 'selection' must have arrows that match up appropriately with the arrows in the more general order. Every such fragment of a partial order always also determines a partial order in its own right. See Figure 2.4.

Generally speaking, partial orders are induced naturally not only on actual objects or situations composed of discernable parts of whatever sort, but also on practically any systems involving various degrees of merely possible determination. For instance, the collection of all possible non-equivalent descriptions of the components of some variable situation (all the different fragments, say, of distinct building-plans that are possible for an architectural site) can be structured by a partial order in which an arrow from one such fragment to another implies that the target contains all the information of the source (and therefore typically *extends* or more fully determines the description).

SETS AS SPECIAL CASES OF PARTIAL ORDERS

Free use has been made of the term 'collection' in the examples above. By 'collection' we mean informally what is designated formally by the mathematical term 'set'. We could define a set independently, but since we have just gone to the trouble of defining partial

Diagrams of Structure: Categories and Functors 81

2.4
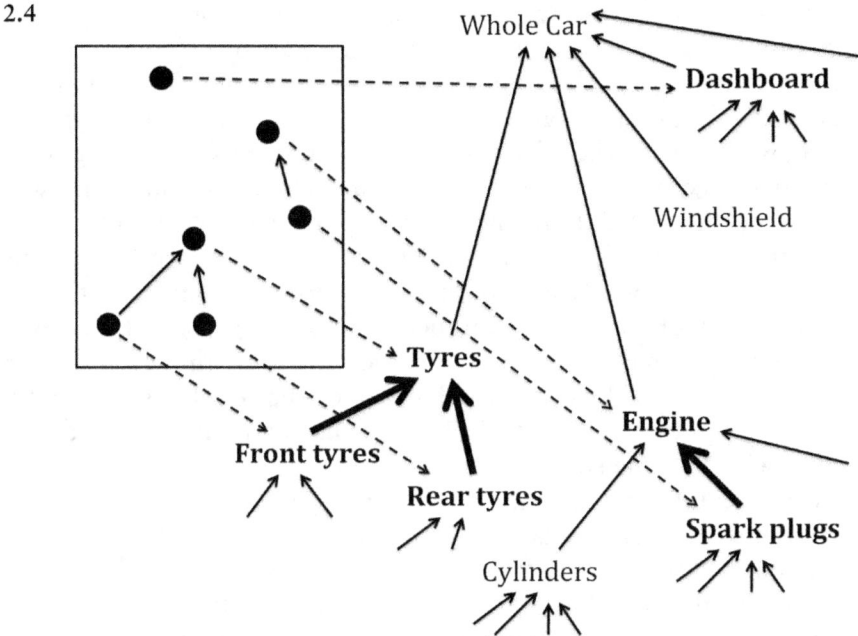

orders, let us simply define a set as a particular type of partial order. A *set*, then, is just anything diagrammed by a partial order (a graph satisfying criteria 1 through 4 above) that in addition meets the following 'set' criterion:

(Set) If there is an arrow X→Y, then X=Y.

In other words, no arrow in the graph has two non-identical dots as its source and its target. The set criterion states, then, that the only arrows in the partial order are 'identity arrows' going from dots back to themselves. The reflexivity criterion already ensures that *every* dot will have such an arrow. They have to be there to meet the general conditions of a partial order. In fact, any graph satisfying criteria 1, 2 and Set must be a partial order. What about the transitivity and anti-symmetry criteria? These will be trivially satisfied automatically since there are no arrows between distinct dots, and if no such arrows exist, no arrows can fail to satisfy the relevant properties. So for our purposes a set will be just an unusual sort of partial order, one that has as little order-structure or intrinsic 'directionality' as possible. Such restricted or minimal partial orders look like the maximally free order on the extreme right in Figure 2.3 above. They are distinguished diagrammatically from one another solely by how many dots they have.[3]

Given any such set, we may define a straightforward selection operator, called *subset*, which selects some part of it. This part may consist of one, some, all or none of the dots in the set. If it consists of exactly one, that part is also called an *element*.[4] Just as with graphs above, we will treat the selection of a part of a set as a mapping from a distinct selector set into the set at issue. The important thing will be that no distinct dots in the selector part shall be allowed to be associated by the mapping with the same dot in the target set. Thus in the subset mapping, each dot in the selector must have exactly one arrow going from it to some unique dot in the target set, and no two of these arrows may have the same target dot. Note that even though they are both sets, the conceptual status of the selector set is subtly different from that of the set. It is somewhat more abstract and represents a 'type'. The subset as such is thus actually conceived as any relevantly equivalent *mapping* from this 'type' to the target set.

Subset selections may be seen to *compose* with one another in the sense that a subset of a subset of a set is always also a subset of that set. The dynamics of this relation are made evident by simply 'following the arrows' across the composed mappings. See Figure 2.5.

Each of these acts of selection may itself be represented as a dot in a different collection, a collection of parts or subsets of some given

2.5
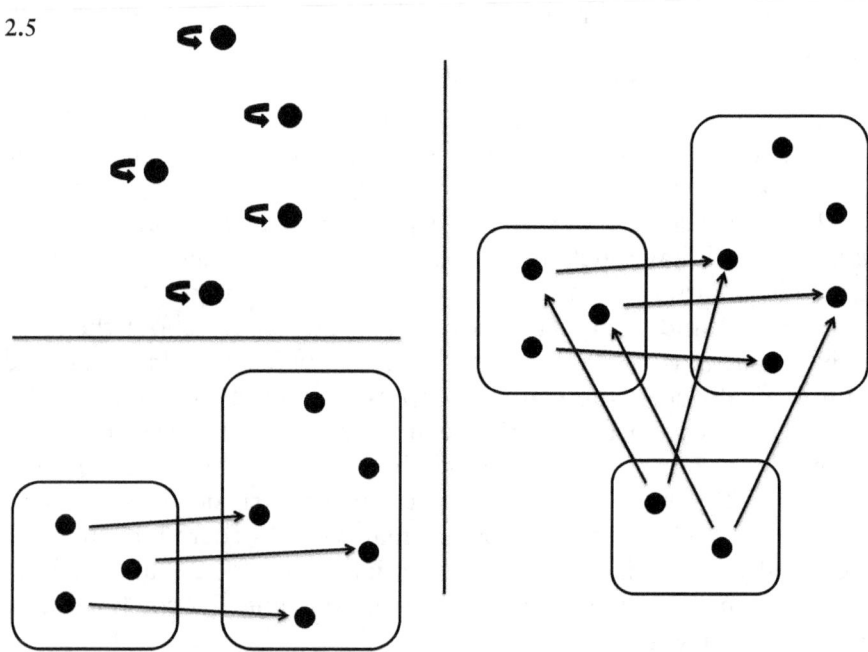

set. Each dot in the new collection will then represent one part (one subset) of the original set. If we gather *all* the subsets of any given set into a new collection in this way, the new collection is called the *powerset* of the original set. In other words, the powerset of any set X is simply the set of all subsets of X, one dot for each relevantly distinct subset mapping. An order-relation may then be defined on this new collection in the following manner: given two dots, say Y and Z, of the new collection, there will be an arrow Y→Z if and only if Y is a subset of Z (if their maps compose in the right way). This order-relation will always constitute a partial order. (Can you prove this? Go back to the criteria that define a partial order and explain how and why the ordered collection of all subsets of any given set necessarily satisfy them. Think of the Chevy.) The relationships between sets, subsets, powersets and partial orders are in general quite rich material for mathematical and philosophical investigation.

SECOND WAY IN: VIA FUNCTIONS

Thirsty or not, let us return to our cocktail party. What exactly did we do when we picked out the property of 'age' with respect to each and every partygoer? First of all, we selected out of the infinite swarm of objects and relations in the room a very definite collection: all and only the partygoers. We then selected a particular kind of property that could be assigned uniquely to each and every member of this collection. Why call this a 'kind of property' rather than just a 'property'? Because each age taken as such is more or less distinct from all the others (recall that we assumed no two partygoers were born at the same instant). There is thus a general 'type' or 'kind' of property, namely *age*, which in fact includes or envelops a variety of particular properties, namely the actual instantiated *ages* of the individual partiers. The induced partial order itself stood in a sense 'between' these two poles of 'type' and 'instance': it represented the relative ordering of the actual ages as a single, unified system without including the informational detail of the exact ages themselves. If we are more concerned with the assignment of a particular age to each partygoer, the determinate mapping as such from each of the elements of one set into another, we are interested in a *function*.

A function is an ordered relation (that is, an arrow) between two sets. The set at the arrow's tail is called the *domain* of the function, and the set at the arrow's head is the function's *codomain*. Typically, a function may be thought of either as the assignment to each and every domain-element of values or properties labelled by elements in the codomain (exactly one value or property for each element of the domain) or as the sorting of all the elements of the domain into exclusive kinds or types labelled by codomain-elements.[5]

Recall that the partial order induced on partygoers generalised a variety of related types of properties: age, time of birth, exact moment of first birthday, etc. Each of these specific types induces a different function, either because it implies a different codomain (numbers versus times, for instance) or because it assigns different values in the codomain (for example, moments of birth versus moments of first birthdays).

The graph notation of dots and arrows applies naturally to functions at two different levels. See Figure 2.6. At the first level (pictured above the line on each side in the diagram), the domain and codomain are pictured as framed collections of dots and a given function is represented as a family of arrows, exactly one for each element of the domain, with their tails at dots in the domain and their heads at dots in the codomain. But we may also consider collections of dots, each of which represents a set, with arrows going from one dot to another (or from a dot to itself) representing particular functions from one set into another (or a set into itself). At this second level

2.6

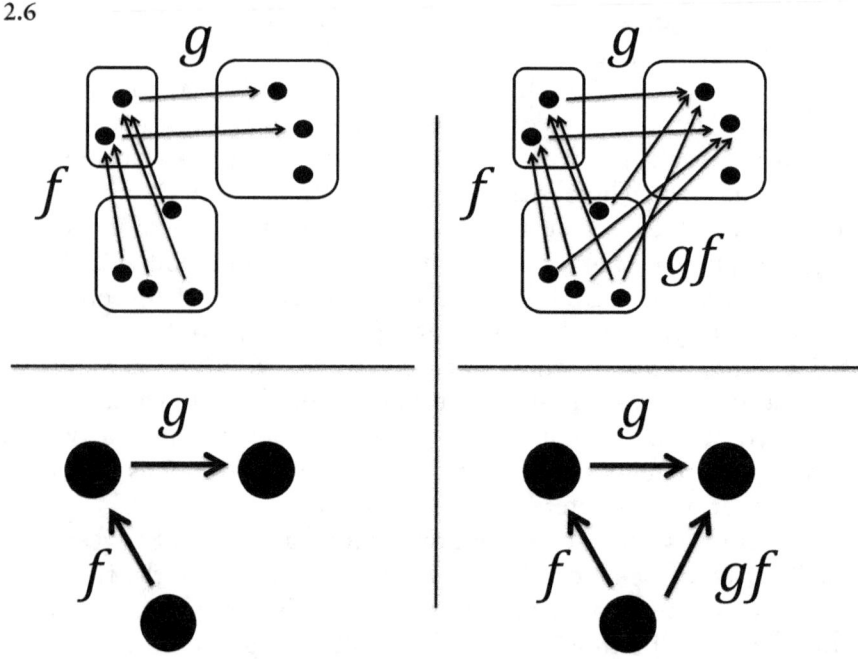

(pictured below the lines on each side), a single dot represents an entire collection and a single arrow represents the entire family of arrows that define a function at the previous level. If the first level provides a relatively ostensive or 'internal' picture of the dynamics of a given function, the second level represents functions between sets in a more abstract and 'external' way. We will call any graph at the second level a *graph of functions*.

Notice that graphs of functions may in general be more complicated than graphs of partial orders. In particular, in graphs of functions, there may be multiple arrows going from one dot to another, and there may be arrows going in both directions between dots; that is, for two dots X and Y, there may be arrows X→Y as well as arrows Y→X. This means that generally criteria 1 and 4 above for partial orders do not hold. (Under what conditions are graphs of functions among sets *also* partial orders?) However, graphs of functions do exhibit certain regular characteristics, or at least may be extended in well-defined ways to ensure this. In particular, they may always be extended in a unique way to meet structural criteria closely related to criteria 2 and 3 above for partial orders.

For one thing, every set may be uniquely associated with an identity function that takes each element of the set to itself. The internal picture of this function appears exactly as the partial-order representation of the set. The external picture of an identity function represents the set as a single loop-arrow from the dot representing the set into itself. It is typically not the only such arrow. How is it distinguished? From a purely external point of view, it is necessary to examine the function's compositions with other functions (see below). For any graph of a system of functions, we may require that this unique identity-function arrow be added to the diagram if it is not already there. Doing so ensures that a variant of the reflexivity criterion above (criterion 2) is met, with the important difference that the unique identity arrow is not in general the only arrow that goes from a dot to itself, since criterion 1 has been relaxed.

Another thing that we may do with functions is to *compose* them, much in the same way that subset selections were seen to compose with one another. In fact the earlier composition of subset selections now appears as a restricted case of the more general notion of composition of functions. It is necessary simply to relax the restriction that no two 'internal' arrows may have the same target-dot. The representation of functions as arrows between dots makes this easy to see. Essentially, a composition of functions then corresponds to a *path* of arrows in a graph of functions. Any such path determines a unique composition, and hence a unique (possible) arrow. In Figure 2.6, the function gf is the composition of g following f (compare the right and left sides of the diagram).

If for some given graph of functions the requirement is imposed that for any pair f and g of head-to-tail arrows the arrow gf representing the function that composes f and g must also be pictured in the graph, then what results is a kind of generalisation of the transitivity criterion (criterion 3) for partial orders. All pathways of arrows will be uniquely represented by a single arrow. Interestingly, for any series of compositions (that is, for pathways of three or more arrows) the order of individual composition-pairs is irrelevant. Formally, $h(gf) = (hg)f$. Any graph of functions may be uniquely extended by introducing any identity and composition arrows that may be missing from it. We will call such a graph a *regular* graph of functions. Because such an extension is uniquely determined in any given case, it is convenient to treat every graph of functions as already implicitly regular. This is directly analogous notationally to 'dropping' the reflexivity and transitivity arrows in partial orders above.

The above concerns apply to arbitrary graphs of functions. What if as a special type of case we are interested in the graph of *all* the possible functions between sets for some given collection of sets? A graph of this kind will be called a *complete* graph of functions. We are then guaranteed to have as many arrows from any dot X to any dot Y as there are distinct functions from the set represented by X to the set represented by Y. This will imply in particular that every dot will have as many loop-arrows from itself to itself as there are functions for which that set is both domain and codomain. One of these, of course, will be the identity-function. Because identity-functions and composition-functions are always well-defined, the arrows representing these functions will inevitably be present in any complete graph of functions and their presence will guarantee that the function-based versions of the criteria of reflexivity and transitivity as described above will be met. In other words, given any collection of sets, the 'external' graph of those sets and all functions among them will automatically be both 'reflexive' and 'transitive' in the functional sense of identities and compositions. This implies, then, that every complete graph of functions is necessarily regular. Consider the complete graph below in Figure 2.7 of functions among sets with one, two and three elements, where two of the individual arrows (functions) have been selected and their 'internal' structure

2.7

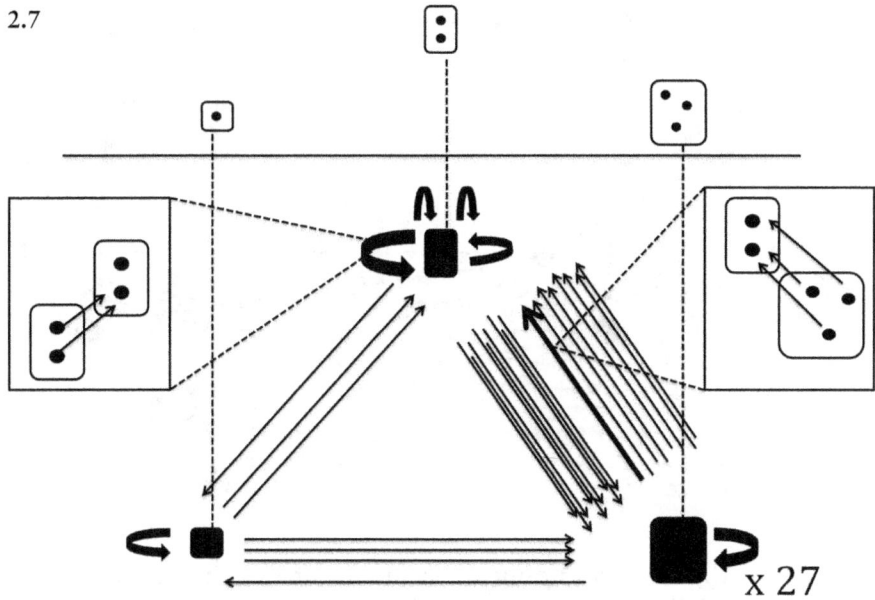

shown. For any collection of sets whatsoever, a complete graph of functions may be naturally induced on them in a similar way.[6]

The relationships between the internal and external diagrams of functions are deep and sometimes surprising. The internal 'content' of a function may in general be recovered solely from the external graphical 'form' of maps and their compositions, if necessary by introducing additional sets and functions to the corresponding graph. Yet this is true only up to the general 'shape' of the function in which all the 'internal' dots of the sets involved are treated as interchangeable. What this means is that we may take two essentially different conceptual perspectives on sets and functions, closely related to the difference between 'internal' and 'external' diagrammatic representations. From the first, more abstract perspective, sets with the same externally determined structure are simply identified. What this means essentially is that if two sets have the same number of elements (in set theoretical terminology, the same cardinality) they are treated as a single dot. Thus from this perspective different dots in graphs of functions must have different cardinalities, or numbers of elements. From the second perspective, every internally distinct set is treated as a distinct graphical dot. Sets themselves from this point of view are distinguished not by their structure (their compositional potential) but by their inner content, even if this content is not

2.8

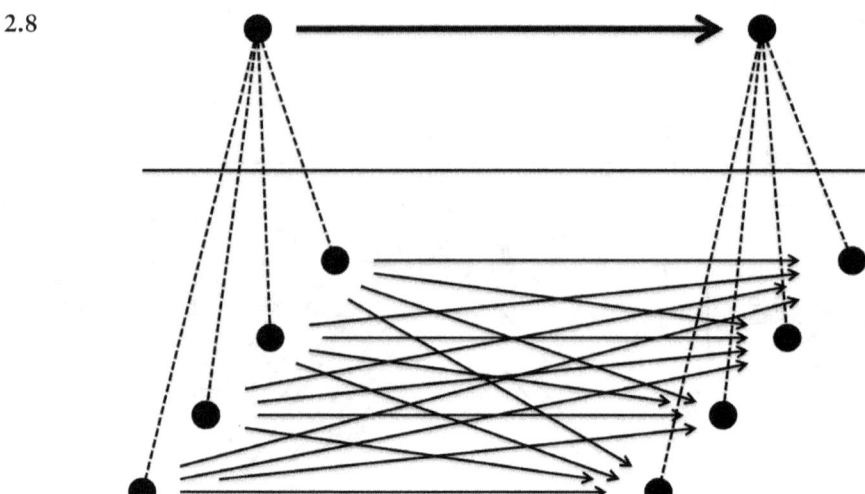

'visible' in the corresponding diagram. In effect, diagrammatically speaking, their internal dots – whether presented explicitly or not – should be understood as selections of individual elements from some independent domain (such as a chosen model of ZFC set theory or a barnyard of chickens). This second point of view is essentially that of Fregean extensionality. The relation between the two perspectives is schematised in the diagram above in Figure 2.8, where a single arbitrary function seen from the more abstract perspective above the line is 'projected' onto the class of all the equivalent functions below the line as viewed from the second, extensional perspective. Note the similarity between this diagram and the diagram of affective potentiality in Spinoza from the previous chapter.

CATEGORIES

We are now in a position to define categories in a general way. The nature of a category may be taken initially to be an abstraction or diagrammatic selection made from two of the types of graphs discussed above, partial orders and regular graphs of functions. This implies that without being aware of it, we have nonetheless already been working within category theory for some time now, although only in certain restricted or specialised modes. All of the previous examples of partial orders were already examples of categories, because all partial orders are (representable as) categories. And all of the examples of regular graphs of functions were already categories

Diagrams of Structure: Categories and Functors

as well. All that is necessary now is to select explicitly the properties relevantly common to partial orders and regular graphs of functions and thus to abstract away from the extraneous ones.

First of all, then, we know that partial orders and regular graphs of functions may be understood as specific types of directed graphs, that is, they are collections of dots connected by arrows in certain regulated ways. So, too, a category from this perspective is simply a type of directed graph. What additional criteria must it satisfy? Closely related to criteria 2 and 3 for partial orders above (and their analogues in graphs of functions), categories are constrained by three general criteria that we will designate as axioms C1, C2 and C3.

(C1) (Composition) For any two arrows f and g that meet 'head-to-tail' (that is, the same dot is the target of f and the source of g), there is exactly one arrow called the 'composition' of f and g that goes from the source of f to the target of g. This composition arrow is written gf (read 'g following f').

(C2) (Identity) Every dot has an arrow called its 'identity' that is compositionally inert. That is, for every dot X, there is an arrow i: X→X such that for any arrow a going into or out of X, the composition of a with i (either ia or ai) is a itself.

(C3) (Associativity) For any two overlapping composition arrows gf and hg, the composition of h following gf is the same as the composition of hg following f, or $h(gf)=(hg)f$.

These axioms are schematised in the diagrams below in Figure 2.9, where hollow dots and hollow arrows informally represent 'any

2.9

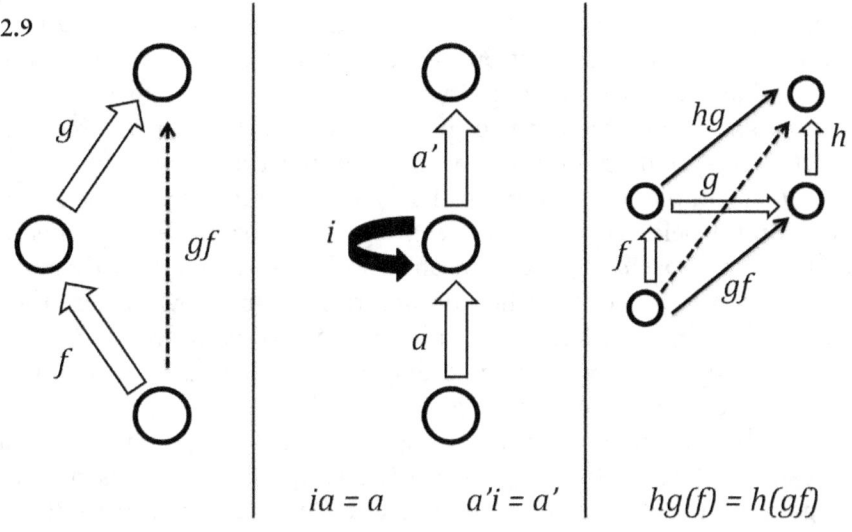

$ia = a$ $a'i = a'$ $hg(f) = h(gf)$

such' dots or arrows and a dashed arrow represents 'there exists exactly one such arrow' in the relevant context.

The three axioms C1–C3 may be summarised in a pair of intuitive rules of thumb concerning paths of arrows, that is, arbitrary sequences of arrows connected head to tail in categorical diagrams. In any category:

1. Every path of arrows is equivalent to a unique arrow.
2. Paths of arrows are indifferent to identities.

The first rule of thumb consolidates the composition and associativity axioms. Of course, it is technically necessary to stipulate that the unique arrow equivalent to any given path must go from the path's first source dot to its last target. In practice, this is always easy to keep in mind because of the evident 'arrow-like' character of such paths. The second rule of thumb reminds us that identity arrows may be arbitrarily added or subtracted from pathways without altering them, that is, without altering the composition arrows they determine. These are precisely the reasons that justified the more convenient and intuitive notation for partial orders introduced above in Figure 2.3, which we will continue to use in fashioning categorical diagrams.

Conceptually, a category may be thought of as a collection of objects embedded in a network of (typically overlapping and multi-directional) partial orders that distribute and interfere with one another in a certain coherent, rule-governed way. The graph notation of dots and arrows lends itself naturally to representing arbitrary parts of such systems as formal diagrams. A *diagram* D in a category C is the selection of a directed graph from among the dots and arrows of C. A diagram is said to *commute* or to be *commutative* if all possible paths of its arrows with the same source and target correspond to the same unique composition arrow. In Figure 2.10 for example, the upper left diagram commutes if, as labelled in the diagram below it, $h=gf$ and $k=jh=jgf$. Two or more diagrams in the same category *compose* with one another to form a new diagram when they are 'glued' together along any dots or arrows where they overlap. The bottom left diagram in Figure 2.10 is, in this sense, the composition of the two 'triangle diagrams' $h=gf$ and $k=jh$ as glued together along h and its source and target dots.

Probably the most important aspect of category theory from a philosophical perspective is that it offers a highly subtle instrument for gauging the degrees of identity and difference between elements

2.10

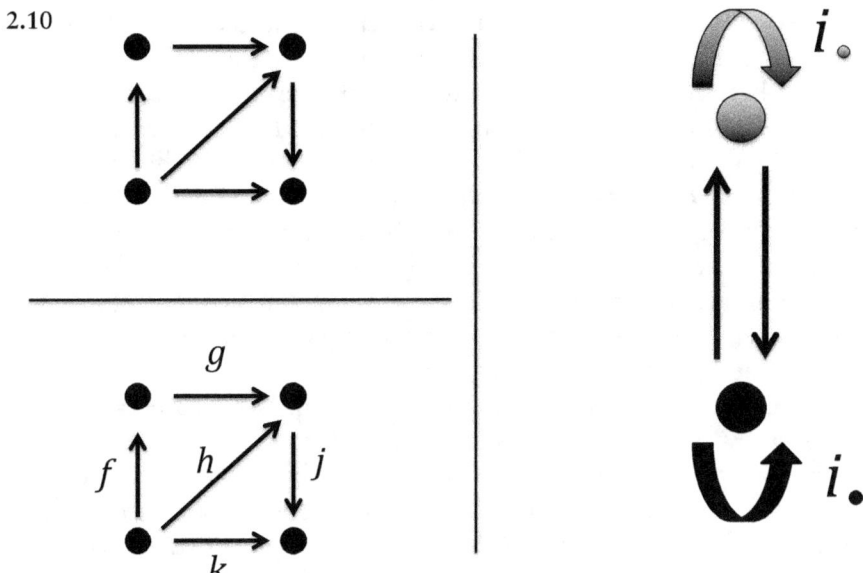

of an abstract domain. In this regard, one of the most important concepts of category theory is that of *isomorphism*. In general, theorems in category theory are proven 'up to isomorphism', meaning that if a result is proven for some object X, then this same result applies to any object that is isomorphic to X. What this means in practice is that within any given category, if two objects are isomorphic, then they are for all practical and consequential purposes 'the same'. Isomorphism is a generalisation and controlled relaxation of strict identity within the 'pragmatic' context of categories where ordered arrows matter more than independent dots.

Two objects X and Y in a category **C** are *isomorphic* if there are arrows $f: X \to Y$ and $g: Y \to X$ such that the composition arrow *fg* is the identity arrow on Y and the composition arrow *gf* is the identity arrow on X. More simply, two objects or dots in a category are isomorphic if a diagram selecting them that is structured like that on the right of Figure 2.10 exists and is commutative (where the *i* arrows are the respective identities). This entails as a special case that every object is isomorphic to itself (just take both *f* and *g* in the definition to be the identity arrow on whatever object). Upon reflection, it should be clear why this definition entails that isomorphic objects are for all practical purposes the same from the standpoint of the category of which they are a part. Because of the axiom of composition, any object that is connected to some other object by at least one arrow is necessarily connected to all the objects connected to the latter by arrows going in the same direction. In short, then, the stipulated relation between the pair of arrows that ensures two objects in a category are isomorphic ensures at the same time that all arrows-in and arrows-out with respect to those objects are effectively the same with respect to all other objects in the category. Both the arrows-in and the arrows-out of two isomorphic objects must exactly mirror one another. Since arrows and their path-compositions alone determine relative difference and hence relative sameness in a category, isomorphic objects are thus themselves 'effectively' or 'consequentially' the same in the context of the category as a whole.

For any category it is possible to 'shrink' the category to its *skeleton* by identifying all isomorphic objects.[7] Since the systems of arrows in and out of two isomorphic objects are distinguished *only* by the inconsequential difference between those objects themselves, the 'collapse' of this difference as a result of identifying the two isomorphic objects simply snaps their already matching arrow-systems into one, like the slipping into alignment of congruent figures engraved separately on two panes of glass.

Universal mapping properties

Recall the earlier example of partygoers ordered by age. We were able to identify the youngest and oldest individuals at the party solely by noting distinctive properties of the induced system of arrows. Such 'arrows-only' characterisations are instances of a highly useful tool in investigating categories. A *universal mapping property* or *UMP* is a property of an object in a category defined in terms of that object's interactions with *all* other objects in the category via arrows. For example, an *initial object* in a category **C** is an object such that there is exactly one arrow from that object to every object in **C**. In a dual fashion, a *terminal object* is an object such that there is exactly one arrow from every object into it. See the upper right and upper left diagrams in Figure 2.11 respectively, where the hollow dot stands for any dot in the category and the dashed arrow means 'exactly one arrow exists'. A simple proof shows that initial and terminal objects are unique up to isomorphism: consider two initial objects I_1 and I_2. By the definition of initial object, there is exactly one arrow $I_1 \to I_2$ and one arrow $I_2 \to I_1$. Also, by the same definition there is exactly one arrow $I_1 \to I_1$ and one arrow $I_2 \to I_2$. These latter arrows must be the identities, since identity arrows exist for all objects. Therefore a diagram like that on the right in Figure 2.10 above exists and is commutative for I_1 and I_2. The same proof applies immediately to terminal objects.

More generally, the *limit* of a diagram D in some category C is defined as a dot L in C that stands in a special relationship to D, namely, it satisfies two criteria:

(1) There are unique arrows from L into each dot of D that compose commutatively with all the arrows of D. Technically, these arrows should be considered part of the limit L as well. That is, L is more precisely a 'cone-like' object consisting of a single dot with multiple arrows coming from it, exactly one for each dot in D, such that all triangles of arrows commute in the extended diagram that composes L and D.

(2) If any other object K in the category *also* meets criterion (1), then there exists exactly one arrow in the ambient category C from K into L that carries K's own commutative diagram commutatively into that of L.

The first criterion establishes a certain positionality of the limit-object L vis-à-vis the selected diagram at issue: it is sufficiently connected to the diagram D via arrows and compositions that it is able to coordinate all the information contained in D in a single coherent manner. This coherence is expressed through the commutativity of the composition of L and D. The second criterion ensures that the limit-object L possesses a certain universal status for structures of its diagrammatic 'type'. In a strikingly Platonic fashion, a limit is such that all appropriate 'rivals' must 'participate' in it via uniquely determined arrows.[8]

To illustrate, consider the diagram on the bottom left of Figure 2.11 as the selection from some arbitrary category C of three particular dots and two arrows connecting them according to the specific 'head to head' pattern shown (two arrows with the same target). The larger dot in the centre diagram taken together with the three arrows coming from it, each of which goes to one of the dots in the previous diagram, will be a limit L for that diagram if two conditions are met: first, the centre diagram commutes (all the pathways from the larger dot to the dot at the lower left compose to the same unique arrow); and second, for any other dot that exists in C connected to arrows that form a similar commutative diagram as in the centre diagram here, there is exactly one arrow in C from it into the larger dot such that the entire resulting diagram commutes. This second condition is represented in the rightmost diagram by the hollow dot (meaning *for*

2.11

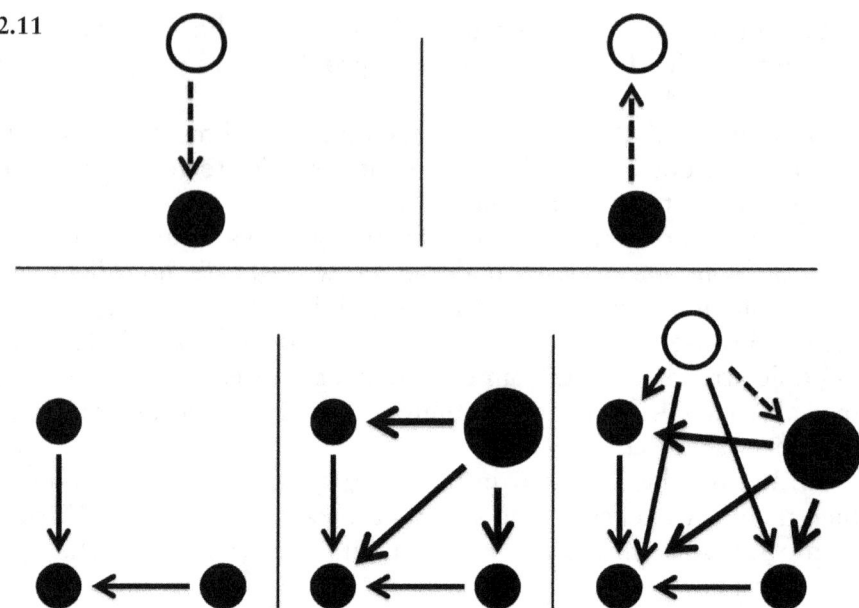

any such object) and the dotted arrow from it into L (meaning *there exists exactly one such arrow*).

If this explanation seems somewhat confusing, consider the leftmost diagram as some selected piece of the earlier graph of partygoers ordered by age. It thus represents two partygoers, each of whom is 'as old or older than' some third partygoer. A dot like the larger dot in the centre diagram will be constrained in this category to represent some partygoer who is 'as old or older than' all three. It may very well be the case that multiple 'candidates' meet this requirement depending on which three dots in the category were selected by the leftmost diagram. How do we choose among them? It will be necessary to find the *one* candidate such that *every such* candidate is 'as old or older than' he or she. This will satisfy the 'local universal' property represented in the rightmost diagram. A moment's reflection should be sufficient to convince the reader that the only possible solution will be the oldest of the three partygoers selected by the diagram at the left.

Functors

Just as when we examined partial orders and systems of functions we had been working within the framework of category theory without

Diagrams of Structure: Categories and Functors

being aware of it, we have been making use of special mappings between categories called *functors* without being explicit or formal about doing so. In particular what we called a 'selection' above may be understood as a kind of functor between categories. More generally, a functor is any mapping from one category into another that takes every dot in the source category into some dot in the target category and every arrow in the source category into some arrow in the target category *such that the identity and composition of arrows is preserved* across the mapping.

From a more contracted or external point of view, a functor may be diagrammed as simply an arrow from one dot to another, where each dot represents a category. See Figure 2.12 below the line. From a more explicit or internal perspective that carries more diagrammatic information, each of the two categories may be pictured in the now familiar way as framed systems of dots and arrows, and the functor from the source category to the target will be represented as a family of arrows with tails in the source category and heads in the target category, one for each dot and one for each arrow in the source category, taking dots in the source category to dots in the target category and arrows in the source category to arrows in the target category. See Figure 2.12 above the line, and note especially how the two non-identity arrows in the source category are mapped

2.12

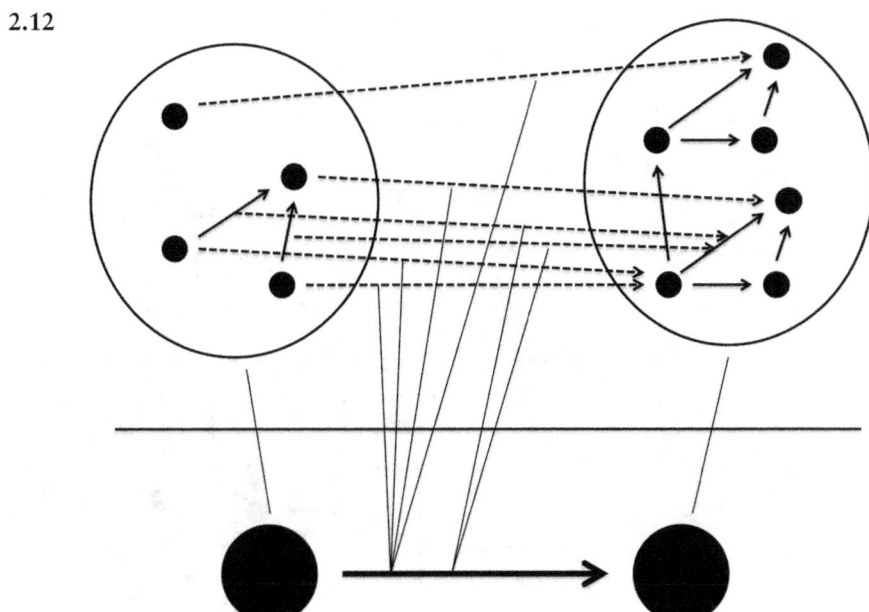

to the same arrow in the target category and how this constrains the two distinct source-dots of those arrows to be mapped by the functor to the same dot (identity arrow mappings are implicit).

More formally, a *functor* $F: \mathbf{C} \to \mathbf{D}$ from category **C** to category **D** is a map that maps every dot of **C** to some dot of **D** and every arrow of **C** to some arrow of **D**, such that

(1) Identity arrows are preserved: if a dot X in **C** is mapped by F to $F(X)$ in **D**, then the identity arrow i_X on X must be mapped to the identity arrow $i_{F(X)}$ on $F(X)$.

(2) Composition of arrows is preserved: for any two arrows g and h in **C** with a composition-arrow hg, the arrow $F(hg)$ in **D** must be the composition $F(h)F(g)$.

Intuitively, a functor stamps or selects an *image* of one category inside another. Some differences among objects and among arrows in the source category may collapse into identities in the image – thus some information (that is, differential structure) may be lost via the mapping – but no *new* differences are allowed to be introduced: no objects (dots) may 'split' into two in the target image, and no arrows are permitted to 'break' or 'tear' from their original systems of compositional relations.

Let us look at functors from three fundamental categories, as easy as **1**, **2**, **3**. We will conceive of the images of functors from these categories as the possible diagrammatic 'semantics' their internal 'syntax' is capable of signifying. Compare the following descriptions with the functors diagrammed in Figure 2.13.

2.13

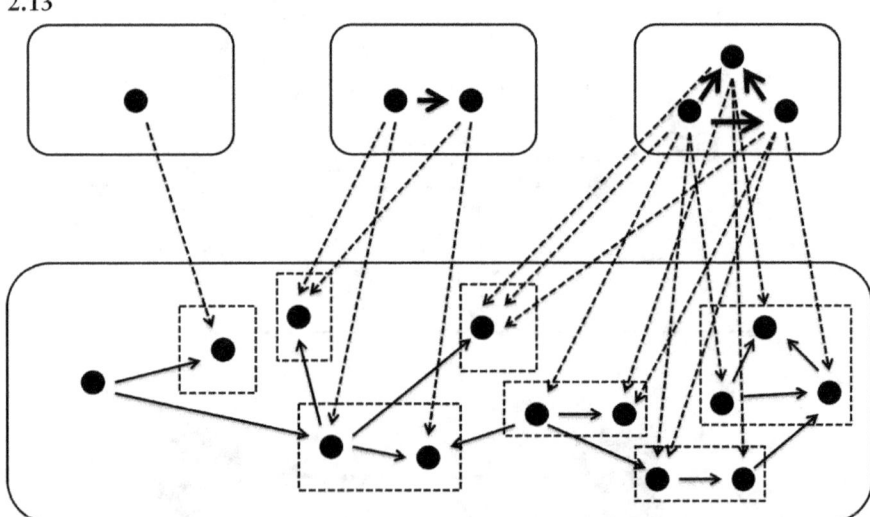

Diagrams of Structure: Categories and Functors

First, we consider the category **1**, consisting of just one dot and the one arrow required by the Identity axiom C2. What does this category represent? In a word, *something*. Or from a slightly different perspective, *anything at all*. If we presume that each thing is identical to itself (no small presumption in some philosophical circles), then the category **1** is just the diagrammatic representation of any particular thing whatsoever, considered in abstraction from the various systems of relation in which it may be embedded. Look back at the non-standard definition of a set that we cobbled together in the section on partial orders. A set according to that definition is just a collection of **1**s. Such a collection is also a category. We may conceive it as a category that contains no more 'internal' information than we are able to extract by examining the possible functors from **1** into it. In a certain sense, such a category is *nothing but* the collection of such functors. In general, functors from **1** into any category simply select dots (objects) in that category.

The only slightly more complicated category called **2** represents a pair of things each 'equipped' with its own identity. But unlike the category that consists of merely two copies of **1**, this category also includes a single arrow that effectively *orders* the two objects. Using arrows alone, it is possible to distinguish the two dots: one is determined as 'the dot at the tail of the only non-identity arrow', and the other is determined as 'the dot at the head of the only non-identity arrow'. We may call these the initial and the terminal dot respectively in this category. Note that these may be selected and distinguished by means of (the only two possible) functors from **1** into **2**.

Functors from **2** into any category **C** map the pair of dots in **2** into corresponding dots in **C** and map the one arrow from the initial to the terminal dot in **2** into a single arrow between the dots selected in **C**. In short, functors from **2** select a single arrow in the target category. Here it is important to recall that the two dots that are distinct in **2** may 'collapse' to a single dot in the target, thus losing their distinctiveness in the image of **2** within the target category. In such a case, the arrow selected by the functor from **2** will necessarily be an arrow in the target category whose own source and target are the same dot (which however may or may not be the identity arrow on that dot).

What does **3** represent? Three distinct things, each with its own identity, and among these an order-structure composed of three arrows differentiating an initial, a medial and a terminal object.

Functors from 3 into whatever category select a single compositional 'triangle' in that category, that is, three arrows – say f, g and h – such that $gf=h$. Just as the distinct dots in 2 may in some functors collapse into a single dot in the target category, the dots in 3 may collapse as well, with the difference that with three dots there are more possibilities for collapse, more degrees of coincidental freedom. Any such collapse, however, must respect the composition of arrows, which means that there are effectively just four structural 'types' of functors with 3 as the source category.

Historically, people were counting and doing arithmetic for quite some time before the number zero came to light. There are good pragmatic reasons for this: the first useful numbers are one, two and three. The utility of zero only appears later.[9] In any case, whether justified or not, we have reserved the introduction of 0, the 'empty category' until now. There is not a lot to say about this category. It does not represent anything at all. Alternatively, with a shift in perspective we may say that it in fact represents *nothing*.[10] In any case, this category is occasionally of use, due to its simple and distinctive properties. Are there any functors from 0 into other categories? At first glance it would appear that the answer is no. A functor is a structurally regulated map from dots to dots and from arrows to arrows across categories. Since 0 has neither dots nor arrows, how can it support any functors? Certainly there cannot be any functors from a typical category **C** with its various dots and arrows *into* 0, since it is impossible to map the dots and arrows of **C** into those of 0; there just aren't any there to 'target'. But look again carefully at the definition of a functor. A functor is specified when a mapping takes any and all dots and arrows of a source category into dots and arrows of a target category according to certain criteria of coherence. A unique 'empty' mapping trivially takes *any and all* dots and arrows of 0 into any chosen category whatsoever, simply because there are none there in 0 to be taken. Thus exactly one 'empty' functor exists from 0 into whatever target category.

Interestingly, this entails that although consisting of nothing and thus involving neither dots nor arrows and in this way appearing as the very representative and even essence of emptiness, the category 0 is nonetheless capable of consistently sustaining a single functorial arrow from itself to itself. This is perhaps the purest mathematical model of emergence *ex nihilo*, compared to which the empty set of set theory appears as a simple wilful decision, a merely contingent stipulation and not a truly necessary creative expression.

Examples of Categories

Mathematics and reality are full of categories. We conclude the present chapter by listing just a few important examples and types.

(1) Sets and functions: There is first of all the category of all sets and all functions among them, designated **Sets**. There are also what were above called the regular graphs of functions, each of which is a category. Each of these is a fragment or subcategory of **Sets**. In addition, each set itself may be considered to be a category. This is why it was convenient earlier to define sets as restricted partial orders. When sets are considered as categories in this way, each function between two sets may be represented as a functor between the two corresponding categories.

(2) Partial orders: There is a category **Orders** of all partial orders with arrows between them representing order-preserving maps. Also, every partial order is itself a category, as already discussed. This includes maximally free partial orders, or sets, as just described, but also for each set a spectrum of increasingly structured (decreasingly free) orders, with its maximally unfree pole at linear or total orders defined on each set. An important subclass of partial orders are *lattices*, which are essentially partial orders such that every pair of dots has a limit 'below' it in the order (called the *meet* or *greatest lower bound*) and a limit 'above' it in the order (called the *join* or *least upper bound*). See Figure 2.14. These structures are ubiquitous in logic, topology and ordinary experience.

(3) Preorders: What if we relax the restriction on 'loops' or 'cycles' in our partial orders (criterion 4)? Note that if a cycle exists, it is necessarily a 'two-way' cycle – why? (Consider the consequences of criterion 3). Such relaxed partial orders are called *preorders*. Every such preorder may be understood as itself a category, and there is also the category **Preorders** (an extension or supercategory of **Orders**) with all preorders as dots and all order-preserving maps between preorders as arrows. Loops or cycles in a preorder may be treated as collapsing to a single dot in a corresponding partial order (this defines a functor), since all the arrows into and out of each of the dots comprising every loop or cycle are necessarily the same. Indeed, isomorphism may be understood as a generalisation of this functorial 'collapsing' property that applies in any category. In addition, every category **C** may be 'reduced' to a canonical preorder C_{pre} by carrying over all the dots of C into C_{pre} and stipulating that for any two objects X and Y of C, a *single arrow* X→Y exists in C_{pre} if and only if *any arrows* X→Y exist in C.

2.14

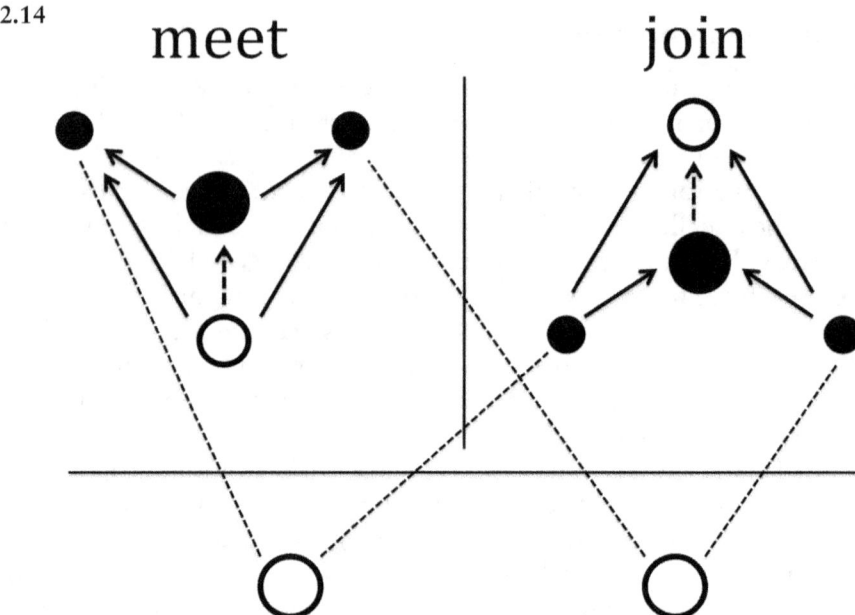

Preorders are less restricted and hence more general than partial orders and thus define a larger class of models. One important type of preorder is that of systems of logical inference. Consider a collection of *statements* represented – as by now should be habitual – by a collection of dots, one for each statement. Now consider drawing an arrow from one dot to another if and only if the statement represented by the target dot is a legitimate logical *inference* from the statement represented by the source dot, that is, X→Y just if statement X logically implies statement Y. Under ordinary assumptions about logical inference, we are assured that the resultant graph meets criteria (2) and (3) above for partial orders. Every statement implies itself (reflexivity), and for any statements P, Q and R, if P implies Q and Q implies R, then P implies R (transitivity). Criterion (1) is also met, by stipulation, since we do not distinguish among more than one 'kind' of inference: either P implies Q or not, but we do not allow for two distinct ways that P might imply Q. But note that in general criterion (4) will *not* be satisfied. It is perfectly acceptable for P to imply Q and Q also to imply P. In fact, this is the very definition of logical equivalence. In categorical terms, logical equivalence is inferential isomorphism.

(4) Categories: Finally, there is the category of categories, which we designate **Categories**. Its dots are categories and its arrows are

Diagrams of Structure: Categories and Functors

functors. Functors between categories interact with one another much as functions between sets do. For instance, just as a function arrow into a given set may be composed with any function arrow out of that same set to determine a third function (given two functions $f: A \to B$ and $g: B \to C$, where A, B and C are sets, there always exists the composition function $gf: A \to C$), a functor going into a given category may be composed with any functor out of that same category to determine a third functor (given two functors $F: \mathbf{A} \to \mathbf{B}$ and $G: \mathbf{B} \to \mathbf{C}$, where **A**, **B** and **C** are categories, there always exists the composition functor $GF: \mathbf{A} \to \mathbf{C}$). Similarly, just as every set comes equipped with an identity function that maps each element to itself (given a set S, there is a function i_S such that $i_S(x)=x$ for all elements x of S) and this identity function serves as the identity arrow in **Sets** and its subcategories, every category comes equipped with an identity functor mapping each object and each arrow of the category to itself (given a category **C**, there is a functor $I_\mathbf{C}$ such that $I_\mathbf{C}(X)=X$ for all objects X of **C** and $I_\mathbf{C}(f)=f$ for all arrows f of **C**). In addition, these compositions and identities perform as required by the categorical axioms. In particular, the composition of functors is associative. This means that there are well-defined categories whose objects are categories themselves and whose arrows are functors between categories (analogous to regular graphs of functions). Indeed for any given collection of categories, we have the naturally induced category whose objects are the given categories and whose arrows are all the functors between those categories (analogous to complete graphs of functions).

The category **Categories** expresses the structure of all categories and all functors among them. Is there any way to find our bearings among this tangled structure of tangled structures? We have already defined several of the dots of this category/meta-category. In particular, our categories **0** and **1** play special roles in it. For any category whatsoever, call it **C**, there is exactly one functor $\mathbf{0} \to \mathbf{C}$ and exactly one functor $\mathbf{C} \to \mathbf{1}$. Notice that these functors go in 'opposite directions', the one going into **C** and the other coming from **C**. Among the many diagrams we might select within **Categories**, then, are those schematised in Figure 2.15, where the hollow circle above the line ranges universally across all categories and the dashed arrows signify 'exactly one functor exists'.

A single complex object composed of unimaginably many 'individuals' (dots as categories) and all the possible structurally consistent 'relations' among them (arrows as functors), infinitely stretched out as it were between initial **0** and terminal **1** – perhaps this structure is

2.15

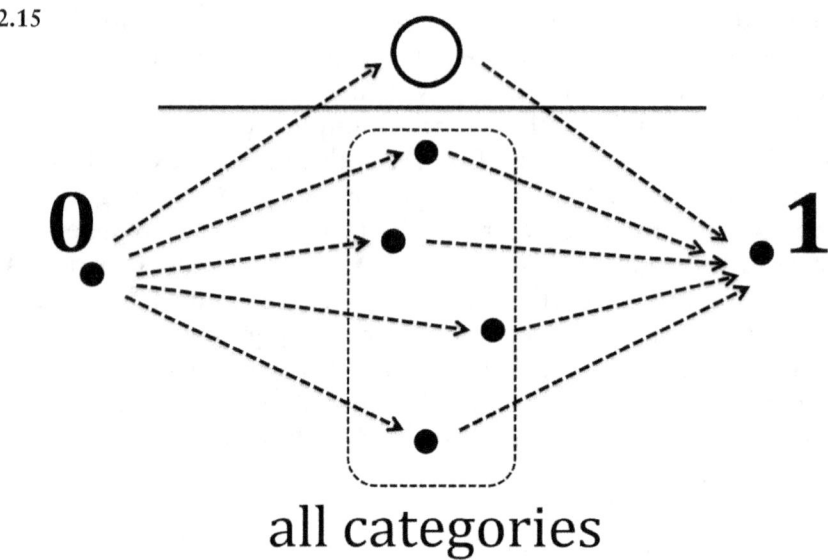

all categories

rich enough to model the absolutely infinite relational ontology presented in Spinoza's *Ethics*.

Notes

1. At a methodological level, note that this particular example fulfils its exemplary and ostensive functions by instantiating all the relevant differences and variations at issue while more or less minimising redundancies.
2. In effect, it can be mapped (in very many ways incidentally) onto a finite continuous line segment while preserving all the relevant differences among the dots without introducing any new arrows between them. Mathematically we can name this paradigmatic order of finite continuity [0,1]. This notation is meant to represent the set of real numbers between zero and one, the square brackets signifying that this is a 'closed interval', that is, an interval that includes its endpoints. Much can be done with this little line.
3. Things become only marginally more complicated when considering infinite sets of various orders.
4. The identification of set-elements as merely certain kinds of set-parts is characteristic of the categorical approach to sets. In contrast, the importance of the difference in kind between elements and parts (subsets) is a major feature of standard set theory, as explained and developed in an ontological register throughout Badiou's *Being and Event*.
5. Lawvere and Schanuel, *Conceptual Mathematics*, pp. 81–5.

6. For infinite collections of sets or collections involving infinite sets, complete graphs of functions of course cannot be 'materially' constructed, even in principle. Nevertheless – certain technical issues in set theory and model theory aside – their induced complete graphs of functions remain thoroughly determined. Diagrams may be (and in mathematics typically are) abstract, that is, selected from within an abstract domain of objects and relations.
7. Technically, there are in general many such skeletons, depending on which objects in the category the isomorphic objects collapse into in the skeleton. Nonetheless, all the resultant skeletons are essentially (structurally) the same.
8. See David Ellerman, 'Category Theory and Concrete Universals'.
9. See Brian Rotman, *Signifying Nothing*.
10. Heideggereans, Badiousians, mereologists and Lebowskians will appreciate the ensuing semantic subtleties.

CHAPTER 3

Peirce and Semiotic Immanence

> It seems a strange thing, when one comes to ponder over it, that a sign should leave its interpreter to supply a part of its meaning; but the explanation of the phenomenon lies in the fact that the entire universe, – not merely the universe of existents, but all that wider universe, embracing the universe of existents as a part, the universe which we are all accustomed to refer to as 'the truth', – that all this universe is perfused with signs, if it is not composed exclusively of signs.
>
> C. S. Peirce, 'The Basis of Pragmaticism'

In his 1868 article for the *Journal of Speculative Philosophy*, 'Some Consequences of Four Incapacities', Charles Peirce lays out a systematic rejection of the principles of Cartesianism. His rationale consists of the assertion and defence of the 'four incapacities' of his title, four powers that the Cartesian tradition has in one way or another presumed to exist and which Peirce himself denies the philosophical inquirer (and by extension, the community of inquirers) to possess. Peirce summarises his anti-Cartesian quartet as follows:

> 1. We have no power of Introspection, but all knowledge of the internal world is derived by hypothetical reasoning from our knowledge of external facts.
> 2. We have no power of Intuition, but every cognition is determined logically by previous cognitions.
> 3. We have no power of thinking without signs.
> 4. We have no conception of the absolutely incognizable.[1]

It is worth citing Peirce's defence of the fourth and final claim at some length since in it he raises a number of issues that will be crucial in what follows. Essentially, in justifying his rejection of any concept of the 'absolutely incognizable', Peirce moves from an initial conception of the mind-independent thing-in-itself that serves as a sort of ideal original limit of cognitive experience to a terminal understanding of the mind-independent real as a futural projection made on the basis of thought's presumptive tendency to exclude progressively the idiosyncratic aspects of individual cognitions. In other words, he orders the conceptual dynamics of thought itself in terms of a continuum or open interval stretched from the minimally to the maximally general, yet comprising neither endpoint within it. Thus an orientation immanent to thought is described that nonetheless sits between two poles of 'objective' mind-independence that cognition approaches as asymptotic limits, the first being posited to exist prior to the mind's activity and instigating it; the second being no longer dependent on any particular mind and thus ideally completing the cognitive process. In Peirce's words:

> At any moment we are in possession of certain information, that is, of cognitions which have been logically derived by induction and hypothesis from previous cognitions which are less general, less distinct, and of which we have a less lively consciousness. These in their turn have been derived from others still less general, less distinct, and less vivid; and so on back to the ideal first, which is quite singular, and quite out of consciousness. This ideal first is the particular thing-in-itself. It does not exist *as such*. That is, there is no thing which is in-itself in the sense of not being relative to the mind, though things which are relative to the mind doubtless are, apart from that relation. The cognitions which thus reach us by this infinite series of inductions and hypotheses (which though infinite *a parte ante logice*, is yet as one continuous process not without a beginning *in time*) are of two kinds, the true and the untrue, or cognitions whose objects are *real* and those whose objects are *unreal*. And what do we mean by the real? It is a conception which we must first have had when we discovered that there was an unreal, an illusion; that is, when we first corrected ourselves. Now the distinction for which alone this fact logically called, was between an *ens* relative to private inward determinations, to the negations belonging to idiosyncrasy, and an *ens* such as would stand in the long run. The real, then, is that which, sooner or later, information and reasoning would finally result in, and which is therefore independent of the vagaries of me and you.[2]

Thus, Peirce concludes, 'since no cognition of ours is absolutely determinate, generals must have a real existence'.[3] This line of argumentation is in effect what makes Peirce – swimming against the powerful tide of nearly all modern philosophy – a scholastic realist rather than a nominalist. The dynamism and immanent orientation of all thinking towards increasing generality reduces to contradiction any notion of concepts as merely arbitrary and inert 'names'.

Against the received notion that scholastic realism posits illegitimate 'metaphysical fictions', Peirce points out that 'a realist is simply one who knows no more recondite reality than that which is represented in a true representation'.[4] In other words, for Peirce the real is not what is wholly external or independent of thought, but is on the contrary that upon which thought itself has the tendency to converge *independently of any particular cognitive event or site*. Thought is a self-magnetising arrow, and the concept of the absolutely incognizable is as self-refuting a notion as that of an extended space composed entirely of inextensive points.

Like Spinoza, then, Peirce rejects modes of (apparent) explanation that in fact merely refer the thing to be explained to some mystery or some singular 'unknown X'. However Peirce is certainly no rationalist in the standard mould, in the sense of endorsing an essential epistemological, or more broadly philosophical priority of logical concepts and formal deduction to the hazards and vagaries of sensible reality, even if he indeed asserts that 'every cognition is determined logically by previous cognitions'. Few if any philosophers have more thoroughly rooted their thought in the rich soil of worldly experience than Peirce, giving due consideration to the real capacities of our surroundings to surprise and to instigate us to think. No one has done more to make room in the modern tradition of philosophy for vagueness, guesses, hunches and to show how essential such blurred structures and informal practices are to good scientific inquiry. By giving name to the 'fallacy of misplaced concreteness', Whitehead diagnosed one of the most profound, because most frequently overlooked, pitfalls of philosophy. Anachronistically, the prognosis for this disorder – which from an immanent standpoint amounts to an irrational fear of thinking as such – is to be found with Peirce and his unique conjunction of semiotics, metaphysics and pragmatic epistemology.

Indeed, in a different text Peirce reflects on the Molièrean canard of the learned doctor who ascribes 'dormitive virtue' to opium, thereby 'explaining' why it produces the effects it does. Yet rather than sharing Molière's contempt for such empty and pretentious talk, Peirce finds in it – or rather in the tactic of explanation it illustrates – a kernel of insight worthy of serious philosophical consideration. Peirce writes:

> [E]verybody is supposed to know well enough that the transformation from a *concrete predicate* to an abstract noun in an oblique case, is a mere transformation of language that leaves the thought

absolutely untouched. I knew this as well as everybody else until I had arrived at that point in my analysis of mathematics where I found that this despised juggle of abstraction is an essential part of almost every really helpful part of mathematics; and since then what I used to know so very clearly does not appear to be at all so.[5]

For Peirce, mathematics is involved in the study of any necessary consequential relations whatsoever, and the helpfulness of what he calls the 'despised juggle of abstraction' is thus applicable to a much more extensive range of phenomena than just numerical quantities or mathematics in the conventional sense. It is a component, rather, of all processes of reasoning, even the most ordinary. What matters here to Peirce is the power essential to mathematical thinking that turns relations and properties into things. This power, Peirce sees, is in fact at the root of all systematic questioning. In order to investigate the unknown and thereby to gain knowledge, it is necessary first to make a pair of presumptions: something must be presumed there to be known in the first place, and something must be presumed doable that will appropriately disclose it. If the former presumption fails, then inquiry will turn out empty. If the latter, then inquiry will be hopelessly blind. Simply to begin any process of inquiry, one must indicate at least in the projected mode of concrete possibility the invisible reason for the visible given, the potentially lawlike intelligibility of the as yet merely sensed or hoped for. This ability to stipulate an index of the unknown ('there must be *something* at work here') stands at the very core of what it means to seek explanation and more broadly understanding.[6] It involves a generic instance of what Peirce calls the act of 'hypostatic abstraction': 'that process whereby we regard a thought as a thing'.[7] The 'unknown X' is here not an explanatory answer but rather a diagrammatic condition for *seeking* such answers.

In this regard, Peirce conceives a continuum relating the known and the unknown, as well as the sensible and the intelligible. Late in his life, Peirce chose Synechism as the most comprehensive name for his philosophical system because it connotes both continuity and relationality, his most fundamental concepts. More importantly, it suggests a general explanation of relations in terms of how they might be grounded in the structure of the continuum itself. Hookway glosses:

> When we reason about a continuum – about time or a continuous process – we use existential quantifiers to pick out parts of the

continuum and we reason about the relational properties of the elements that we refer to. So to speak, we find a relational structure in the continuum and that provides a focus of our reasoning. However, no one relational structure captures the nature of the continuum, and we cannot quantify over all of the elements of the continuum. The relational structures we reason about are, in a sense, determined by the nature of the continuum we are reasoning about, but they do not exhaust its character.[8]

If the mathematics of category theory provides an infinite universe of structure and relation rich enough potentially to model the absolute infinity of the Spinozist Nature-God, with Peirce we begin to understand just how this structural universe might be put to philosophical work. The relevant conceptual framework for Peirce is that of an immanent nature composed of semiotic processes, and the ensuing investigative method is that of diagrammatic practice.

Dyadic and Triadic Relations

With Peirce as with Spinoza, a relation between metaphysical immanence and the power of signification is at the heart of our investigation. Yet whereas with Spinoza immanence and signification were prima facie at odds and had to be reconciled through a practical conception of logical form, with Peirce the two are intimately correlated at the very basis of his philosophy. For Peirce, the structure of what is ultimately real is semiotic, or sign-like. At the centre of Peirce's philosophy is a structural coordination, a strict homology, between the ultimate categories of experience conceived as kinds of relation and the most basic types of signs. To the relational categories of firstness, secondness and thirdness correspond the fundamental sign-types of icon, index and symbol, respectively. This homology underwrites Peirce's claim that 'all this universe is perfused with signs, if it is not composed exclusively of signs'.[9]

Perhaps Peirce's greatest achievement as a philosopher was to invert the traditional prioritisation of objects over relations in philosophical questioning and to show in a rigorous way how a consistent unification of its traditional themes thereby becomes possible. By starting with and remaining within relations at every step of philosophical inquiry, Peirce instituted a novel form of philosophical immanence, the immanence of signs. Beginning in signs, proceeding through signs, Peirce ends in signs too. The following exposition begins by using Peirce's distinction between dyadic and triadic relations to help explain the difference between Peirce's own semiotic theory and the more familiar notion of signs that comes out of the Saussurean tradition. In using Peirce's distinction between dyadic and triadic signs as a way to approach his thought more generally, we are guided especially by the work of Ochs, Sheriff and Deely, all of whom share a common therapeutic or reconstructive emphasis with respect to the philosophical tradition.[10]

For Peirce all signs are ultimately composed of triadic relations, as we will see, but this does not imply that they are always adequately conceived as such. Indeed, misconceptions concerning the real being of signs – in particular the late medieval victory of nominalism and the carrying over of its dyadic model of concepts and signs into Cartesian and post-Cartesian modernity – are for Peirce at the root of a host of egregious philosophical errors. For this reason, a more adequate understanding of signs as irreducibly triadic relations holds out promise to remedy some of the more negative aspects of the nominalist and Cartesian legacies.

To begin with, we may understand some of the limitations of a metaphysics based only on dyadic relations as these limitations appear through a dyadic understanding of signs. Such an understanding may function on both a naïve, intuitive level as well as in more sophisticated theories of signification such as those developed in structuralist linguistics. At the most basic level, a sign is understood on such a view to indicate or represent some referent. Something points to something else: smoke indicates fire. The precise relationship binding the one to the other need not be specified – it may be causal or imaginative, natural, metaphorical or socially conventional – but at this level, what defines a sign as such is the two-term relation, X indicates Y, connecting the second thing to the first. When human language is interpreted at this basic level we find a simple (nominalist) relationship between *words* and *things*; both the word itself and the thing indicated thereby are conceived as things in the world, and the relation between them is the habitual association of one with the other. Saussure's innovation in linguistic science at the turn of the twentieth century was to locate and analyse a second dyadic relation within the word, or verbal sign itself. This internal dyad is then understood to constitute a second functional level for the understanding of linguistic signs. It is the interior or subjective dimension of human language as determined by an internally coherent set of differential relations that taken together constitute an ideal system of meanings.[11] The two terms a single word-sign relates in this system are then not things in

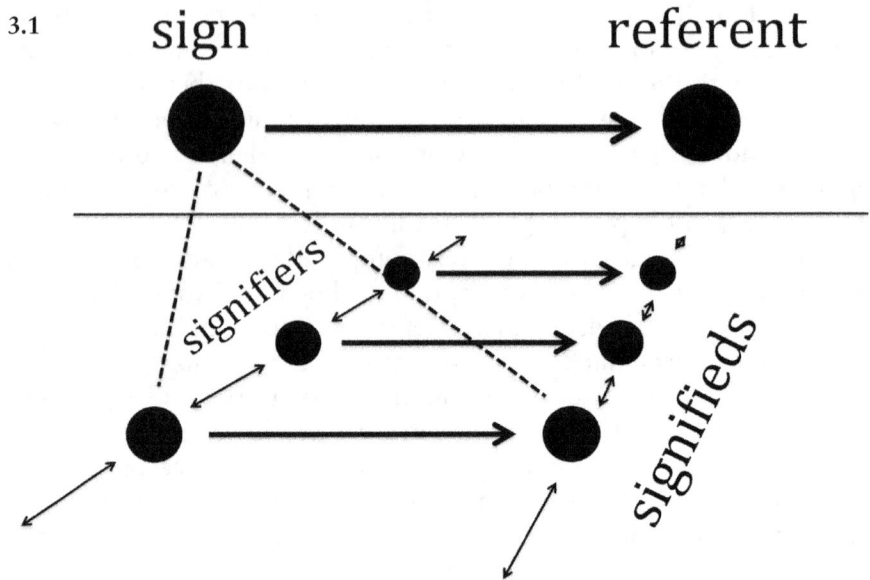

3.1

the world, but subjective idealities – a *word-image* and a *concept*. Here the signifying relationship itself becomes primary, and its two terms are defined on the basis of that relation itself. The sign is the very relation, and the two terms it relates are conceived as *signifier* and *signified*, which are further organised into parallel systems, somewhat as pictured in Figure 3.1.[12]

What allows for the constructive theorisation of this second, ideal level in Saussure is the positing of the dyadic sign-relation as an *arbitrary* relation.[13] This specifically linguistic model of the conventional sign then becomes applicable more generally to a variety of linguistic and non-linguistic cultural codes: consumer products, physical posture, architecture, etc. The dyadic logic of signifier and signified provides a general template for conceiving of abstract meaning as such – this is why Saussure believes that human language conceived dyadically provides the best initial model for the more general science of 'semiology':

> Signs that are wholly arbitrary realize better than the others the ideal of the semiological process; that is why language, the most complex and universal of all systems of expression, is also the most characteristic; in this sense linguistics can become the master-pattern for all branches of semiology although language is only one particular semiological system.[14]

Conceiving of the relation between signifier and signified as 'wholly arbitrary' provides the dyadic model's strength and general applicability. One theoretical advantage of this model thus consists in its ideal bracketing of the complex and individuated history that brings any particular sign into being. The dyadic model abstracts from the concrete history of actual signs and sign-systems to provide an image of the ideal, general signifying structure that all signs possess formally as representations of sense. It is this highly generalised, formal power that has allowed the dyadic conception of signs to find such universal application in the structuralist and semiological analyses of culture. Rather than reducing the unlimited variety of cultural phenomena to a single abstract formula, this approach provides a general theoretical model that can be applied in different cases according to the specificity of whatever meaningful context happens to be under consideration. In this way the dyadic model is universal in principle.

What defines the arbitrariness of the sign for this conception is its capacity to be used, comprehended and interpreted by an abstract or underdetermined subject. In this way the representational dyad is reflectively grounded in the egoic structures of consciousness, abstract interiority and autonomous individuality. The structure of the dyadic sign – the signifying relation of signifier to signified – is in principle accessible in the same way to any observer or 'reader'. In the decoding of the sign, the one for whom the sign signifies remains in principle detached from the event of signification as such – one is 'free' with respect to the meaning the sign discloses. This is why the Saussurean model has been so successfully applied to written texts: the detachment of the signifier/signified relation from the subject who interprets the sign maps closely onto the ordinary reading habits of most readers.[15] Just as I remain free to pick up or put down a novel at will, to skip over boring passages or revisit an especially pleasing scene, as an interpreter of dyadic signs I am free to take or leave the sign's meaning as *I* wish. Thus dyadic signs tend to reinforce a subject-as-sovereign model of mentality.

The meaning presents itself to me as a represented content; this content remains detached from the interpreting gaze that views it. Because of this detachment of the sign's meaning from the one for whom it becomes meaningful, a dyadic sign can make no claim on a given subject which that subject would not have the power to override or ignore at will. Hence not only is the relation between signifier and signified considered arbitrary in the dyadic sign, but the encounter of a particular sign with a given interpretive subject is understood to be arbitrary as well. In this way the dyadic model considers signs like books collected in a library: as a potential reader, one is free to peruse the spines and to choose whatever reading material serves one's own purposes.[16] From this detachment of meaning from subjective freedom follows the always potentially public and universal character of dyadic representations. Since dyadic representations can be conceived independently of the particular subject who reads or interprets them, these representations may typically be publicly communicated and exchanged.

Yet for all its analytical power, the dyadic conception of signs has two major drawbacks. It cannot account for the effective power of particular signifiers to give rise in concrete contexts to specific meanings (why does X, and not Y, signify Z?), and it is unable to include the actual history that both establishes and transforms sign-conventions in the structure of the signs themselves (how does the X–Z relation develop as a historical or traditional formation?). These drawbacks are closely related to one another, and both are entailed by the conception of the arbitrary nature of the sign-relation.

In any socially meaningful sign, a collective and generally long-term contraction of habit has formed the relation between signifier and signified as a *real* relation in the world. The contraction of a habit in the context of social action and communication develops a real relation between two terms that need not have any prior basis in the nature of the two terms themselves. This relation is 'arbitrary', then, only in the sense that it could not have been foreseen. Once the relation is established *in fact* for a given community of sign-users and is therefore recognisable as an actually effective sign, its arbitrariness refers at that point only to the formal structure of the linked terms and no longer to the actual relation as such.[17] In other words, the arbitrariness of dyadic sign-relations is relative to the structure of the dyadic model itself. Signs are viewed as arbitrary by virtue of being analysed or conceived as dyadic representations.

A habitual action only appears arbitrary when considered from the standpoint of purely abstract possibility. From the standpoint of actual use, habitual signs constitute relations by no means arbitrary in fact. Knowing how a given sign actually and effectively signifies a particular meaning or action would be equivalent to knowing its specific history. Actual signification would then be understood as a process of coming to be this one particular sign-relation rather than some other. Asking what a sign is would become equivalent to asking how it has been formed, that is, what has made it work successfully enough to establish itself and endure over time. The field of possibility within which a formal sign-relation is judged to be arbitrary thus loses its import when the actual, historical effectiveness of a given sign is at stake.

To maintain the arbitrariness of the sign even in the context of a long-established communicative context is to deny the relationship between signification and habit. Yet signs are not only meaningful; they are also effective.[18] Any concern for a sign's actual effectiveness has to address a broader set of philosophical questions surrounding contingency and necessity, possibility and actuality, history, force and causality. When signs are understood according to the dyadic model, everything but their formal signifying function is bracketed. All the relational complexity involved in these other aspects of the sign risks being obscured or ignored.

From the dyadic model of the sign, we turn accordingly to signification understood as a unified and irreducibly triadic process of interpretation; on this model, a sign is necessarily involved with the history of habits to which it gives rise.[19] Instead of a two-sided signifier/signified relation, we are led to the three-part schema of sign, object and interpretant as developed by Peirce.

Among the many more or less equivalent definitions of the triadic sign scattered throughout Peirce's writings, one taken from his relatively late (1907) unpublished 'letter' on pragmatism is admirably exact and comparatively clear:

> I will say that a sign is anything, of whatsoever mode of being, which mediates between an object and an interpretant; since it is both determined by the object *relatively to the interpretant*, and determines the interpretant *in reference to the object*, in such wise as to cause the interpretant to be determined by the object through the mediation of this 'sign'.[20]

The technique of the composition of arrows used in category theory models this triadic relation well. A sign stands in some relation to something else, its object, such that by being brought into relation with the sign in some appropriate way, some third thing is brought into an appropriately 'composed' relation to the object. Roughly speaking, an interpretant is brought into relation with the object by means of the sign. Importantly, Peirce uses one term – 'sign' – to represent both one component of the triadic relation (essentially the

3.2

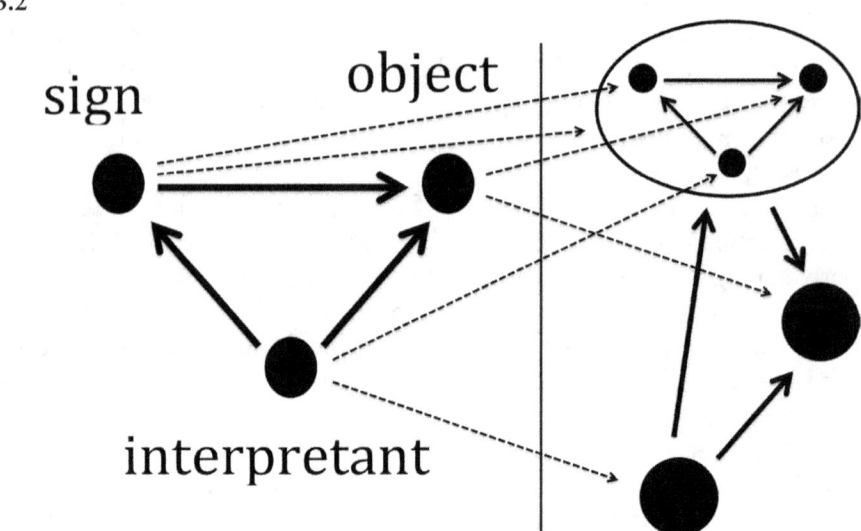

mediator between interpretant and object) and the entire relation itself (the ordered unity of the interpretant-sign-object complex). When Peirce means to specify the former, more restricted or local role of the sign, he sometimes uses the terminology of 'representamen' or 'sign-vehicle'. See Figure 3.2: The mappings from Peirce's general sign-schema on the left to two different instantiations of it on the right show how an entire sign-object-interpretant complex (the oval on the upper right) may itself become the sign-vehicle for a separate, higher-order sign relation (the whole right side of the diagram).

Conceiving of signs in such a way requires a logic of immanent triadic relations.[21] Indeed, for Peirce the transition between triadic relations and triadic signification is seamless; all triadic relations are already necessarily signifying. As Peirce puts it, 'every genuine triadic relation involves meaning'.[22] The basic signifying relation for Pierce is always the triadic relation itself, and in its most general form it appears as the triadic relation between three components that by virtue of the relation that structures them play distinctive roles in the relation as 'sign', 'object' and 'interpretant'.[23]

A logic of triadic relations was developed by Peirce as the cornerstone of his conception of semiotics. Peirce's model bases signification on a genuinely three-term relation, one that cannot be reduced to a sum or hierarchical nesting of dyadic relations. Peirce argues that triadic relations cannot be formed from any assemblage of dyadic relations alone, demonstrating the truth of this claim in part by representing dyadic and triadic relations visually as diagrammatic graphs.[24] Because dyadic relations have only two terms, they can be connected to each other only in a linear series or chain (which may, however, form a circle) no matter how many dyadic 'links' there may be available to colligate. From linkings of dyads, only dyads (or closed monads) can result. A triadic relation, on the contrary, directly and irreducibly links three separate terms in a single relation, and relations with four, five or any number of terms may be easily generated from linkages between triadic relations.[25]

Peirce demonstrates the importance of this difference by showing how it is reflected in certain everyday concepts. His favoured examples for illustrating triadic relations are those of *giving* and *praising*. The relation of 'giving' requires three terms in order for it to exist at all, and the single relation between the three terms cannot be broken up into smaller components. As Peirce puts it:

> Take, for example, the relation of *giving*. A *gives* B to C. This does not consist in A's throwing B away and its accidentally hitting C, like the date-stone, which hit the Jinnee in the eye. If that were all, it would not be a genuine triadic relation, but merely one dyadic relation followed by another.[26]

Peirce's point is that the concept 'giving' (or the sense of the infinitive 'to give') involves an irreducibly triadic relation which cannot be analysed into a simple conjunction of dyadic relations. When A gives B to C, the relation between A and C is in play just as much as the pairs of relations between A and B on the one hand, and B and C on the other. A *single* relation joins A, B and C together in a complex but unified event. The same structure is evident in the form: A praises B to C. The co-implication of all of these relations in a single event, the arising of a new three-term relation in which they cohere as constituents of an irreducible whole, is precisely what defines the triadic relation as such. In either case, however, A, B and C need not be separate individuals. The relation itself – the act of gift or praise – potentially modalises a single individual into more than one distinct term, if for example Joe praises Mary to Mary. In this act, Mary as object of praise is differentiated semiotically from Mary as interlocutor of Joe. The relation itself remains triadic although only two distinct individuals are involved.

The triadic relational model of giving is represented categorically by the diagram in Figure 3.3, which shows functors from the category 3 into the isomorphic sign-category 'giving' which then

3.3

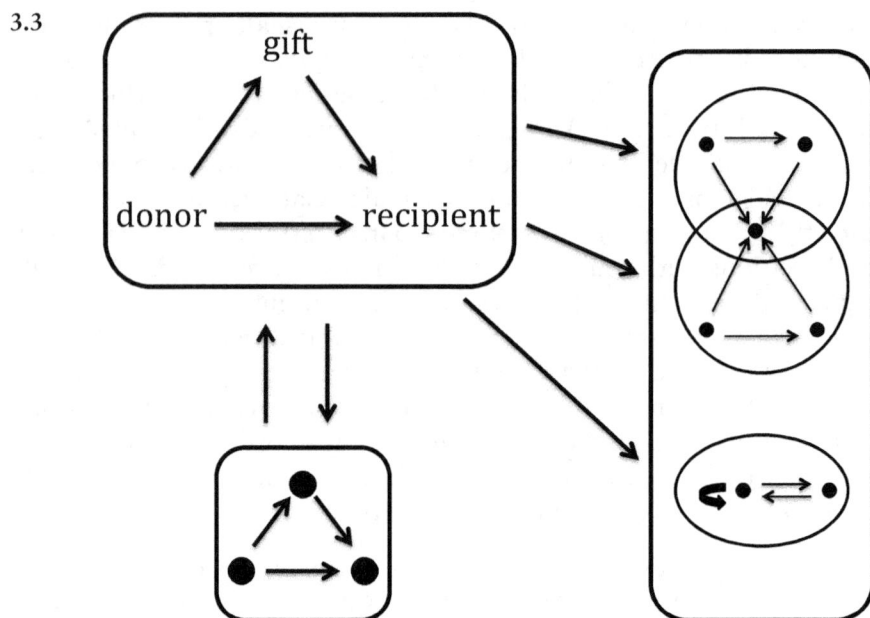

compose with functors from this latter category into whatever categorical fragment of the world might be at issue. Particular acts of giving then correspond to functors from the relatively abstract category 'giving' (itself a specification of the more general category-type 3) into some worldly category representing individuals and their various relations. Collapsing of dots in the image of the composition of the functors here corresponds to cases in which a single individual plays two or more roles in the gift-relation. In the semantics indicated in the diagram, one individual is the recipient of two gifts from two different donors, and another individual gives himself or herself a gift.

Metaphysics as semiotics

Peirce clarifies and extends the idea of triadic relations on the basis of his fundamental phenomenological or 'phaeneroscopical' categories of firstness, secondness and thirdness.[27] While *firstness* for Peirce designates a pure and undifferentiated quality (pure 'redness', for example), and *secondness* refers to the brute, interruptive fact of a real event (for example, the blindly interruptive reaction to a ringing telephone when it disturbs the continuity of a daydream), *thirdness* provides a synthesis of quality and reaction in anticipation of further development or potential meaning ('that must be Steve'). In Peirce's words, thirdness 'is that which is what it is by virtue of imparting a quality to reactions in the future'.[28] This projective synthesis is for Peirce the domain of meaning, mediated reflection, conscious activity and thought in general.

In this regard, it may be possible to misinterpret the 'futural' character of thirdness. Thirdness is not simply a matter of what is to come; it is a constitutive structure of temporality in general as a meaningfully ordered stream of experience and practice. It refers to all experienced continuity in time, to lived duration as the experience of orientation towards an indeterminate but not arbitrary future. Thirdness thus includes any practical involvement in any meaningful process.[29] Such involvement always has a futural dimension, but it possesses this on the basis of a projective continuity with the past and the present. Essential to our purposes here is Peirce's inference from the logic of dyadic and triadic relations to the claim that thirdness cannot be reduced to either qualitative firstness, reactive secondness, or any simple conjunction of these. Thirdness is a category of experience *sui generis*. In consequence, the temporal dimension of meaningful practice is itself irreducible, since it cannot be analysed into more basic components, of which it would be the mere consequence, effect or sum. In other words, the specifically temporal feature of thought cannot be modelled accurately by a purely qualitative immediacy ('firstness'), or an instantaneously interruptive snapshot, or representation of thinking ('secondness'), but only by means of a continuous, temporally ordered and open-ended process itself ('thirdness'). Such a process opens up possibilities by integrating new and more highly-differentiated relations into those already composing it at any given stage.

The key thing to note about Peirce's model is that the practice of interpreting the sign (thirdness as activity or habit) is necessarily involved in the form of the sign itself (thirdness as general sign-relation). Every act of interpretation feeds back into the relevant sign's triadic structure, thereby initiating a new set of conditions for further events of interpretation. Because of this, the process exhibited in the triadic relation maintains both an operative closure and a developmental openness.[30] On the one hand, every triadic relation is a kind of 'closed circle', since any operation that would interpret or revise a given triadic relation occurs structurally as a moment within that relation itself. The triadic structure anticipates and includes its ongoing correction in light of new experience, and to engage a triadic relation critically is therefore necessarily to move within that relation's own movement, participating constructively in that relation's own process. Yet on the other hand, this very closure guarantees in principle an unending process of further interpretation whose potential contours and limits can never be fully determined in advance. This then is the very essence of Peirce's semiotic immanence: thirdness at once presupposes and entails itself and indeed *is* nothing other than the continuity of its self-operation.[31] Not unlike Heideggerian Dasein, the 'ecstatic' or externally relational structures of thrownness from the past and projection into the future are constitutive here internally of the 'thing itself'.[32]

Applying Peirce's semiotic model to particular cases, triadic signification is thus marked in each instance by a unique style or method of performance.[33] Every thirdness is a *singular* thirdness, a concrete enactment. Yet the Peircean model – precisely *as* model – therefore still appears to miss something. What it misses it misses by virtue of its being a model, that is, a general representation or form. The specifically triadic character of a signifying process must be understood as the irreducibly performative dimension of that process, the unique way in which a particular act of meaning is in fact accomplished. Strictly speaking, then, a triadic 'logic' is not a logic at all in the sense of an abstract model. It cannot be applied merely theoretically (like looking through a lens), but can only be concretely and experientially performed in a way that changes the performer herself (like learning to tango). The difference consists in the quality of the relation between activity and object in each case: viewing through a lens presumes a relatively dissociated and passive object whose image or representation becomes available thereby to the subject's active gaze, while practising the tango binds activity and object into the unity of a single, complex undertaking.[34] Such an undertaking can only occur in determinate and self-implicating contexts of meaning. It is thus necessary to 'step into' a triadic relation in order to manifest that relation as such, or rather one must carry forward and develop a relation already at least minimally present. The relations themselves serve then as both self-enabling and self-critical models. Triadic signs presuppose themselves and yet imply their own insufficiency and in consequence call for their further development and supplementation in ongoing interpretation.

We have seen how Peirce uses the act of 'giving' to exemplify triadic relations. There is an essential difference, however, between diagramming the relation of giving and actually taking part in this relation itself. Defining 'gift' in a general way or pointing out that this or that object is a gift is not the same as knocking on the new neighbour's door with a freshly-baked cake in one's hands. When one 'steps into' the relation of giving in such a context, it becomes impossible both in principle and in fact to separate oneself from the meanings and unforeseeable outcomes which the gift-relation generates. To say that a given sign is triadic is to suggest that only through such a performative risk and immersion does that sign exist as what it is and in this way produce the meanings that it does. It is only the performative and participatory dimension of triadic signs that guarantees the *unity* of the triadic relation and thereby distinguishes semiosis from other externally three-part concepts or structures. The unity of triadic relation can be examined and comprehended only 'from within', by participating in the relation itself, and *gift* becomes in this way at once exemplar and type of triadic relation.

Theories of gift and exchange tend to consider gift-giving from the standpoint of a neutral observer who would in principle be capable of viewing all sides of a transaction simultaneously – this is precisely what makes them *theories*, not *gifts*.[35] Gift and receipt, expenditure and consumption, display and recognition, bestowal and gratitude: these various perspectives on the flow of exchange remain simultaneously visible to a theory that represents or models the gift even if aspects of these same transactions are necessarily concealed from the actors themselves. Yet as a real participant in the act of a gift, one 'knows' the event as either giver or recipient. One may stand outside the event and observe both sides at once, but one will never gain access thereby to the immanent relationality of the event itself. Real participation in the event forecloses a neutral or purely theoretical stance, and by the same token to take such a stance removes one from direct participation. It is impossible, for instance, both to be genuinely grateful for a gift and at one and the same moment to question the motives of the giver. To receive a gift as such requires a certain non-theoretical participation in relation to the one who gives. If there exists any knowledge specific to the direct, participatory experience of being either a giver or a recipient, then the theoretical stance remains blind to it.[36] This may suggest why Peirce himself uses the example of 'giving' to demonstrate triadic relations as such. Acts of giving are quintessentially demonstrative of thirdness, and – one might add – rational or exemplary demonstrations become formal analogues of gifts.

All this is to show that the triadic sign may be *experienced* or *participated in* as triadic, but can only be theoretically *modelled* at the expense of losing its triadic quality. As opposed to the tendency towards generalisation and formal summary in dyadic signs, triadic signification tends to increase rather than reduce the amount of complexity in a given system. This is because thirdness is at once 'an irreducible unanalyzable conception' and a figure of processual complexity.[37] Instead of a correlation between two terms, it elicits a process of explication with and among others through a succession of terms and their expanding network of relations. While dyadic representation may be adequately described as a 'slippage' or 'unending substitution' of one term for another, triadic processes typically develop continuously and ampliatively. By their very nature they tend to conserve, extend and reproduce themselves. They cannot be arbitrarily chosen, but must be found already at work minimally in a discourse or activity in which one is already engaged. Because of this, triadic signification cannot be abstracted from the particularities of its immediate context. While any object whatsoever may serve as an abstract example of a gift (in the lesson, say, of a foreign language class), actually to give another person a gift – true *giving* as distinguished from the representation of *a gift in general* – presupposes the particularities and complexities of a real network of relations that are already in place (even those of 'complete strangers'). This pre-existing complex of relations provides the parameters and conditions of possibility for the gift's actual significance. A gift of peaches to some passer-by is not a gift of peaches to one's lover. In any real act of giving, there can be no *anyone* and for that reason no gift *in general*.

Since triadic signification only emerges in this way from within a concrete context already rich with relations, if a triadic sign is genuinely to exceed the dyadic structure of mere nominalist representation, its own movement and articulations must possess at least the relevant relational 'grain' or 'resolution' appropriate to its content. Without this self-modelling iconicity, it would simply collapse into the nominalist's or structuralist's dyadic sign. Considered in a dyadic fashion, a word represents a class of physical objects, for example, by establishing a 'many-to-one' correspondence of infinite aspects, possibilities and parts to a single name. Triadic processes, on the contrary, tend to resist both simplification and generality. A schematic outline of their form or structure almost inevitably misses their essential character. The appreciation of an 'abstract' late Jackson Pollock painting, for instance, requires that special attention be paid to the actual configuration of the paint particles as they have spattered and aleatorically dispersed across the canvas. This grain can only be accurately reproduced by the painting itself.[38] The fractal structure of mathematical forms such as Julia sets and the well-known Mandelbrot set provide other examples. The analysis of such structures requires an unending mapping of 'many-to-more' in which the impetus and orientation of investigation feed back into the detail of the structure and generate increased complexity by and for the investigative process.[39] In such cases, the discernment of distinct levels of finer and finer detail lead not to an overall summary viewpoint, but instead to further demands for even more detailed specification at all scales.

The logic that emerges from these considerations is a logic of diagrammatic signification in an enriched sense that still largely remains to be clarified. For Peirce it is not a matter of simply rejecting dyadic representation but rather of working to overturn its prioritisation and dominance as a general model of intellectual inquiry. On this view, the functioning of the dyadic sign should be understood from within the broader perspective of triadic relations as no more than a special and limiting case. The dynamics of diagrammatic signification are meant to manifest in an exemplary way how this may in fact be accomplished. Thinking from within the semiotic context of diagrammatic relations allows, then, the linguistic sign in particular to emerge as a merely regional and material specification of a much larger class of triadic relational processes rather than serving as a paradigm or foundation for thought.

Diagrammatic signs

What follows is a constructive attempt, based on Peirce's triadic semiotics, to sketch a broadly Peircean theory of diagrammatic signs.[40] It is meant to serve as a conceptual preparation for the more formal categorical theory of diagrammatic signs based on presheaves that will be developed in Chapter 4. The schema presented here is intended to follow quite closely the logic of scientific experiment, since Peirce's triadic conception of the sign is strongly linked to his defence of scientific pragmatism as well as other aspects of his philosophy of science. Indeed, his voluminous writings on scientific method and experimentation are probably best approached as a kind of regional application of and commentary on his more general semiotics. Scientific experiment, from this vantage point, appears as a controlled and particularly efficient method for manipulating certain types of signs. These obviously cannot be dyadic or nominalist signs, since science comes to know the natural world, not the arbitrary world of conventional meaning, but this does not imply that there is no element of conventionality or choice whatsoever in scientific work. In fact, the activity of scientific experiment involves all three of Peirce's fundamental kinds of sign – icon, index, symbol – in a unified fashion with each type of sign playing a distinctive role in the overall process.

From this point of view, what makes scientific experimentation uniquely effective in generating knowledge is that it proceeds in a particular diagrammatic way that is grounded in the relations among icons, indices and symbols. Scientific experiments from this perspective are in fact best understood as conforming to a determinate multi-phase diagrammatic structure. Conversely, any similarly structured diagrams will possess an intrinsically epistemic bearing; they will be, so to speak, magnetised by knowing. Yet such an epistemic orientation involves a conception of knowledge that plunges deeply and extensively into metaphysics, like knowledge in Spinoza, in the sense that degrees of knowledge thereby tend to extend effectively into all degrees of being. In this sense, diagrams will appear as the procedurally integrative type of sign that makes semiotic immanence possible. Interestingly, the stages of the diagrammatic procedure as outlined below move in a direction contrary to that of Peirce's ordering of icon, index and symbol as expressing firstness, secondness and thirdness respectively. This may suggest a certain Aristotelian duality at work between a semiotic order of being and a diagrammatic order of knowing. In any case, the following presentation can be little more than a rough sketch, and while it should be kept in mind that the genuinely diagrammatic sign always comprises the continuous unity of a certain duration and process, we will somewhat artificially analyse it here into three distinct phases: selection, experimentation and evaluation.

Phase one is that of selection. This first phase establishes the basic parameters of the diagram by deciding upon its proximal elements and its distal range. It may be further subdivided into two parts or subphases. The first subphase identifies those aspects of the ambient environment that are relevant to the current context of inquiry. Within some real system of relations (for instance, the spatial and temporal relations of some physical space) certain parts and relations are picked out as especially salient for some question or purpose.

Often these may be grouped naturally into various kinds or types. In a Venn diagram drawn on a napkin, for example, any enclosed region that might be pointed at or scribbled in becomes potentially relevant as a determinate part of the diagram. In a scientific experiment, an apparatus may be arranged, for instance in a laboratory, with certain components of the apparatus attended to and others disregarded. A biologist is perhaps interested in the sterility of a Petri dish, for example, but not its particular size.

At the same time, either explicitly or implicitly a mapping is established that takes each relevant selected (or selectable) part or feature of the diagram to a corresponding part of some semantic domain. This second subphase of the selection phase assigns, either implicitly or explicitly, to each designatable part of the diagram something that that part represents or maps onto. This may be no more than the given diagrammatic component itself, but more typically it will consist of a class of relevantly similar kinds of thing that each component of the diagram is understood individually to represent under a certain interpretation. Regions of a Venn diagram might correspond to demographic groups within a chosen population, for instance, or a spore sample in a lab experiment might implicitly represent all other spores of its same natural kind under comparable conditions.

Normally, then, the relation between the parts of the diagram and their intended semantics is an iconic one. The selected structure of the diagram at some appropriate level of analysis is mirrored in the selected structure of the semantic domain. And the very act of selection itself suggests an indexical component in play to the extent that the relevant parts and features of the diagram are directly 'picked out' from among others. Nonetheless, the dominant semiotic type structuring this phase as a whole is the combination of conventionality, regularity and habit that Peirce designates as the 'thirdness' constitutive of *symbols*. Every selection is an act of intelligence to one degree or another, and this initial phase presupposes continuity above all with past patterns of selection and projected possibilities of innovation and correction.

Phase two involves diagrammatic experimentation. The biologist scatters the spores on the dish and waits. A driver traces possible routes on a roadmap with her finger. Galileo releases the balls on a ramp and watches them roll. This second phase thus involves manipulating the diagram or simply examining it in some new way in such a manner that changes in its constitutive parts and relations or in how these are perceived correspond to similarly structured modifications in its selected domain of semantics. This may, for example, include writing, erasing, moving, extending or varying the system of parts as determined in the first phase, or it may simply involve waiting as some causal process naturally occurs.

Such forms of experimentation themselves occur along a spectrum of purposive control, from inaction or aimless doodling to the strictly rule-bound following of formal procedures, but in any case there is some degree of conventionality (or 'symbolicity') in play as in the first phase. And the iconicity implicit in the relation between the diagrammatic 'syntax' and its intended semantics inevitably conditions the experimenter's actual manipulations. Nonetheless from the perspective of the process as a whole, the dominant feature of this second phase is its indexicality, its 'secondness'. Experimentation is above all a concrete process of action and reaction operating directly on the diagram itself in whatever domain of reality the diagram's parts have been inscribed or selected.[41]

The third phase – evaluation – consists of a qualitative dispositional change that occurs based on the immediate effects, for instance those of direct observation, of the actions of the previous experimental stage. Rearranging or erasing some of the diagram's parts, loosening their restrictions by allowing them to vary along selected parameters or supplementing them with new constructions; all of these operations alter the diagram and reorder its constituent relations. When the parts of the diagram change in various ways, the relations among these parts change accordingly: new relations appear; old relations disappear or are transformed in light of new information. These changes themselves become manifest as a direct result of experimental action and may be directly perceived through inspection of the modified diagram.[42] In light of these changes, certain hypotheses might then suggest themselves, necessary deductive consequences might be noted, new questions might be formulated, and so on. The scientist checks the Petri dish after three days and notes the rate of fungal growth. Her hypothesis is falsified and she frowns. The driver concludes that passing through the desert is best and gets back on the highway headed south.

The passive or receptive character of the perceived changes and newly formed relations in the diagram marks a continuation and yet also a reversal in the evaluative phase of the indexicality that dominated the previous stage of experimentation. The resultant diagram and its component structures impose themselves willy nilly on the experimenter, and its features are given as a direct secondness, not chosen. Also, the conventionality or symbolicity of the first phase of selection remains at work, particularly through the mapping it had established between the diagram's explicit structure and its semantics. The dominant tenor of the third phase, however, is that of iconicity, Peircean 'firstness'. The basic result of the diagrammatic procedure is the direct perception of an essential relational coordination, a 'felt quality' of the structural connection between what has changed in the diagram and what has correspondingly changed in its semantics. What emerges naturally in the semantics is an iconic image of what is observed directly in the selected and modified parts of the diagram, and this icon becomes itself the basis of a qualitative, experiential 'difference' between the states of the diagram before and after its experimentation.

Considered in a more general sense, the final stage of evaluation need not involve conscious or perceptual experience at all. It need only involve some variation, some differential in an established habit, pattern or tendency.[43] Indeed each of the three diagrammatic phases may be reinterpreted as part of a purely structural process that makes no reference whatsoever to intentionality or thought in the ordinary sense. Selection, if it is not a conscious choice, may be simply a local causal interaction (a snowflake 'selects' the leaf on which it alights). And experimentation, if it is not a process of deliberate manipulation, may be simply the unfolding of a natural process (the snowflake melts). This then allows for a quite general application of this schema of diagrammatic signification to the natural world, making perhaps somewhat more plausible Peirce's universalisation of signs, what we have here called semiotic immanence. The relations among the three phases are sketched in an intuitive way in Figure 3.4.

What exactly is the structure of diagrammatic signification according to this selection-experimentation-evaluation model? Succinctly put, it is Peirce's triadic sign-schema made internally relational. Selection corresponds to the relation of interpretant to sign, experimentation to the relation of sign to object, and evaluation to the composition of the latter relation following the former. If in the terms of Peirce's general sign-schema we consider the entire diagrammatic process delineated here as a complex yet unified sign-vehicle, the object to which this sign then corresponds is neither the semantic domain of possible instantiations (this was already established or implicitly invoked in the first stage) nor the actual change in this semantic field. It is rather the *relation* between the change or differential in the 'object' semantics on the one hand and

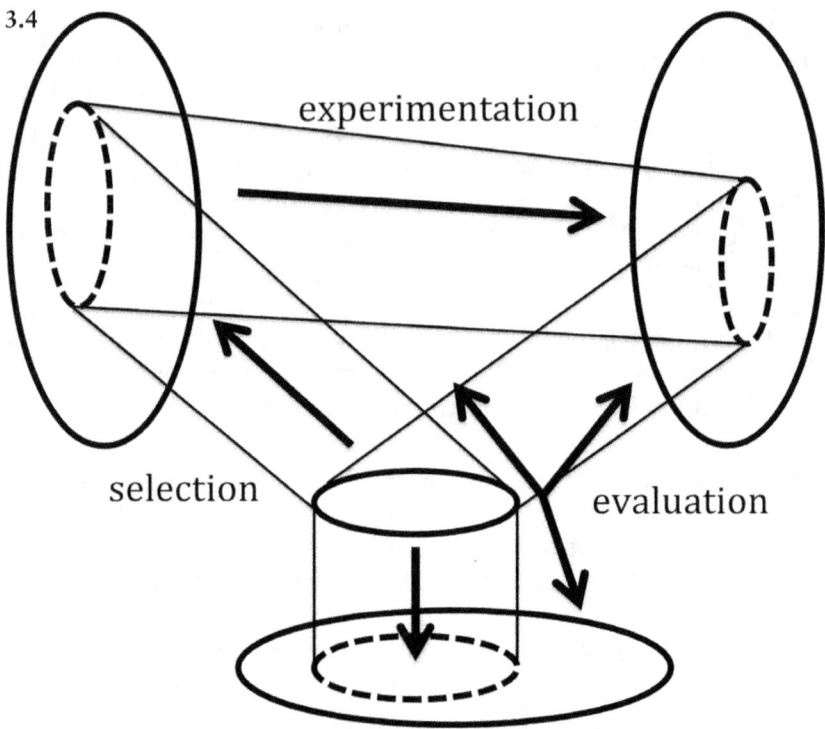

3.4

the experimentation on the diagram 'sign' on the other. The 'interpretant' in turn is then none other than the variable change in habit produced in a higher-order experimental 'subject' that incorporates this relation into the larger constellation of habits and dispositions that already constitute it. There is in this way an implicit or virtual perpendicular dimension through which the diagram carries itself beyond itself, 'bootstrapping' itself as it were into another order of relational consistency.

Understood in this fashion, the diagrammatic sign becomes neither primarily the occasion or cause of a meaning nor the second-order modelling of such a meaning. Instead, the diagrammatic sign functions as an open-ended, performative and ungeneralisable aspect of actual communicative and practical relations that takes place 'between' first-order instantiation and second-order reflection. What such relations are thereby able to reveal only becomes fully apparent from within the activity of such practices themselves and the actual relations that determine them, just as one only comes truly to know the infinitive 'to give' by actually participating in the relation itself in one or another of its constituent roles. The sense of such a triadic relation thus appears each time as specific to the form and context of a particular diagram.⁴⁴

A diagram thus works by modifying previously established habits of acting and thinking, at least in some minimal way. This would suggest that its object might be knowable not in itself, but through consideration of effects wrought upon subsequent thought and practice. Its meaning therefore could not be modelled directly, but only experimentally induced and inferred. Diagrammatic signifying processes must be understood as unique, unforeseeably (but not arbitrarily) active and pragmatically structured in just such a way.⁴⁵ For Peirce's conception, every triadic process would share something of the structure of a diagram in this sense. The entirety of Peirce's semiotic immanence depends upon a singular and infinite distribution of real relations that are themselves actively relational. In fact, as conceived in the context of Peirce's thought, the singularity of a triadic relation is always intrinsically plural, complex and evolutive.⁴⁶ Considered as triadic processes, diagrams are thus communicative and broadly epistemic relations that cannot be known objectively 'in themselves' (i.e. as abstracted from relation) because 'in themselves' they are thoroughly perspectival and relational. They can, however, be participated in.

There is a sharp contrast, then, between the diagrammatic model of experience grounded in Peircean semiotics and that proposed by phenomenology, despite their partial convergence within the sphere of what Peirce calls 'phaeneroscopy'. To help make this clear and to anticipate somewhat Deleuze's critique of phenomenology that will appear in Chapter 5, it is useful to contrast the Peircean conception of relations with Husserl's discussion of relations in his relatively late work *Experience and Judgment*. Husserl considers only dyadic relations (such as 'greater than' and 'less than') and in so doing comes to the conclusion that while such relations indeed serve as determinations of their terms (which Husserl here calls *substrates* on the basis of a model of experience derived, albeit with important modifications, from an essentially subject-predicate grammar of objectual judgements), those determinations remain on a separate level exterior to what they relate – they are not concrete determinations of the substrates themselves. In other words, there are substrates on the one hand and relations on the other, and to enter into or participate in relations does not change or determine what the substrates *essentially* are. Husserl writes:

> [T]he relational determinations certainly appear as determinations of the substrates: it is the substrate which manifests itself as greater or smaller, etc.; but these determinations do *not* appear as *attached to, or in, the unity* between the two members of the relation, as would have to be the case if relational contemplation were an explication of the unity. Rather, the relational determinations emerge *on the ground* of the pregiven; this unity itself does not become thematic, but only the object considered according to the mode of relation.[47]

In other words, for Husserl – echoing phenomenologically Hume's metaphysics of the externality of relations – terms always precede relations and relational determinations do not essentially modify the terms they relate.[48] Peircean semiotics, on the contrary, conceives of triadic relations – signs – precisely as relations such that what Husserl here calls 'relational contemplation' would be in fact necessarily 'an explication of the unity [of and among the members of the relation]'. Since the 'contemplation' of triadic relations implies their enactment or performance, to contemplate a triadic relation would be to participate in it such that one is oneself transformed. The 'unity' thus explicated is the unity of the relation itself – a unity that is irreducibly triadic, or signifying as well as actively dynamic, or transformational.

From Modern Ideas to Postmodern Signs

Peirce's thought anticipates in several ways the concerns of postmodern philosophy, particularly in its critique of Enlightenment and specifically Cartesian foundationalism, its emphasis on the social and communicative production of knowledge, the role of the body and the unconscious in thought, and the essential role of signs in experience.[49] Peirce himself was critical of the methods of modern philosophy and understood himself as working in part to correct its errors and oversights. Deely argues that Peirce's semiotic represents a comprehensive way of thinking sufficiently distinct from the modern paradigm to warrant its being considered definitively 'postmodern'. In this respect Deely sees Peirce's philosophy as not just one additional set of philosophical arguments, methods and themes but as providing a unique way to reconsider and reread the philosophical tradition along its entirety (and according to the differences of its linguistic, cultural and historical sub-traditions).[50] For Deely, one of the primary advantages of a semiotic basis for philosophy is that it allows us to conceive of the history of philosophy as a living tradition, one in which historically sedimented texts continue to find new relevance in unforeseen contexts. The texts of the history of philosophy from this standpoint emerge as semiotic reserves with which we as readers and enactors co-participate in processes of semiosis. Considered in this way, philosophical texts are no longer objectified as archives of fixed meaning to be analysed and commented upon from a detached perspective. Rather, the interests and motivations of later readers – the real problems of existence and meaning with which we question philosophical texts – remain bound up essentially with what those texts disclose. Deely's conclusion is summarised in the following passage:

> Reality is not only what it is, but also what it will be; and in this becoming we are participants through semiosis. The classical ideal of the detached observer gives place to the semiotic reality of the participant in creation, for which thought itself turns out to be essential.[51]

In this passage 'the classical ideal' is distinguished from 'semiotic reality' above all in terms of the relation of the interpreter to the act and content of interpretation. To the 'detached observer' corresponds the dyadic sign and the interpretative framework of representation it entails. The 'participant in creation', on the other hand, is conceived on the basis of triadic processes of signification. Following Deely's conception, for instance, a triadic interpretation of the problem of hermeneutics and programmatics in Spinoza's *Ethics* would suggest that the geometrical form of Spinoza's work implies a constructive task relative to later contexts in which it might be effective.

Deely traces the postmodern 'way of signs' back to Locke's 1690 proposal in the *Essay concerning Human Understanding* to make of '*semiotica*' 'another sort of Logick and Critick, than what we have been hitherto acquainted with'.[52] There Deely notes how Locke's proposed conception of the logic of signs differs from other divisions of knowledge in which logic becomes simply one branch of science among others: '[W]hereas the earlier divisions separated logic in one way or another from the other branches of knowledge, Locke proposes in contrast *a distinction which unites*.'[53] Deely clarifies the importance of this difference as follows:

> Logic as semiotic – that is to say, as *a* semiotic, a part within semiotics – is not just one among other, separated sciences or 'bodies of knowledge'. On the contrary, it is a discipline which affects all knowledge expressible in language, and explores the

dimension common to all such forms of knowledge precisely as their objects enter into and form the substance of human experience through the ever growing and shifting network of sign relations in which experience consists and which language translates into discursive expression.[54]

As understood by Deely, this conception of semiotic as a 'distinction which unites' combines the 'speculative' branch of knowledge ('of things which are what they are by nature') and the 'practical' ('of things which are what they are owing to human thought or action'). The speculative and practical are combined in a logic of signs that investigates 'the *means* whereby knowledge, whether speculative or practical, is acquired, elaborated, and shared'.[55] Yet Deely's apparent restriction of this to 'knowledge expressible in language' seems much too narrow. What of scientific knowledge expressible only in mathematics, such as the state superpositions and tensor products of quantum mechanics? Or of the forms of experience and knowledge propagated by visualisation techniques in Buddhist tantra or Ignatian spiritual exercises? These practices exceed language but are nonetheless capable of being grasped by the semiotics of diagrams.

If we take Peirce's notion of triadic signification as a hypothesis, we see that our ideas of language and subjectivity become correspondingly transformed. These ideas become signifying components of the interpretation itself. The model of the Cartesian subject is then no longer feasible for such a strategy of reading. What Spinoza critiqued as the 'kingdom within a kingdom' model of conscious human activity preserves the inner kingdom of the subject from any contamination by the meanings and signs transpiring beyond its border in the outer kingdom of the world. With triadic signification however, the subjective inner kingdom loses its impermeable boundary and thus its sovereignty. Subjectivity becomes diagrammatic.

Peirce's reflections on triadic relations thus provide one model or example of how philosophical thought and practice might be conceived outside of a Cartesian paradigm of subjectivity. To be consistent and effective, however, a semiotic reading must *do* the work it calls for. The success or failure of such a reading, and more importantly, the directions of inquiry a semiotic approach will take and the conclusions it may lead to, cannot be fully determined in advance of the reading itself. This incapacity to preconceive the contours of method and result is not a merely contingent aspect of reading in this manner, but is part and parcel of the semiotic method as such.

Conceived through triadic relations, diagrammatic practice should be understood not simply according to its semantics but at least equally in terms of how its thought is communicated and what effects it tends to produce in a variety of communicative contexts. Since these effects can only be produced through determinate readings and particular projects, the possibilities and virtues of a semiotic reading are balanced by an inevitable limitation in their actual extension, although not in their potential applicability. Since a semiotic reading is activated only in terms of a particular situation with its already-constitutive relations, the results gained in such a reading will be operative initially only in that local context, although with an intrinsic tendency to 'spread' outward. The possible extension to other contexts is never foreclosed, but such extension always demands the work of additional interpretive practice. Every diagram thus marshals a more or less determinate programme by fashioning a more or less reliable and enduring cognitive tool.

One of Peirce's innovations in philosophy was to treat the efficient use of resources in any theoretical inquiry (time, money, materials) as an important theoretical issue in its own right.[56] One aspect of this concern was his long-standing interest in the problems of philosophical and scientific terminology and his proposal for a rationally grounded 'ethics of terminology'. In light of the preceding analysis and with an eye to the overall proposal of diagrammatic immanence, we might broaden Peirce's notion of an ethics of terminology to include an *ethics of diagrammatic notation*. Given the theoretical status of diagrams as programmes of controlled experimentation, it becomes an important task for philosophy to consider the kinds of diagrams most conducive to philosophy's own ends. One question worth posing is: are there general types or characteristics of diagrammatic notation that lead naturally to more efficient communication and more epistemically effective experimentation?

As desiderata, we might point first of all to the utility of clearly marked differences within the diagram. Because a diagram functions by coordinating certain selected features of the ambient environment with some range of intended 'application' or 'meaning', the more definitively marked the parts of the diagram are, the more exact and explicit the structural coordination between syntax and semantics may potentially be. In this way, a maximisation of efficient iconicity will usually be correlated with a minimisation of irrelevant diagrammatic information. Crisp lines are seldom mistaken for thick objects. Of course, for certain purposes intentionally blurred or indistinct differences are very useful, and often necessary. This must be taken into account as well.

In addition, effective diagrams will typically exhibit a definite overall unity of structure. This is essentially an esthetic criterion that probably cannot be applied mechanically, although the requirement that a partial order category have a terminal object is a helpful formal analogue. Peirce himself, strongly influenced by Schiller, claimed that 'an object, to be esthetically good must have a multitude of parts so related to one another as to impart a positive simple immediate quality to their totality'.[57] In other words, a firstness (an icon) should emerge naturally from the diagram's collection of related parts. At some level of description or experience, a good diagram should cohere into a single quality, the dark interior of a single dot.

Finally, effective diagrams will typically be well-integrated with whatever relevant practical technology, including perceptual technology, is involved in the diagrammatic process. It is important in this regard for contemporary philosophy to keep in mind the wide array of perceptual and cognitive capacities past forms of philosophy have incorporated into the development of the tradition, as well as the new horizons opened by such things as computerised data-processing, graphic interfaces and virtual environments.

In conclusion, it is worth emphasising how easy it can be to miss the radicality of Peirce's pragmatism, or 'pragmaticism'. Just as Spinoza's account of individuation falls stillborn if one presumes at the very outset that one already knows what things there are in the world (it is after all quite 'obvious') and one seeks little more than justification for one's own prior ontological prejudices, Peirce's semiotic pragmatism risks collapsing into triviality if it is not understood to require a fairly thoroughgoing revision of our usual understanding of thought itself. By nature we are habit-governed, mostly blind and deeply conservative creatures. Under reasonable assumptions, these characteristics become practically *a priori* conditions for cognitional beings. Because thought moulds itself as a more or less distorted icon of the process of its production, we human thinkers tend to accept far too readily a self-authorised role of sovereign intentional agent disposing freely with objects splayed for inquiry and use before our gaze. But thought is not only a picture-tool; it is also, both more delicately and more profoundly, the real intrication of a determinate trajectory and a structural milieu through which that trajectory passes. Thought's essential displacement always harbours within the continuity that tracks it infinitely more than the local connections that nonetheless define it. Every movement of thinking finds itself absorbed into a space of variable pathways and at the same time marks discrete concretisations of possibility and real futurity as selectably determinate events *for* further thought. Semiotic immanence as the diagrammatic space of universal thirdness ensures that larger collective processes in which particular cognitive accomplishments and individual actions appear as no more than variable components always in fact structure those components themselves as relative shifts and continuous variations of signs. The diagram is behind you.

Notes

1. 'Some Consequences of Four Incapacities', in Philip Wiener, ed., *Charles S. Peirce: Selected Writings*, p. 41. This article is a continuation of 'Questions Concerning Certain Faculties Claimed for Man' which appeared in the same issue.
2. Ibid., pp. 68–9.
3. Ibid., p. 69.
4. Ibid.
5. Charles Peirce, *Collected Papers*, 5.534 cited in Jay Zeman, 'Peirce on Abstraction', p. 212.
6. Consider the difference between the statements 'binarism is bad', a definite judgement which unless made ironically quickly reduces to either hypocrisy or self-condemnation, and 'something is bad about binarism', more like the expression of a hunch tending towards further inquiry.
7. 'The Basis of Pragmaticism', in *The Essential Peirce*, vol. 2, p. 394. This manuscript appears to be a separate draft of the same paper cited by Zeman in the earlier note.
8. Christopher Hookway, *Peirce*, p. 178.
9. *The Essential Peirce*, vol. 2, p. 394.
10. Peter Ochs, *Peirce, Pragmatism and the Logic of Scripture*. This work provides a detailed reading of Peirce's overall project in light of a series of methodologically reflective levels. It is to Ochs I owe my original introduction to Peirce's thought. Engaging Peirce from the perspective of literary theory, Sheriff distinguishes Saussurean structuralism as a 'structural theory of "gaps" (the theoretical absence of meaning)' from Gadamerian hermeneutics and Wittgensteinian language philosophy as 'philosophies of "grounds" (modes of meaning)'. For Sheriff it is only 'a theory of signs that can relate phenomenology and ontology, modes of consciousness and modes of being', that is, Peirce's semiotic theory with its triadic structure of sign-object-interpretant which is

capable both of rigorously differentiating the two modes and of making clear sense of the latter. John K. Sheriff, *The Fate of Meaning*, p. 54. In his *Four Ages of Understanding*, John Deely distinguishes between ideas and signs, but since our vocabulary draws on Spinoza and ideas in his sense are meant to be any intellectual or reasoning mode, we distinguish here instead between two kinds of ideas corresponding to two kinds of signs. Dyadic signs constitute what Deely calls ideas, and triadic signs here are the 'signs' Deely distinguishes from ideas. In *Four Ages of Understanding*, Deely differentiates modernity and postmodernity as taking the 'way of ideas' and the 'way of signs' respectively. Thus according to the terminology employed here, modern forms of thought are dyadic, postmodern triadic.
11. Saussure distinguishes *langue* as the systematic and structural form of language from *langage* as the actual language as a cultural and historical fact. Ferdinand de Saussure, *Course in General Linguistics*, p. 9.
12. Ibid., pp. 65–7.
13. Ibid., pp. 67–70.
14. Ibid., p. 68.
15. Although as Sheriff shows, the extension of Saussure's model to textual units of meaning larger than sentences (such as paragraphs, chapters, entire literary works) gave rise to distinct problems for structuralist literary theory. Dyadic models of signification break down at the point that the 'signified' becomes too complex to be conceived as a single, indivisible intuition or concept. It is largely because Peirce's semiotic approach is more effective in this regard that Sheriff recommends it. *The Fate of Meaning*, pp. 11–18.
16. This rather schematic picture of dyadic signs is complicated by the use of Saussure in certain forms of structuralism in which subjectivity is itself understood as a mere effect of underlying oppositional structures.
17. Saussure himself emphasises that linguistic signs cannot be changed wilfully. Yet for Saussure this only reaffirms the essential contingency of the signifying relation itself. *Course in General Linguistics*, pp. 71–4.
18. The difficulty of reconciling language and force is one major impetus for Derrida's philosophy of deconstruction. In 'Force and Signification' Derrida writes: 'Force is the other of language without which language would not be what it is'; and 'one would seek in vain a concept in phenomenology which would permit the conceptualization of intensity or force. The conceptualization not only of direction but of power, not only the *in* but the *tension* of intentionality.' Jacques Derrida, *Writing and Difference*, p. 27. See also the work of François Laruelle, especially in the period he calls Philosophy I, including *Machines textuelles* and *Au-delà du principe de pouvoir*.
19. In Saussurean linguistics, this movement corresponds to the diachronic analysis of the sign (see *Course in General Linguistics*, p. 81). Peirce's

triadic signification effectively traces a diagonal line, drawing into intimate, performative relation the theoretically independent axes of synchrony and diachrony as they function in the Saussurean model.
20. Peirce, 'Pragmatism', ch. 28 in *The Essential Peirce*, vol. 2, p. 410. Needless to say, Peirce's semiotic theory extends far beyond anything that may be elaborated or even adequately summarised here. An excellent survey may be found in T.L. Short, *Peirce's Theory of Signs*.
21. In set-theoretic terms a triadic relation is simply a set of ordered triples, just as a dyadic relation is a set of ordered pairs. What remains opaque in this way of formulating the issue is precisely how the *relation* itself becomes different in kind when it involves more than two terms. For set theory, the irreducible unity of the triadic relation remains inaccessible. In fact an ordered triple is defined as just a type of ordered pair (one for which the second element is itself an ordered pair). Ultimately, it is this unity which constitutes the continuous duration of triadic thought as a process in time. It is here that Peirce's analyses become necessary, and the logic of triadic relations must be developed as a semiotic, and then ultimately as a theory of iconic logical graphs (Peirce's gamma graphs).
22. *Philosophical Writings of Peirce*, p. 91.
23. Sheriff, *The Fate of Meaning*, pp. 55–62. It is important to note that the 'interpretant' is *not* a subject who interprets, but rather something more like the formation of a general habit. See the discussion in Ochs, *Peirce, Pragmatism and the Logic of Scripture*, pp. 188–91.
24. See the analysis in Ochs, *Peirce, Pragmatism and the Logic of Scripture*, pp. 207–28. For a general discussion of Peirce's Existential Graphs, see Don D. Roberts, *The Existential Graphs of Charles S. Peirce*. A more recent and specialised account (bracketing the gamma graphs) is given in Sun-Joo Shin, *The Iconic Logic of Peirce's Graphs*. A very good brief introduction to the graphs is found in Ahti-Veikko Pietarinen, 'Existential Graphs: What a Diagrammatic Logic of Cognition Might Look Like'.
25. See Ochs, *Peirce, Pragmatism and the Logic of Scripture*, pp. 208–23.
26. *Philosophical Writings of Peirce*, p. 92.
27. A clear summary may be found in Sheriff, *The Fate of Meaning*, pp. 62–6. The fullest account of these categories and their links to other aspects of Peirce's thought is given in Peirce's series of spring 1903 Harvard lectures. See chs 10–13 in *The Essential Peirce*, vol. 2. These lectures are interpreted by Ochs in ch. 6 of *Peirce, Pragmatism and the Logic of Scripture*.
28. *Philosophical Writings of Peirce*, p. 91.
29. Sheriff shows how for a Peircean conception past signifying processes may themselves become reactualised as the objects of later signs: 'Any sign or collection of signs that a person has experienced in the past can become an object in the representamen-object-interpretant relationship

that allows signs to be represented, that is, to have meaning. [. . .] Every sign is interpreted by a subsequent sign or thought in which the relation-of-the-sign-to-its-object becomes the object of the new sign'. *The Fate of Meaning*, p. 61.
30. Peirce's semiotic shares this quality with the communicative systems-theory model developed by Niklas Luhmann on the basis of G. Spencer Brown's logical calculus, which is essentially equivalent formally to Peirce's EG-alpha, although with a logically dual interpretation. See Luhmann, *Social Systems*, and Spencer Brown, *The Laws of Form*.
31. See Peirce's discussion of the 'perfect sign' in note 25 to 'The Basis of Pragmaticism', *The Essential Peirce*, vol. 2, p. 545.
32. See, of course, Heidegger, *Being and Time*.
33. To say that triadic signification is 'marked' by these characteristics is to say that such characteristics establish an existential index (in Peirce's sense) of a triadic sign. They are 'marks' in the sense that G. Spencer Brown's logical calculus invokes as the origin of possible value: 'Let a state distinguished by the distinction be marked with a mark of distinction.' *Laws of Form*, p. 4.
34. It is here that Peirce's semiotic links directly to the pragmatic element of his philosophy.
35. The classic theory of gift and exchange is Marcel Mauss, *The Gift: The Form and Reason for Exchange in Archaic Societies*.
36. Bourdieu has brought to light a component of exchange that cannot be accounted for by neutral, theoretical models in his discussion of *habitus*. See his *Outline of a Theory of Practice*. Bourdieu's discussion of language, disposition and form in *Language and Symbolic Power* is also relevant to these concerns.
37. Peirce, 'The Categories Defended', in *The Essential Peirce*, vol. 2, p. 176. Peirce explains: '[Thirdness] is complex in the sense that different features may be discriminated in it, but the peculiar idea of *complexity* that it contains, although it has complexity as its object, is an unanalyzable idea.'
38. Henri Maldiney, *Regard Parole Espace*, p. 160, cited in Jose Gil, *Metamorphoses of the Body*, pp. 133, 319 n.
39. The mathematically inclined reader is advised to examine *coalgebras* in this regard. See Barwise and Moss, *Vicious Circles*, part 5.
40. The connections between Peirce's notion of the diagram and Husserlian phenomenology are investigated at length in Stjernfelt, *Diagrammatology*. This book is an important background source for much of what follows.
41. As Reviel Netz has shown in his analysis of diagrammatic methods in ancient Greek geometry, it is this indexical character of diagrams and the potentialities it harbours that distinguishes diagrammatic representation most clearly from other forms of representation.

42. A thorough analysis of the inner workings of this stage of the process would require a lengthy detour through Peirce's semiotic account of perception. What is essential is that Peirce conceives of perception as both hypothetical and inferential in character. Like Bergson, Peirce situates the perceptual act within an unbroken continuity stretched between receptive and active poles. One 'sees' to the extent that one moves or is prepared to move, acts or is prepared to act with respect to what is 'seen'. In short, perception is essentially abductive.
43. See Justus Buchler's concept of alescence in *Metaphysics of Natural Complexes*, ch. II, and especially his analysis of the universal duality between prevalence and alescence.
44. In Peirce, this aspect of diagrammatic processes becomes fully visible only at the level of the 'gamma graphs', or third level of existential graphs. It is here that the thought-processes of philosophers tend to be singularised according to the social and communicative contexts in which their patterns of thought have developed. In ch. 8 of *Peirce, Pragmatism and the Logic of Scripture*, Ochs demonstrates the logic through which readings of repair communicate across Peirce's own successive revisionings of pragmatic philosophy (culminating in the existential graphs) and the practices of Scriptural communities. More generally, '[p]hilosophers specializing in the critique of medicine or of theoretical physics will deliver their correctives to common sense through the way that they write within the discourses of medicine or physics, and so on' (p. 323).
45. It is this dimension of triadic signification that directly links Peirce's semiotic theory to his 'pragmaticism'. See the 'Prolegomena to an Apology for Pragmaticism' in *Peirce on Signs*, pp. 249–52.
46. At the most formal level, this complex inherence of multiplicity within singularity is developed in Peirce's understanding of the mathematical continuum – the relations between and possible abstractability of points in and from a line. See Hilary Putnam, 'Peirce's Continuum', in Ketner, ed., *Peirce and Contemporary Thought*. I am grateful to Ochs for introducing me to this line of thought in Peirce.
47. Husserl, *Experience and Judgment*, p. 155.
48. More recently, Badiou has made this dyadic notion of relation central to his own 'phenomenology' as the logic of appearance opposed to the 'ontology' of the pure multiple expressed in set theory. See Badiou, *Logics of Worlds*.
49. All of these features are evident as early as Peirce's 1868 articles written for the *Journal of Speculative Philosophy*, and they are elaborated together over the next four and a half decades of Peirce's career. In particular, Peirce's argument that all processes of reasoning and even of perception are constituted through signification and never simple intuition anticipates Derrida's important criticisms of the idea of

signification in Husserl's phenomenology as developed in *Speech and Phenomena* and later works.
50. Deely undertakes this ambitious genealogical project in *Four Ages of Understanding*.
51. John Deely, *New Beginnings*, p. 246.
52. John Locke, *Essay concerning Human Understanding*, ch. 20, quoted in Deely, *Four Ages of Understanding*, p. 594. This section repeats and develops Deely's earlier discussion of Locke in *New Beginnings*, pp. 109–43.
53. Deely, *Four Ages of Understanding*, p. 606.
54. Ibid.
55. Ibid.
56. See the discussion in Nicholas Rescher, *Peirce's Philosophy of Science*, ch. 4.
57. CP 5.132 cited in Hookway, *Peirce*, p. 112.

CHAPTER 4

Diagrams of Variation: Functor Categories and Presheaves

The problems of representation and reference under conditions of radical immanence are particularly striking, as both of these appear to require at least a minimal transcendence in order to function at all. The category-theoretical framework continued in this chapter addresses these abstract yet still strictly philosophical problems from a purely formal standpoint in which the 'interiority' and 'exteriority' of categorical determinations serve as a basis for reconceiving the internal and external relations of entities understood as diagrammatically structured. The key insight is a continuation and extension of that begun in Chapter 2, namely that within the framework of category theory categories themselves may appear as objects with well-defined systems of relations to one another via functors. Such systems of objects and relations may themselves constitute categories in their own right. This formal 'immanence' – the collapse of meta-systems and meta-relations into the same type of diagrammatically tractable systems and relations – may itself be lifted to the level of functors themselves: whereas functors in category theory are essentially maps between categories, natural transformations are structure-preserving maps between functors (maps between maps of systems of maps). Thus the relation between functors and natural transformations is a useful general model of the distinction between systems of relations and systems of meta-relations that yet treats these in a structurally identical manner. Examples in this chapter are developed in terms of demonstrating the ways in which the diagrammatic and structural methods of category theory thus model immanence, building up to a formal model of diagrammatic signification based in presheaves, a type of functor, and the functor categories – presheaf categories – that are constructed from them. This model will cast the Peircean characterisation of diagrammatic semiotics from the previous chapter in a categorical context.

Consider an abstract 'slice' of the cocktail party encountered in Chapter 2, selecting from among its innumerable constituent things,

140 *Diagrammatic Immanence*

4.1

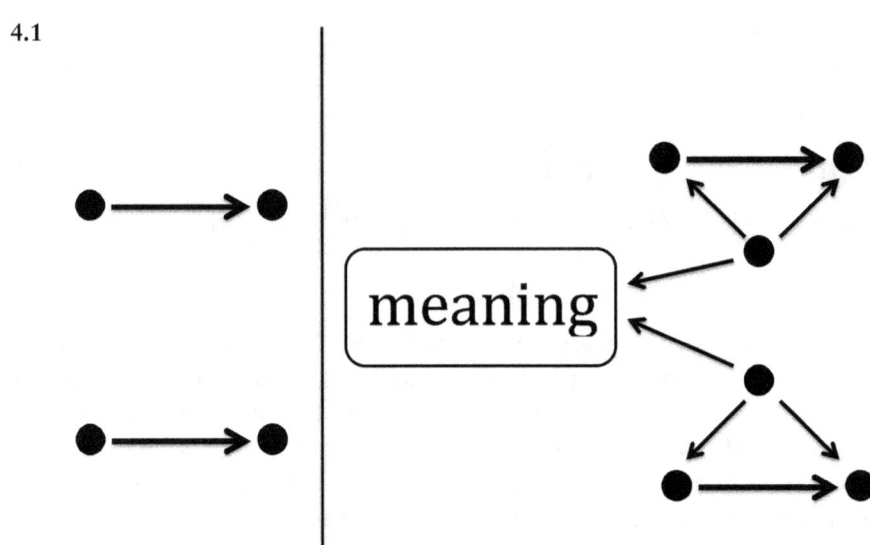

properties and relations two couples in the midst of two conversations. With dots representing people and arrows standing for the relation 'is speaking to', we have a diagram like that on the left in Figure 4.1.

What are they discussing? The diagram does not tell us. In general, signifying relations appear categorically as arrows that may be 'exposed' by some third object with a pair of arrows coming from it that represents a meaning or system of meanings via composition, as in the commutative diagram on the right in Figure 4.1.[1] If the category in which such a diagram appears is internally organised as a system of meanings, then the third object in the diagram should ideally be the limit for the signifying arrow in that category. But what is the internal structure of a 'system of meanings'? If it is a category, what are its dots and arrows? A meaning of whatever sort is necessarily determined by its position in a space of various intersecting structures, each with its own rich tangle of relations. Each of the 'single' topics being discussed opens up internally into a complex arrangement of mappings between words, sentences, semantics, phonemes – all the systematic orders of differential relations that structuralism has taught us to recognise. And these orders are themselves embedded in actual material and historical processes.

The seemingly intractable complexity of actual language (*parole* and not only *langue*) is one of the reasons linguistic semantics have tended to resist mathematical and logical formalisation so stubbornly. Meaning is enacted in singular events and in this way resists

Diagrams of Variation: Functor Categories and Presheaves

abstract treatment. Yet at the same time, meaning presupposes translatability. All the singular grain of the interlocking systems of some actual conversational exchange connects potentially to the systems of innumerable others. Any adequate categorical representation of linguistic events and, more generally, semiotic processes must be both rigorous and flexible enough to track the logical and structural underpinnings of meaning and at the same time facilitate the blurrings and affordances of translation.

No doubt signification is an especially rich and complex form of relation. We have already seen how the interplay of natural language and inferential form in Spinoza's *Ethics* functions as a problem and test-case for his metaphysics of immanence and his account of individuation. We have also seen how Peirce's sophisticated theory of signs relies on a general theory of categories of relations and in particular on the distinction between dyadic and triadic relations. This chapter aims at the formulation within category theory of a general semiotic theory of diagrams in the sense and spirit of Peirce as previously outlined. The most important components of the construction, as already suggested, will be the category theoretical notions of presheaves and presheaf categories. First, in what follows, the general concept of a functor category is sketched. Then, after defining presheaves and elaborating some examples, it will be a straightforward matter to define presheaf categories as functor categories whose functors are presheaves. These latter objects will then constitute a rich fabric of many-layered relations out of which a general theory of diagrams may be cut.

FROM FUNCTORS TO FUNCTOR CATEGORIES

Recall from Chapter 2 that a 'functor' is an arrow from one category to another that represents a 'structure-preserving' mapping of dots onto dots (that is, objects onto objects) and arrows onto arrows (that is, dyadic relations onto dyadic relations). To say that a functor 'preserves structure' is to require that mappings of identity arrows onto identity arrows follow the mappings of dots, in other words if dot X in category **C** is mapped to dot Y in category **D** by a given functor, then the identity arrow associated with dot X must be mapped to the identity arrow on dot Y by the same functor. Furthermore, it is to require that arrow-composition be preserved across the mapping: if f and g are arrows in category **C** and the arrow h is the composition gf (g following f), then f, g and h must be mapped by the functor to arrows in category **D**, say k, l and m respectively, such that m is the composition lk. This ensures that the triadic continuity enshrined in the transitivity of arrows is also mapped accordingly.

In keeping with the general mathematical approach of categories (and in the philosophical background, the metaphysics of immanence), there is no need to hold here to a strict or absolute division between objects and relations. Although a functor is essentially a kind of relational mapping of one category into another, we may freely understand this mapping to be itself a determinate type of object. A functor then is a certain well-behaved relation between categories, where categories are themselves structured systems of relations. So a functor is a systematic relational coordination of systematic relational coordinations. From the standard philosophical perspective that privileges objects over relations, such meta-relations must necessarily appear as high-level abstractions whose existence would be by this very token especially dubious or problematic. From the categorical (and immanentist) perspective, however, degrees of abstraction vary independently of degrees or levels of reality. It is the intrinsic consistency of relations at whatever scale that determines what is real, not a distance metric from some supposedly foundational base level.

Into the highly structured, intricate space of functors, we will simply send our trusty dot of selection. An arrow sending this dot into the 'space' of functors (however this space turns out to be structured internally) picks out some particular functor, say, the functor **2→Sets** that takes the simple partial order and category **2** into the category of sets and functions, itself thereby selecting some particular function inside **Sets**, say, the function 'age in years' from partygoers to real numbers from Chapter 2. Our chosen object is thus a specific mapping or selection by one category of its 'image' inside another.

Now it is a matter of considering categories of such objects. A *functor category* will therefore be a category whose dots represent functors. Since in general we want all the objects of a category to share certain relevant features in order to facilitate the category's cohesion, we will work with cases in which all of the objects at stake are functors from a single definite category to some other single definite category. In other words, the objects should be functors from **C** to **D** for some fixed pair of categories, **C** and **D**. Each of the functors at issue will be represented (that is, selected) by a unique dot in the new category. If functors themselves are diagrammed by arrows between category-dots in **Categories**, then functor categories

Diagrams of Variation: Functor Categories and Presheaves

'lift' such arrows to unique dots in different kinds of categories with new kinds of arrows.[2] There is really nothing more surprising in this than that relations at any given level of investigation may become objects of systematic investigation in their own right at another. In Figure 4.2, the three functors from the category **1** to the category **3** are represented 'internally' in the upper frame. In the middle frame, the same three functors are represented 'externally' as they appear in the category **Categories** where **1** and **3** both collapse to mere dots. The functors appear as arrows between them. The bottom frame expresses how the three arrows (the functors) in the middle frame may themselves become dots in a new category, the category of functors from **1** to **3**. The arrows in this category are natural transformations, which will be described below. Note that the bottom frame has exactly the same structure as the category **3** in the upper frame. This is one case of a more general result. It is easily shown that every category is in fact isomorphic to the functor category of functors from **1** into it, with all natural transformations between them.

So much then for the objects, or dots, in a functor category. They are functors. What are the arrows? An arrow from one dot

4.2

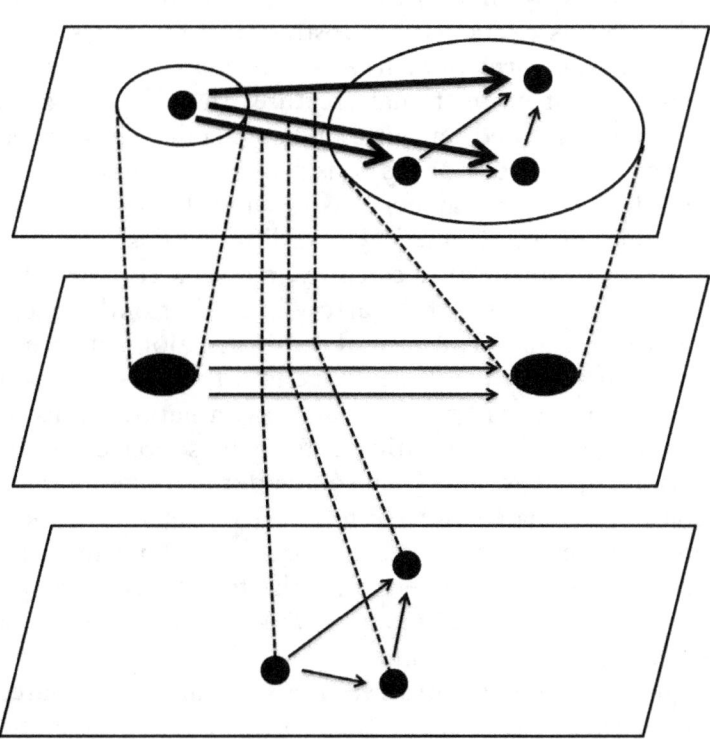

4.3

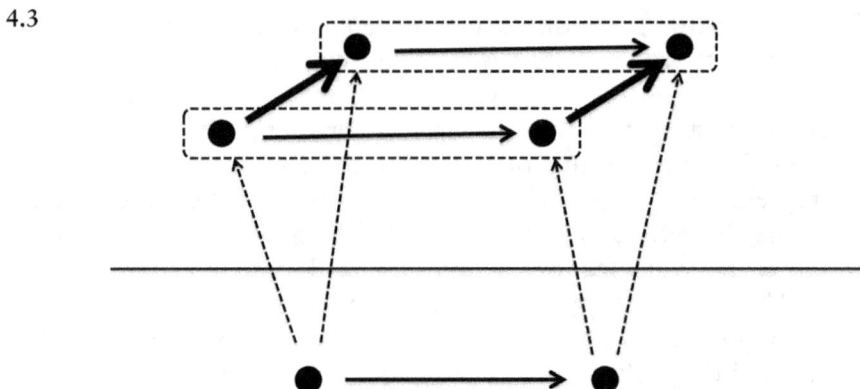

to another in this sort of category will represent a map from one functor to another functor. Understanding what such an arrow conceptually *is* involves probably the first genuinely difficult thinking of the present work. To grasp the essence of what an arrow from one functor to another designates is to conceive of a determinate and well-regulated relation between two determinate and well-regulated relations between two systems of determinate and well-regulated relations. As exotic as this abstract beast might seem, it is called a *natural transformation*. It was mostly for the sake of determining these meta-meta-relational creatures that Eilenberg and Mac Lane originally invented categories in their seminal 1945 paper. Figure 4.3 gives an initial idea of the construction. Consider an arrow between two dots in some category, as pictured below the line. Two different functors, represented by two different dashed arrows, carry that arrow into some other category, represented above the line. There are thus two copies of the arrow in the bottom category 'imaged' in the top category. The natural transformation between the two functors 'shifts' or 'slides' one image into the other, using arrows available in the top category. In this way, a natural transformation may be thought of as translating dots in the source category into arrows in the target category. Each source-dot becomes a target-arrow, each object is translated into a difference (or a relation, depending on one's point of view). Of course, these cannot be just any arrows, but they must be ones that cohere with the two functors they differentiate/relate in an appropriate way. In this case, the square of arrows in the top category must commute.

Just as a functor preserves the structure of its source-category as organised in that category's constituent system of arrows across the mapping that takes it into the functor's target-category (in a relative fashion subject to the possible local collapse of information or difference), a natural transformation preserves (relatively) the structure of a given functor as it 'varies' or 'transforms' into another functor with the same categorical source and target. If a functor may be understood as a kind of image of its source-category inside its target-category (with some possible collapsing of dots and/or arrows but no splitting or tearing), a natural transformation may be understood as a well-behaved map from one such image to another, constructed with arrows inside the target-category. Thus it forms a sort of 'oriented prism' in the target-category (with functorial images of the source-category at the bottom and the top of the prism). From a slightly more abstract perspective, if a functor from C to D is thought of as the 'selection' of a structure of type C inside D, a natural transformation selects a cohesive mapping or transformation inside D that uses arrows in D to 'carry' one such C-structure into another, where both of these C-structures are themselves systems of dots and arrows selected in D by functors from C.

See Figure 4.4. The two functors are represented 'externally' by the lower and upper thick arrows from C to D. The 'internal' images

4.4

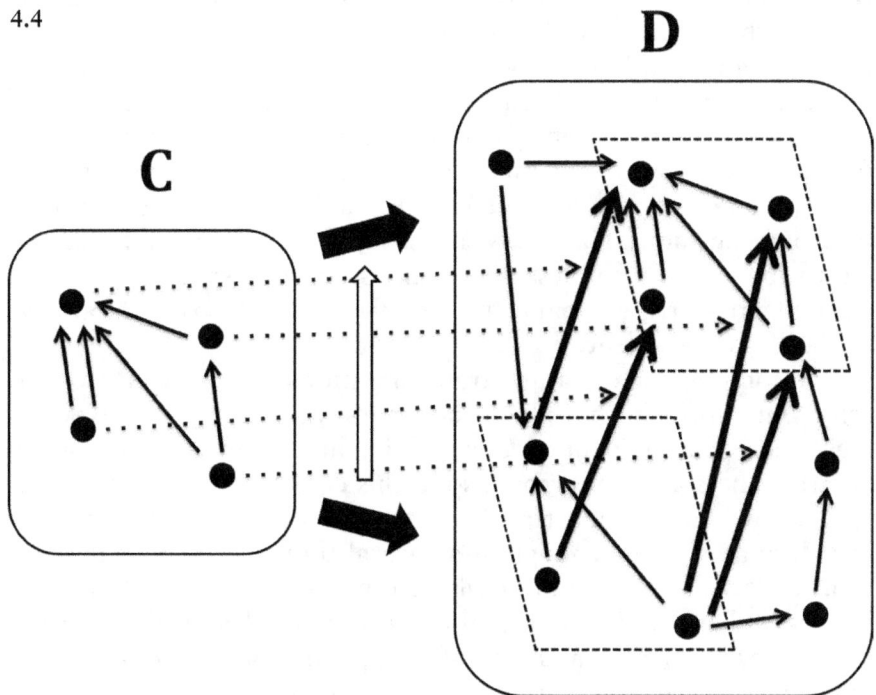

of **C** they select in **D** are indicated by the dashed frames inside **D** (the reader should check that these in fact determine functors from **C**). The natural transformation is represented 'externally' by the hollow upward arrow between the two thick black arrows, and 'internally' by the mapping of dotted arrows from the four dots in **C** to the four slightly thicker arrows selected inside **D**. These selected arrows may be seen to carry the lower dashed frame in **D** into the upper, and it should be remembered that all the relevant compositions in the resulting 'prism' must commute appropriately.

So the dots of our proposed category are defined: functors. And so are its arrows: natural transformations. How do we know that these definitions actually work together to define a category in the proper sense? Remember the three categorical axioms. If we can show that (C1) pairs of head-to-tail arrows always compose to uniquely determine arrows on the whole path, that (C2) every dot has an identity arrow, and that (C3) composition is associative for pathways of arbitrary length, then we are assured that our dots and the arrows between them constitute a mathematical category.

First, we will verify the identity axiom, C2. Take any arbitrary functor $F: \mathbf{C} \to \mathbf{D}$. We can always relate F to itself by 'cloning' it, that is, by considering two identical copies of F and then relating one copy to the other with identity arrows in **D**. In effect, this identity natural transformation converts each **C**-image-*object* carried by F into **D** into the identity *arrow* on that object in **D**. It is thus a sort of 'meta-identity arrow' composed of identity arrows. The conversion of each of the dots in the image of **C** into an identity arrow simply selects the identity arrow (in **D**) corresponding to each one of these functor-image dots. The arrows in the image of **C** living in **D** according to the functor F necessarily compose in the expected way with these identity arrows, thanks to the rule of thumb 'paths of arrows are indifferent to identities'.

The composition of natural transformations is a bit trickier to conceive, but in principle it follows the same straightforward 'bookkeeping' logic as that of identity. Composition means 'an arrow following an arrow nets another arrow', so in this case a natural transformation following a natural transformation should net another natural transformation. Sure enough, if a natural transformation is thought of as an oriented prism in **D** whose top and bottom are functorial images of **C** in **D**, then a natural transformation following a natural transformation is just a 'stack' of two prisms where the top of the first is the same as the bottom of the second. When these two prisms are 'glued together' via the composition of arrows in the target category **D**, a new prism results. In categorical terms this new prism is the natural transformation that is the composition of the first natural transformation followed by the second. Essentially, the composition of arrows in **D** as guaranteed by the composition axiom C1 'carries over' to the natural transformation arrows.

Finally, the requirement of associativity is met by colligating two compositional triangles and checking that the relevant three-arrow pathways do indeed result in the same composition-arrow regardless of the order in which they are composed. If such an associative composition holds within the given category for two arbitrary triangles, then it must hold throughout the category as a whole. In effect, in the present case the associativity axiom 'carries over' from **D** arrow-paths to natural transformation arrow-paths.[3]

PRESHEAVES

Putting functor categories and natural transformations to one side for a moment, it is now time to introduce one of the most important and productive category-theoretical constructions: presheaves. A presheaf is essentially a relation between an arbitrary category **C** and some fragment of the category of sets and functions that 'mirrors', 'represents' or 'realises' **C** in a certain way. In fact, the relation in question is that of a particular type of functor, a *contravariant* functor from **C** into **Sets**. The 'mirroring' relation here is of a special type and is especially important. Somewhat as a mirror 'reverses' left and right in its image, the functor that defines a presheaf reverses the direction of all the arrows in the mapping from **C** into **Sets** while nonetheless preserving their identifying, compositional and associational structures. This reversal of arrows in the target category constitutes what is called the 'contravariance' of the functor.

Intuitively, a presheaf may be pictured as some given category **C** 'laid flat' with a category of sets and functions layered on top of it, with a single set stacked like a column over each dot of **C**. We will refer to the bottom layer as the *base category* and the fragment of **Sets** 'over' it as the *model category*, the reason for this becoming clear in what follows. To each arrow in the base category there will correspond a unique arrow representing a function in the model category, this arrow however going in the opposite direction. Typically, the arrows (functions) in the model category are 'restriction maps'

4.5

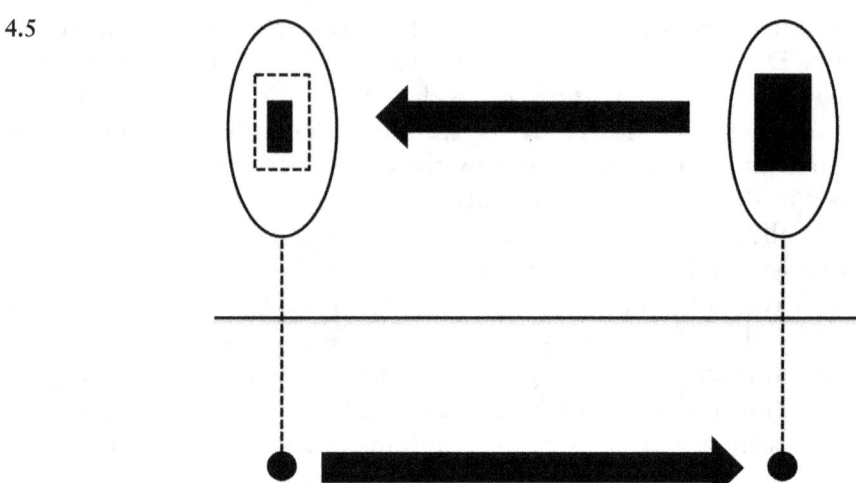

in the sense that they take more extensive structures (the elements of the source-set) over some element in the base to those same structures *as restricted to* the part coded by the corresponding 'lower' element in the basal order. If we limit ourselves to partial-order categories in the base, the contravariance of the functor is readily imaged by contrasting 'flows' in the base and the model: left-to-right in the base, right-to-left in the model. In the diagram pictured in Figure 4.5, the dot on the left in the base is 'below' the dot on the right in terms of the order of the category, and the model over the dot on the left is the same as the model over the dot on the right (the larger rectangle) only 'restricted' to its smaller central region.

A very useful class of examples offers itself at this point: presheaves over topological spaces. Consider a finite space, in the sense of some chunk of our intuitive, familiar three-dimensional environment abstracted of any particular contents. The room you find yourself in right now, for instance. It is a simple matter to consider such a space as a partial order category. Consider all the continuous 'chunks' and 'sub-chunks' of the space. It may be helpful to picture these as spheres of every imaginable size and location, but they may also be of any shape whatsoever. There is a natural category defined over any collection of such chunks and sub-chunks: simply take each such chunk as a dot in the category; an arrow goes from one dot to another in this category if and only if the target dot represents a chunk that completely contains the chunk represented by the source dot. It should be evident why this forms a partial order, and hence a category.

More generally, we may define a *topological space* as a family of

Diagrams of Variation: Functor Categories and Presheaves

objects called *opens* (including unique initial and terminal objects) together with a pair of operators, *intersection* and *union*, defined on them that are required to meet three criteria, which taken together guarantee that the family of opens hangs together in a coherent way. The first two are closure properties imposed on the operators. First, for any pair of opens, their *intersection* must also be in the family. Second, for any arbitrary subset of the family, any denumerable collection of opens whether finite or infinite, the *union* of that subset must also be in the family. Finally, the relation between the intersection and union operators must distribute in the sense, roughly, that the intersection of any single open with any union of a collection of opens must be the same as the union of all the intersections of that single open with each of the opens in the collection.

Although these determinations may be given entirely abstractly such that they apply only to the *operations* defined on the opens, not the opens themselves, usually the role of opens is played by sets, and they are then called 'open sets'. The simplest intuitive example is given by considering collections of subsets of some chosen set S. A *topology on S* is then any collection T of subsets of S that includes the empty set and S itself, and is closed under the basic set-theoretical operations of union and finite intersection on the elements of T. If all this seems a bit confusing, the reader should just think informally of ordinary three-dimensional space and the natural sense in which any way of carving up, say, the space of a small room that would include all the possible overlaps and collections of the carved-up parts are naturally ordered by inclusion in a straightforward manner. For any two 'pieces', X and Y, of the space, just ask: is X completely inside Y, Y completely inside X, or neither?

Any topological space (or a topology) may be understood as a lattice with certain properties. And recall that a lattice is just a special kind of partial order and therefore a category. Consider the open sets of a topological space as the 'parts' of the space, with those parts ordered by inclusion, as sketched above. If the parts are diagrammed as dots in a category, an arrow from one dot to another indicates that the set represented by the source dot is a subset of the set represented by the target dot. Since set inclusion is a reflexive relation (every set is a subset of itself) and a transitive one (any subset of a subset of S is also a subset of S), we are assured of having a partial order and hence a category.

To build a presheaf over such a category, it is a matter of assigning a set to each of its dots (each of the nodes of the lattice). Recall that each dot in our example is a part of a three-dimensional space. What set shall we assign to each part of the space? Let's assign the set of all real-valued functions with the set of points in that part as their domain. In other words, take some function that assigns a single real number to each and every point in the part. For example, if the part is a cubic metre of three-dimensional space, say a chunk of a chilly classroom, such a function might represent a temperature gradient, with each point in the cubic metre mapped to the real number corresponding to its temperature in degrees Celsius. Then consider *all* the possible assignments of real numbers to all points in the part (normally these values would be required to vary continuously). This is a huge collection of possibilities. It represents an enormous amount of information thrown together completely haphazardly. There is no internal structure to the collection of these functions. They constitute a set.

Yet when we stipulate this same sort of mapping (from a given part of space to the set of all real-valued functions on the points of that part) to *all* the parts of the space, an interesting cohesion emerges among all this unstructured data. Consider a cube ten centimetres on each side in one of the corners of our cubic metre. This corner cube is included in the larger part, and it has been assigned the set of all the functions from its points into the real numbers. But this means that every assignment of a real number to every point of the cubic metre (that is, a single element in the set assigned to the larger part) is at the same time an assignment of a real number to each point of the smaller cube. There is therefore a well-defined 'restriction map' that takes each element of the set of functions 'above' the cubic metre (each real-valued function on the large cube) to exactly one element of the set 'above' the smaller corner cube (a real-valued function on the points of the corner cube), namely the element (the function) that takes exactly the same values at each point in the corner cube. This coordination of relations of parts to whole in the base with restrictions of sets from whole to parts in the models is one very useful type of presheaf, definable over any topological space.

In a similarly intuitive fashion, all the possible 'snapshots' capturing a singular configuration of waves on the entire surface of a lake are representable as presheaves of sets of 'local snapshots' over local patches of the surface. The patches will be ordered by inclusion in the base (local to global) and the snapshots ordered by restriction in the models (global to local). Diagrams, like most

Diagrams of Variation: Functor Categories and Presheaves

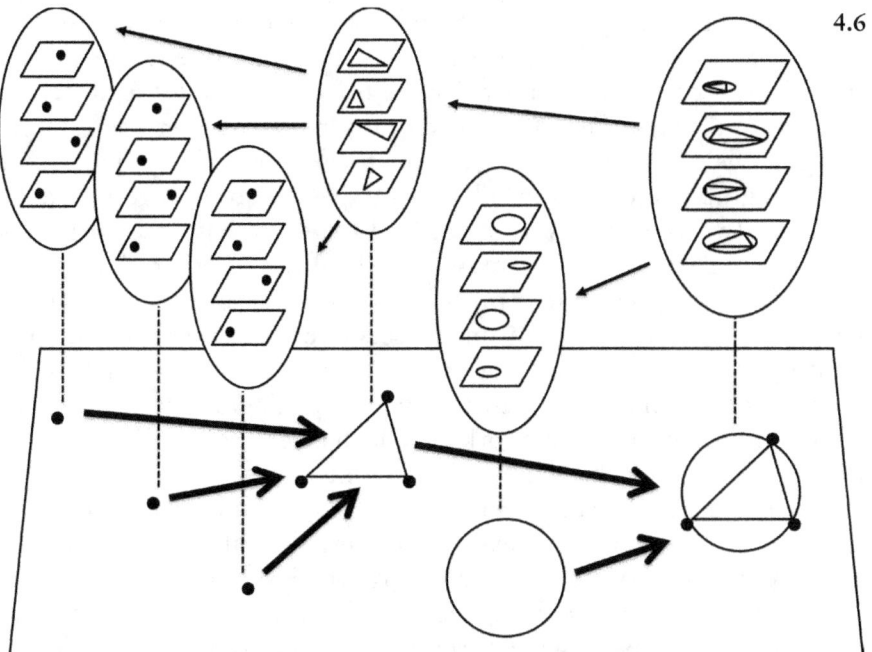

4.6

things, typically have parts organised into a whole. This same approach thus allows us to consider the sets over meaningfully selectable parts of any such diagram as 'local models' of that part of the diagram, with the semantic range of the entire diagram represented as the set over the largest part (the whole as composition of all the diagram's parts). By way of illustration in Figure 4.6, the Euclidean diagram of a triangle inscribed in a circle is represented as a presheaf.[4]

Presheaves in general represent either singular or variable realisations inside **Sets** (the model category) of some determinate system of abstract relations (the base category). Often, these conjugations of purely relational systems and set-theoretical models provide a straightforward way to specify the members of interesting classes of objects. For example, directed graphs – the general kind of dot-and-arrow diagrams introduced at the beginning of Chapter 2 – are expressible as presheaves over a base category with two dots and two parallel non-identity arrows. Given such a presheaf, the elements of the model set corresponding to the dot at the tail of the two arrows in the base represent the dots of the graph, and the elements of the set corresponding to the dot at the head of the two arrows in the base represent the graph's arrows. The pair of functions from the latter set to the former in the model thus take each represented 'arrow' to a pair of 'dots', one for its source and one for its target, providing precisely the data requisite for determining the structure of a unique graph. In other words, any presheaf over that simple category 'is' (uniquely represents up to isomorphism) a particular directed graph, and every graph may be specified by such a presheaf.[5]

Given two presheaves over one and the same base category, it is possible to define a map from one presheaf to the other. A *presheaf map* from a presheaf P to a presheaf Q over the same base category C is a family of functions from the sets over C in P to the sets over C in Q such that the appropriate paths of arrows commute in the manner of a natural transformation. The diagram in Figure 4.7 shows intuitively how it works.[6] The dashed right-to-left arrows in the top half of the diagram represent a family of functions in **Sets** from the model-sets in the presheaf represented on the right to the model-sets in the presheaf on the left that all commute in the appropriate way (visible in the diagram). It should be noted how two of the sets collapse into one across the mapping. This should help to suggest how in general there will be not only many different

4.7

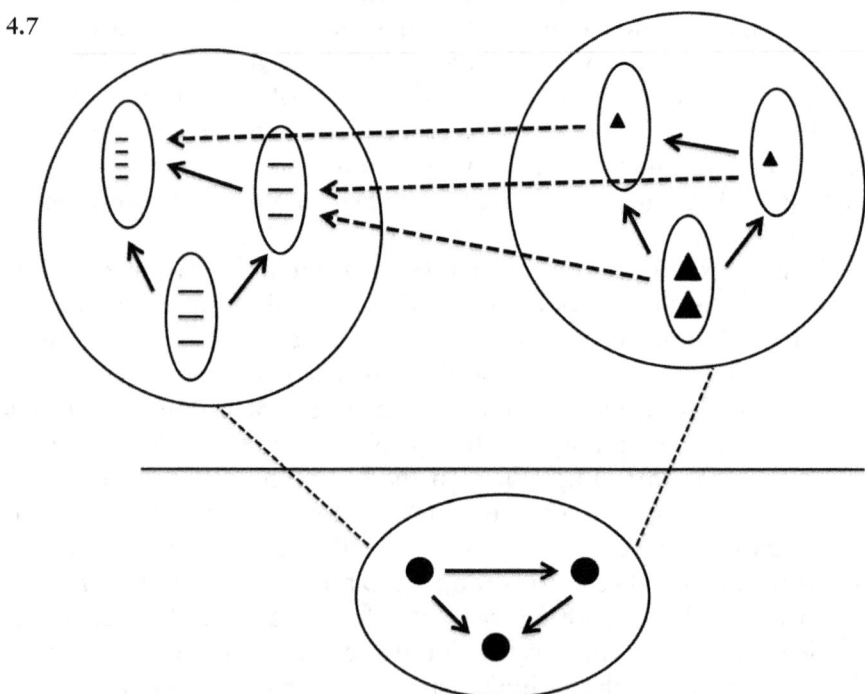

maps but also different *kinds* of different maps between two such presheaves.

FROM PRESHEAVES TO PRESHEAF CATEGORIES

For any category **C**, it is possible to build a variety of presheaves over **C** by taking **C** as the base category and allowing the particular collection of sets and functions (the selection from **Sets**) as the model category to vary. The infinite collection of all such possible presheaves for some given category **C** may then be considered to constitute the objects (the dots) of a well-defined category with arrows between these objects stipulated to be all possible presheaf maps between the presheaves. This category may be designated **Presheaves**$_C$.[7] It is the category of all presheaves over **C** and all natural transformation maps among them. Each category naturally induces such a presheaf category.[8] We may picture the situation informally (ignoring certain technical distinctions) as a relation between two sheets that are, respectively, *whole* and *part* of **Categories:** for every category on the upper sheet, there is an associated category of presheaves on the lower sheet coordinating all of the upper category's possible 'actualisations' or 'realisations' in **Sets**.

In general, a presheaf category represents the system of naturally ordered relations among all the possible realisations in **Sets** of some abstract category. One of the most important results in category theory shows that *any* category may be represented in this way *within* the category of sets and functions. This is *Yoneda's lemma*, which demonstrates that every category may be represented in terms of a distinct embedding into its own presheaf category, that is, the category of contravariant functors from it into the category of sets and functions (and natural transformations between these).[9] Intuitively, Yoneda's lemma shows how any category is structurally equivalent to a certain selection from among the system of relations among the various ways it may be translated into systems of sets and functions between sets. The category itself as a system of virtual relations may be 'found' concretely among the relations between the different possible ways it itself may be 'actualised'. Like other 'representation theorems', Yoneda's lemma guarantees that a certain kind of mathematical structure may always be modelled in a particularly useful way. The representation itself carries all the requisite information about what it represents. This complex but very important mathematical result serves in the present context as an indication of the representational power of category theory with respect to a variety of formal problems surrounding representation, self-reference, operational closure and other concerns that straddle metaphysics, formal logic and mathematics. While the details and proof of the lemma go beyond the reach of the present book, it is a result the importance of which can hardly be overstated in terms of thinking of the variety of what presheaves can do.

A CATEGORICAL THEORY OF DIAGRAMMATIC SIGNS

We have been working with diagrams for some time now, both in a relatively informal philosophical setting as a way to illustrate certain concepts in Spinoza and Peirce and in an increasingly formal setting as we have stocked our arsenal of category theory constructions. With the key notions of presheaf and presheaf category in hand, the way is clear to define a *diagrammatic sign* in a quite general way within category theory itself. The discussion of Peirce's semiotic conception of diagrams in Chapter 3 will serve here as an important guiding thread.

If the structural 'syntax' of a diagram is represented by the dots and arrows of a category, the diagram's 'semantics' may in a relatively straightforward way appear as the sets and functions in a presheaf over that category. The diagram's iconicity is modelled in this way by the functor of the presheaf itself, which ensures that the structure of the syntax is carried over in a relevant manner into the semantics. The most intuitive case is when the diagram's syntax is a static organisation of discrete parts and the semantics over each part is simply the collection of possible 'instances' or 'tokens' of its corresponding syntactical unit. In such a case, the base category of the presheaf is a partial order category (typically with a terminal dot representing the diagrammatic syntax as a whole) and, for each arrow in the partial order, the functions between sets in the semantics take each 'instance' or 'token' of the greater syntactical part ('above' the other in the order-structure) to its natural restriction to the smaller, as in the Euclidean 'circle and triangle' diagram elaborated in Figure 4.6 above. More complex and dynamical diagrams may be constructed by enriching the base category (using categories involving cycles and multiple arrows between dots to represent variable physical systems, for example) and also by making use of the representational flexibility of set theory in the semantics (for instance, by having functions or systems of differential equations as the elements of the model-sets).

What is most important from the Peircean semiotic perspective on diagrams, however, is the triadic relation of sign, object and interpretant. It is the holistic unity of this relation and the manner in which varying any of its terms and subrelations alters the others in corresponding ways that makes the relation itself semiotic and also pragmatic; and it is the possibility of situating all of its terms and subrelations in some common 'space' of effectivity that would underwrite the claim that semiotics may indeed be truly immanent. To be aligned, then, with both a diagrammatic pragmatism and a metaphysics of immanence, the (essentially dyadic) characterisation just given must therefore be extended to a more intrinsically variable and triadic conception.

A *diagrammatic sign*, then, will be a triadic relation represented categorically by a composition-triangle of three functors (*Selection, Experimentation, Evaluation*) between three categories (**Interpretant [Int], Ambient [Amb], Sets**) in the following way:

Selection is a functor **Int→Amb**. Typically, this functor will be an inclusion, but this is not required. *Experimentation* is a contravariant functor **Amb→Sets**, where **Sets** is the category of sets and functions (or some appropriate subcategory of the latter). Informally, this functor only needs to be defined on the subcategory of **Amb** that is 'selected' by the *Selection* functor from **Int**. As a contravariant functor into **Sets**, this functor determines a presheaf, that is, an object of **Presheaves**$_{Amb}$. The selection of the subcategory in **Amb** by *Selection* should be thought of as a diagrammatic substrate or 'base' with the sets assigned to each of its objects in **Sets** by the *Experimentation* functor as 'models' of that component of the diagram. *Evaluation* is then a contravariant functor **Int→Sets**. It is the composition of *Experimentation* following *Selection*, an object in the category **Presheaves**$_{Int}$.

As each of the component functors varies (corresponding to natural transformations in the relevant presheaf categories), the compositional unity that defines the diagrammatic sign as a whole must vary as well. The roles of the three categories and the composition-structure of the three functors are shown in Figure 4.8. It is essentially a compositional triangle of three functors, two of which are presheaves. The diagram illustrates how variation in the experimentation presheaves correlates with variation in the evaluation presheaves. The internal diagrams in each category present a very

4.8

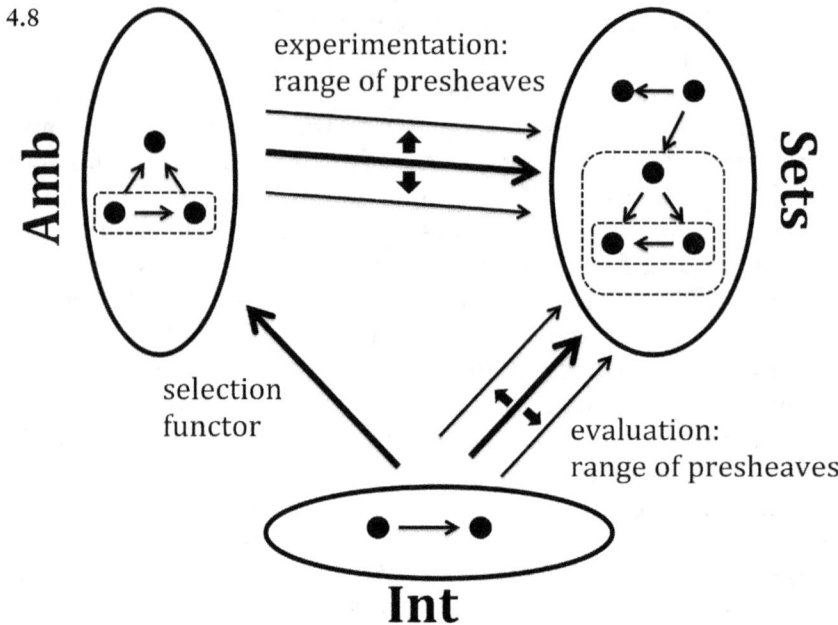

simple example. The images of the functors are pictured with dashed frames (note the contravariance of arrows in the images selected in Sets).

Peirce's Existential Graphs

The dynamics of the proposed theory are exemplified well by Peirce's own system of Existential Graphs (EG).[10] Peirce's logical notation of EG provides a rich field for investigating logical relationships in an iconic and diagrammatic way that coheres naturally with the more general account just given. Because formal logic is so crucial to much contemporary philosophy, it is one important aspect of the current proposal that a rigorous system of representation for propositional, first-order and a variety of higher-order and modal logics is readily available for it. To the possible objection that situating philosophy within diagrammatic immanence would require reinventing the wheel of logical formalism, the proper response is that the wheel has in fact already been reinvented, not to mention in key respects improved. It should be noted here that 'graphs' in Peirce's sense of Existential Graphs are distinct from the 'directed graphs' discussed in Chapter 2, which are diagrammatic systems of dots and arrows.

4.9

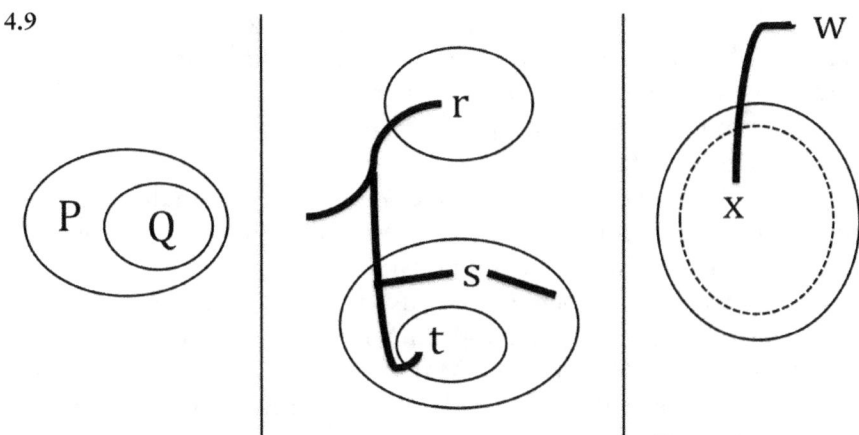

Figure 4.9 presents an example of each of Peirce's three levels of Existential Graphs: alpha, beta and gamma (from left to right). Graphs at each level are inscribed on a blank area that Peirce calls the 'sheet of assertion' or SA, which serves as a sort of transcendental condition as well as a material substrate for the construction of Existential Graphs (EG) and their experimentation. The syntax of the alpha graphs consists of letters or other symbols that represent propositions and oval-shaped 'cuts' representing the negation of the conjunction of the contents of the areas they circumscribe on the SA. Cuts may be nested, but may not intersect. The semantics of the alpha graphs are generated by reading from the outermost area inward, what Peirce called the 'endoporeutic method'. The graph pictured on the left in Figure 4.9 encloses the conjunction of P and the negation of Q (Q alone inside a cut) in a cut in the outermost area of the SA. It thus signifies 'not (P and not-Q)' or, equivalently, P implies Q.

The graph in the centre of Figure 4.9 is an instance of Peirce's EG-beta. At this level, which corresponds to first-order predicative logic, the syntax of 'cuts' as negation is conserved and a new convention – the 'line of identity' – is introduced in order to handle quantification. The line of identity is essentially an existential quantifier; it signifies 'something exists'. Its continuity signifies its identity in a strikingly iconic way. When enclosed in a negating 'cut', the line of identity becomes a negative universal quantifier: 'nothing exists'. When attached to a predicate, it attributes the predicate to the 'something' or the 'nothing'. Two-place and higher-place relations join multiple lines of identity according to the logic of the relational predicate represented. Thus the beta graph shown represents the claim that 'something exists that is not-*r* and if that something stands in relation *s* to anything, then it is not-*t*'. Peirce's beta graphs have been proven to be logically equivalent to first-order logic in its more standard linear notation.

Finally the gamma graphs, which Peirce never finalised in any single version, introduce the convention of a dashed cut representing the *possible* negation of its conjunctive contents as well as (in various drafts) a variety of higher-order conventions for representing characteristics of graphs themselves and for regulating the introduction of new notational conventions. Making use of the dashed cut alone, together with the conventions of the beta graphs, it is possible to institute deductive rules corresponding to the familiar modal logics of S4, S5 and many others. In the gamma graph pictured on the right in Figure 4.9, it is claimed that something exists that is *w* and it is not the case that that same thing is possibly not-*x*. Equivalently, something *w* and necessarily *x* exists.

These hasty remarks and simple examples barely scratch the surface of Peirce's system, and there is obviously much more to be said. Without going into the details of Peirce's three-level system of EG and its rules of deduction that at each level allow for the topological transformation of one graph into others in ways that preserve the original graph's truth-value, it is still possible to briefly sketch how the semantics for the EG diagrams may be efficiently represented by presheaves. Figure 4.10 explicates the EG-alpha graph pictured on the left in Figure 4.9. The internal topological structure of the graph is represented by the partial order that serves as the base category of the presheaf. In a manner that should be quite clear upon inspection and comparison with the original graph, this partial order simply distinguishes the various syntactically relevant 'parts' of the graph and their nested ordering within areas enclosed by cuts. The graph as a whole is represented by the terminal object of the partial order. In the 'stack' of cuts-only graphs above each element of the partial order are all the possible combinations made by replacing the propositional variables P and Q with the empty cut (representing the value 'false') or the blank SA itself (representing the value 'true') for that given part of the graph. These stacks are thus the sets assigned to each element of the partial order by a canonical presheaf functor. The functions from one of these sets to the next as defined by the functor are the evident restrictions from larger to smaller parts of the graph. The internal structure

4.10

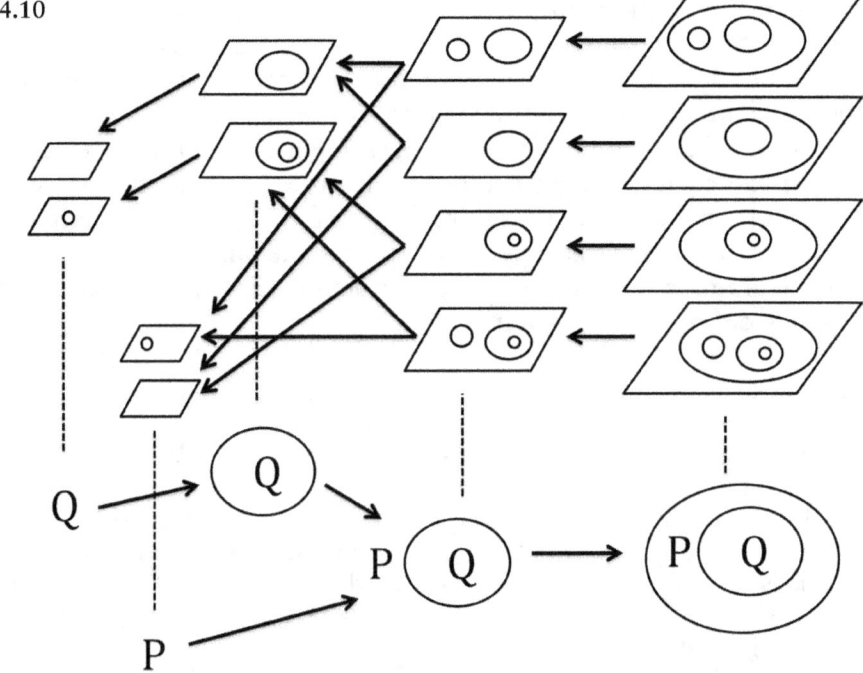

of these functions is pictured by the arrows in the model category section of the diagram. The logical dynamics of this simple alpha graph (the 'truth function table' for a generic material conditional) may be read directly off the functions that determine the diagram's models.

Obviously as Existential Graphs become more complex, the internal structure of the semantics embodied in such presheaves becomes increasingly difficult to represent or visually interpret fully. But this is precisely the advantage of turning to the more abstract 'external' modes of representation available within category theory. Not only the semantics of alpha graphs but equally those of beta and gamma may be diagrammed by presheaves. Such presheaves naturally relate to one another in a variety of ways, in particular in ways that correspond to the transformational deduction rules that make Peirce's EG such an efficient logical calculus. Even more generally, the basic method illustrated here of treating diagrams as partial orders with their semantics registered as sets defined by presheaf functors takes Peirce's EG as just one special case (albeit one that is general enough to model all of propositional, first-order and common modal logics) of a thoroughly diagrammatic syntax-semantics relation. Note that topological variations in the graphs (variations in their corresponding *Selection* functors, where the role of the category **Amb** is played by the sheet of assertion represented as a topological space) induce logically interesting variations in the *Experimentation* and hence *Evaluation* presheaves. These changes themselves may be tracked within the corresponding presheaf categories. In conjunction with Yoneda's lemma, many intriguing levels of analysis and experimentation naturally emerge, even for very simple cases of EG-graphs. The diagrammatic sign presheaf construction, of course, applies to a much wider field of possibilities.

Notes

1. The language of 'exposure' is taken from Badiou, *Logics of Worlds*, pp. 313–17.
2. It is here that a more technical treatment would require the introduction of the distinctions among 2-categories, 3-categories and so on. This goes well beyond the scope of the present text. For introductory details, see Lambek and Scott, *Introduction to Higher Order Categorical Logic*.
3. In the liminal world where mathematics and philosophy overlap, two distinct populations are generally found: one made up of those who pull out pen and paper and check the algebraic equations for themselves, working their way back all the way to the fundamental categorical axioms, and one of those who simply check their intuition to whatever intermediate degree of clarity and confusion and take the formal details on faith. Each path consolidates its own set of virtues and intellectual habits. We leave it to the gods and nameless fates to sort out each group's just deserts.
4. This use of presheaves to elaborate the syntax-semantics relation of diagrams is analysed in more detail in Gangle and Caterina, 'The Sheet of Indication'.
5. If desired for mathematical neatness, all the presheaves that represent the same graph may be gathered into an equivalence class. See F. William Lawvere and Stephen H. Schanuel, *Conceptual Mathematics*, pp. 149–51.
6. Details may be found in Marie La Palme Reyes, Gonzalo E. Reyes and Houman Zolfaghari, *Generic Figures and Their Glueings*. Generally, the only technical difficulties here other than the red herrings of set-theory 'size' issues arise from tracking the contravariance of the presheaf functor through the various mappings. This is largely a notational problem. The solution proposed by Reyes, Reyes and Zolfaghari is a helpful first step in this regard.

7. In the literature, this category is usually notated with the 'exponential' notation $\mathbf{Set}^{C(op)}$.
8. Technically, this is only true of so-called 'small' categories, that is, categories the dots of which may be gathered into a set and of which a set may be gathered of all the arrows between any two dots.
9. See Mac Lane, *Categories for the Working Mathematician*, pp. 59–62.
10. See note 24 in Chapter 3 for references linked to Peirce's EG.

CHAPTER 5

Deleuze and Expressive Immanence

> Whether we are trying to understand how consciousness can sleep, how it can be inspired by a past which it has apparently lost, or finally how it can open up again to that past, it is possible to speak of passivity only on the condition that 'to be conscious' does not mean 'to give a meaning', which one projects onto an ungraspable object of knowledge, but to realize a certain distance, a certain variation in a field of existence already instituted, which is always behind us and whose weight, like that of an object in flight, only intervenes in the actions by which we transform it.
>
> Merleau-Ponty, *In Praise of Philosophy*

Jean-Pierre Marquis has made a detailed and convincing case for conceiving the development of category theory as an extension and generalisation of Felix Klein's Erlangen Program in geometry.[1] The Erlangen Program aimed to resituate the entire set of linked problematics concerning general geometrical objecthood and proof around a more abstract and algebraic conception of groups of transformations. In the face of a proliferation of different and at times competing geometries in the mid-nineteenth century, Klein proposed an intrinsically variable and pluralistic reconceptualisation of geometric systems and relations. For Klein's approach, geometries are understood as systems of relations of figures that remain invariant under possible transformations. Or to put it otherwise, geometries are coherent selections of transformations of figures that are allowed to collapse into indifference in order that the remaining transformational differences might be effectively theorised. Geometries thus stipulate what does and does not matter from the standpoint of what turns, slides, shrinks and reflects in a generic space of any and all such figural transformations. *A* geometry (Euclidean, Lobachevskian, Riemannian, projective) becomes an abstract object that is variable and relatively underdetermined in itself, remaining structurally invariant only at the level of certain group-theoretical axioms, properties and operations defining 'indifferent' transformations (effectively, isomorphisms). Then at a second level, the variable differentiations among such systems of variable differentiation schematise a space of possible geometries as such, including utterly non-intuitive, unimaginable and interestingly pathological cases. Within this enriched space, what determines the difference between two systems of geometry (for instance Euclidean and Riemannian) are the different (though often at least partly overlapping) cohesive sets of transformations of figures they separately determine.

Deleuzian thought may be understood to execute a sort of Erlangen Program within contemporary philosophy and especially post-Heideggerian phenomenology. Just as Klein asked geometers to abstract from the qualities of particular geometrical figures and to attend to the global systems of invariance they might conceivably exhibit under slippages, reflections, contractions and explosions, Deleuze impels philosophers to abstract away from the coordinates of common-sense objectivity and clichéd modes of representation (even and especially when these are imported into philosophically 'critical' procedures) in order to attend to the continuities and discontinuities inflecting the real-conceptual processes that generate them. In this, Deleuze is eminently Spinozist, as he himself declaims throughout his oeuvre.

From this perspective, Deleuze's thought is best understood as formally topological in essence. The model of Ideas that Deleuze differentiates from the regulative one of Kant through a kind of quasi-inversion of Platonic-Husserlian *eidei* neither serves a limiting function nor plays the role of original or type with respect to possible copies or tokens. Instead, Ideas are the higher-order thresholds that mark qualitative shifts in the real transformations of actualities themselves. As Bryant puts it, 'Deleuze conceives Ideas topologically as sets of variations or deformations in which one form can pass into another while maintaining a structural identity, rather than as fixed forms to which individuals more or less correspond.'[2] More exactly, Ideas are not mere collections of variations but are rather determinations of the relative cohesiveness of such collections. The Ideas are immanent, ideal, structural conditions determining relations among the variables (the real variations) of some domain: 'what Ideas define is an ideal topological or differential essence characterizing a field of variations or permutations'.[3] The Ideas *define* the field itself, and are at a second remove from the objects or entities the field's transformations map. The model of philosophical experience proposed by

Deleuze is thus one of purely conceptual (second-order) dilations, contractions, inflections, gluings and tearings. These are characteristics of continuous multiplicities, not properties of objects. And as Peirce emphasised, continuity is never composed of points even if points may always be abstracted from continua. Deleuze's conception of Ideas as singularities may be understood in this sense as being in accord with a broadly Peircean approach to metaphysics:

> *A singularity is not a point.* So long as we conceive singularity after the fashion of a point, we remain unable to understand the different properties which Deleuze attributes to them. Rather, we must treat singularities as being a sort of thread, flow, distension, or 'smear.' A singularity is a thread or expanse of becoming. It is a duration.[4]

Bryant earlier points out that it is for this reason that Deleuze's philosophy does not stand in need of a conceptual *schematism* in the manner of Kant, and reiterates Deleuze's own preference for Maimon's critique of Kant and the ambiguous role of the Kantian schemata.[5] This helps us to understand how the 'topological' dimension of Deleuze's thought must be taken in an abstract or purely conceptual fashion. It is by no means a 'spatialisation' in any empirically intuitive sense, no matter how variable or flexible. This same danger of misinterpretation applies to such Deleuzian concepts as the 'fold'. The topological structure of Deleuzian philosophy should in fact be conceived as a relative *indifference* to variation and becoming.[6] Topological relations remain invariant even as figural, positional and metric relations vary. This does not entail however that the variations are simply placeholders in an abstract structure. This is one way that Deleuze may be thought consistently to stand in a relative continuity with phenomenology while at the same remaining critically distinct from it. As in the epigraph from Merleau-Ponty, the Deleuzian relation to experience is always to its sleeping, lost or obscure dimensions. Deleuze's project is to make such aspects of experience philosophically productive *within* experience, and like Merleau-Ponty suggests, the concomitant method for philosophy involves introducing 'a certain distance, a certain variation' from within immanence.[7]

THINKING FROM BLINDNESS

One thing Maimon and Deleuze share in their common critique of Kant is the structural inversion of a certain common-sense duality that is formally quite straightforward but rich in consequences, a bit like Marx's inversion of Hegel, and perhaps not wholly unrelated. In Maimon and Deleuze, the apparently 'derived' term in a conceptual pairing (for instance, the limit of a series) is instead placed in the position of priority and genesis. The limit, singularity, infinitesimal thus takes on an explanatory role. It is *real*, although not actual; it is *ideal*, although not abstract. In Bergsonian terms, it constitutes a *difference in kind* between terms that makes possible their no less determinate *difference in degree*.[8] The former is asymmetrical and irreversible; the latter is symmetric and at least partially reversible.

The categorical analogue of this Maimonian-Deleuzian inversion is precisely the sense in which category theory as a whole may be understood as an extension and generalisation of Klein's Erlangen Program in geometry. The latter treats actual relations of congruence, etc., within *a* geometry as mere effects or consequences of the fundamental group of transformations that determines the geometry globally. In a similar fashion, category theory privileges arrows over objects and arrow-compositions over arrows in the sense that objects in a category are determined foremost by their arrows and arrows by their compositions. Relations constitutively determine what they relate. Rather than functor categories, for example, being viewed as abstractions from more concrete categories, the intrinsic tendency of category theory is to proceed in the other direction: since functor categories are, after all, categories, it makes sense to investigate them first as locally generative limits or singular nodes of intensity in the category of categories (or some fragment thereof). This is why when working within category theory it is often easier to work in a 'top-down' fashion, for instance by 'forgetting' the internal structure of objects (or of categories) and attending only to compositions of arrows (or of functors). If needed, it is frequently possible to represent these more ideal or global structures *inside* the more rigid or local ones (such was essentially the revolutionary approach of Grothendieck to a variety of problems in algebraic topology and other mathematical fields via representable functors). In this sense, category theory remains broadly Platonic and phenomenological in spirit, although no longer in a dualistic way: 'essences' take *relative* priority over 'existents', not because they are more general but because they are more variable and differentiated at their given level of immanent structure. Nonetheless, the 'essences' themselves prove experimentally accessible through transformations and active participations (iconic representations) at 'lower' levels of more invariant structures.

For Deleuze the very possibility of such a structural chiasmus of existential and essential tendencies follows as a *consequence* of metaphysical immanence, which possesses in Deleuze's thought the status of an ever-renewed experimental hypothesis. This helps to shed light on an interesting paradox: much of the most intriguing recent work on Deleuze has come from a Kantian and broadly transcendentalist and even 'rationalist' standpoint, yet Deleuze's project is quite directly opposed to Kant's (even more so than to Hegel).[9] But also, some of the most promising avenues of research in Deleuze have emphasised the esoteric and even occult aspects of Deleuze's thought.[10] Another aspect of the same problem concerns the relative continuity or rupture between Deleuze's earlier solo writings and the later collaborations with Guattari. In general, the latter work proceeds on a more materialist and historical terrain. At the same time – largely due to Guattari – diagrammatic expression and explicit references to Peirce become prevalent in the later writings. Despite the validity of Bryant's point, the old problem of Kantian schematism is not so easily sidestepped. If concepts do not stand in need of some mediating 'form' in order to synthesise with sensible experience, in Deleuze this problematic itself is nonetheless converted into a kind of imperative and the task of contemporary philosophy becomes one of transforming the Kantian schematism into a Nietzschean creative 'power of the false'.

Like Spinoza and Peirce, Deleuze rejects the recourse to mystery in philosophical thinking. For Deleuze such rejection is at heart a Nietzschean gesture of creative thought's essential impiety and is thus grounded in a more fundamental active affirmation. Rather than a negation of mysterious and unknowable transcendence, the gesture here is really one of positively 'casting' immanence. Its negative aspect, its rejection of transcendence, is no more than a secondary and derivative effect of this aleatory cast. Nonetheless, in a Peircean more than a Spinozist spirit Deleuze's thought remains highly sensitive to the unremitting surprise of experience and nature's chaotic turbulence with respect to which ordinary experience and conventional rationality remain always fragile and hypothetical. What in Peirce unfailingly recurs as fallibility, defeasibility and theoretical adjustment on the fly becomes in Deleuze a sustained indifference to common-sense understanding, theoretical clichés and the ordinary representational image of thought.

Barber has shown how philosophy crucially for Deleuze 'is learning to think with a certain blindness'.[11] It is important to hear the word 'with' in this description in its active and not merely conjunctive sense. As Barber clarifies:

> Blindness is no longer that which one experiences as a result of not seeing the light, or as a result of coming back into the world having already seen the light. Blindness, in other words, is no longer the privation of an already existing light. It is rather that by which one learns to see, it is its own, nonconceptual sight, a sight that does not take its cues from the given form of conceptuality.

This grounds what Barber develops as the immanent logic of 're-expression', which is 'a way of articulating an immanent demand for something that would not be limited to what is given'.[12] Some such concept is necessary for any philosophy of immanence that would not simply collapse into an inert positivism. As a methodological principle, it responds to a desire for real difference from the given actual similar to that which frequently drives the philosophies of transcendence, but it structures this desire immanently. In Barber's analysis, this aspect of Deleuze is closely related to his often-overlooked prioritisation of suffering and shame as core affects of contemporary philosophy. Deleuze's Nietzschean affirmation of life is profoundly misconceived if it is not understood as a programme responding to the manifest failures in actual life to revolt sufficiently against the intolerable aspects of the present. In the contemporary world, what is called philosophy by and large accepts its own neutralisation by the decrepit and debt-ridden ambient culture of commodified reality. Simply to maintain itself, philosophy must in general actively collude with the forces structuring the cultural dynamics of the present, yet 'philosophy's collusion with the present state of affairs gives rise to shame, and any exodus from this collusion requires that we conceive and display critically this collusion'.[13] Like blindness, then, shame too for Deleuze is a 'shadow' that must become 'a real condition of thought'.[14]

In Chilean novelist Roberto Bolaño's *Distant Star*, the enigmatic poet and artist Carlos Wieder throws a reception to celebrate his latest exhibition of photographs in the wake of the ascendancy of the Pinochet regime. As the guests mingle at the party, one by one they enter the adjacent room where his latest photographs have been hung, and they emerge one by one in shock, horrified, some vomiting, some simply fleeing the event without a word. It turns out the photographs are images of the bodies of victims tortured and killed in secret police interrogations by collaborators with Pinochet's regime. By exhibiting the photographs in this way, Wieder the artist and documentarian is flaunting his own presence and participation in the acts of political torture, and he 'repeats' the brutality by displaying it to his unsuspecting viewers, each of whom becomes in this way a kind of second-order victim. The entire novelistic scene becomes a diagram of photographic representation as medium of sadistic art.

Bolaño is not only examining the potential complicity of art and fascism in this scene; he is equally indicating the reality of simple indifference and bourgeois complacency in proximity to active evil. An important Deleuzian insight is that under contemporary conditions such proximity is a significant and ubiquitous philosophical factor. It charges what philosophers do and how they think, particularly when they think such moral and political concerns are irrelevant to their 'areas of specialisation'. When Deleuze rails against the stupidity of the use of 'obvious' or 'common sense' instances of recognition or discourse as paradigmatic for philosophy, there is more in play than the otherwise wholly valid point that the obviousness of such discourse stands in need of explanation and should not serve as a ground of 'intuition' without pain of begging practically all important philosophical questions. The point is equally political and moral. There is nothing innocent in the choice of a neutral and seemingly innocuous method or example as used to illustrate some philosophical point. Cocktail party chatter conceals monstrosities, and we must always learn to see and speak differently. This is part of why new expressive tools must be developed – immanently – in and for philosophy.

The tendency in Deleuze to associate blindness with desiring difference is strong enough that it has enabled unfortunate readings like that of Hallward, for whom Deleuze's resistance to the actual is raised to the power of a full-throttle rejection of the world.[15] Deleuze thus risks caricature as a kind of Swedenborgian mystic, afraid to face the world's troubling actuality. What risks these caricatured readings is an indisputable fascination with the unrepresentable impulses at the very origins of thought. Deleuze's is undoubtedly a philosophy of the unthought, of the 'dark precursor' and the violence that 'forces us to think'. But contra Hallward this unthought is not reified or theologised in Deleuze. It is precisely *thought*, soberly, in its very essence as constitutively unthought. If some variant of a form/content, tool/object or meaning/meant distinction remains inescapable for any philosophical thinking, Deleuze works resolutely against every inclination to take the form-, tool- or meaning- pole of such dualities as fully determinative in any 'structural' or a priori manner, as fixed in advance in such a way that the -content, -object or -meant poles of the dualities would reduce to mere indifferent tokens or mimetic instantiations of the possible. If structurally, so to speak, there is some cloud of unknowing in Deleuze's philosophy, it is no cloud into which the thinker would fire, blindly hoping (and in fact really giving up), the dart of thought; it functions rather as an hypothesis of orientation from which any trajectory of thinking becomes susceptible of taking its own constitutive 'blind-spot' of compulsion into account.

The core of Deleuzian method is an experimental conjunction of concept and practice under the hypothesis of immanence as unilateral difference. Under conditions of dyadic representation like those commonly given in and by language, the thought of unilateral difference can only appear as a paradoxical Zen-like *koan* split between contemplative stillness and spontaneous impulse. Or alternately, it finds itself mapped back onto established if not hackneyed philosophical coordinates: limit and approximation, the macro-distinction of dual 'planes', conceptual cataloguing. But under conditions of diagrammatic practice, the paradoxical character of this thought evaporates and its rigour and coherence become veritable operators on real experience, that is, they become manifest as powers or vehicles, vectors of transformation rather than positions or theses.

SPINOZA'S TRIADIC DIFFERENCE

As is well known, in *Difference and Repetition* Deleuze distinguishes between two modes of thinking that tend to condition philosophy, the one ordered through representation and the other structured through difference. These contrasting 'images of thought' are distinguished by Deleuze according to their respective orientations towards *generality* on the one hand and *repetition* on the other. Each of these orientations implies its own form of philosophical practice:

> [A] *Generality* presents two major orders: the qualitative order of resemblances and the quantitative order of equivalences. Cycles and equalities are their respective symbols. But in any case, generality expresses a point of view according to which one term may be exchanged or substituted for another. *The exchange or substitution of particulars defines our conduct in relation to generality.*

[B] *Repetition as a conduct and as a point of view concerns non-exchangeable and non-substitutable singularities. Reflections, echoes, doubles and souls do not belong to the domain of resemblance or equivalence; and it is no more possible to exchange one's soul than it is to substitute real twins for one another. If exchange is the criterion of generality, theft and gift are those of repetition.* [. . .] *To repeat is to behave in a certain manner, but in relation to something unique or singular which has no equal or equivalent.*[16]

General representations make up the terrain of our most familiar, reflexive image of thought. Such representations tend to be easily expressed. Yet philosophy on Deleuze's understanding is or should be oriented through repetition and singularity. The difficulty for Deleuze thus rests not only in carefully distinguishing the two images of thought, but more importantly in finding ways to express the image of difference and repetition in appropriate ways.

The basic method of philosophy shifts accordingly for Deleuze from reflection or recognition to practical relation. In Deleuze's case the importance of this shift away from representational modes of thought consists in affirming the creative potential of philosophy.[17] Deleuze, contrary to the representational conception of philosophy, conceives of thought not as adequate knowledge but in continuity with the creative movements of nature and life.[18] This entails new understandings of philosophical method and practice. Later in *Difference and Repetition* Deleuze specifies the way such modes of practice originate:

> Something in the world forces us to think. This something is an object not of recognition but of a fundamental *encounter*. What is encountered may be Socrates, a temple or a demon. It may be grasped in a range of affective tones: wonder, love, hatred, suffering. In whichever tone, *its primary characteristic is that it can only be sensed*.[19]

In other words, concrete encounter and relation – sense – becomes the irreducible basis and impetus for philosophical thinking. Philosophy begins in experience, but not just any experience. Rather, the beginnings of philosophical thought are signified in those unique experiences that call us up short by indicating something powerful, problematic and unseen beyond themselves:

> The object of encounter [. . .] is not a quality but a sign. It is not a sensible being but the being *of* the sensible. It is not the given but

that by which the given is given. It is therefore in a certain sense the imperceptible [*insensible*].²⁰

By interpreting the philosophical encounter as a sign, Deleuze resituates the notion of philosophical *problems*.

[T]hat which can only be sensed (the *sentiendum* or the being of the sensible) moves the soul, 'perplexes' it – in other words, forces it to pose a problem: as though the object of encounter, the sign, were the bearer of a problem – as though it were a problem.²¹

In particular, Spinoza's *Ethics* provides, for Deleuze, an encounter and a problem of this kind – a creative potential – within the modern philosophical tradition, because of its commitment to an immanent metaphysics. The study of Spinoza's thought was crucial for Deleuze himself in moving from the critique of representation to creative difference, in inventing new forms of thinking.²² The philosophy of Spinoza is not, for Deleuze, just one influence among many; rather, Spinoza's work – particularly the *Ethics* – provides a thread of continuity across Deleuze's otherwise varied output. What does Deleuze find so compelling about Spinoza's *Ethics* in particular and its complex arrangement of propositions and proofs couched in the mixed idiom of late medieval and Cartesian thought? More importantly, what – according to Deleuze – does Spinoza's *Ethics* say to contemporary thinking?

For Deleuze, the conceptual framework of Spinozist immanence helps to generate modes of thinking that stand in sharp contrast to the subjectivist tradition in modern philosophy originating with Descartes and developing through Kant to Husserlian phenomenology and the philosophical arena of Deleuze's own day. Deleuze transforms Spinoza's thought by situating it in a context quite different from that of early modern philosophy. Deleuze reads Spinoza in light of philosophical problems that were not those of Spinoza's own day but to which Deleuze finds Spinoza's thinking nonetheless capable of response – especially those of language and subjectivity. In the intellectual context that gave rise in France to postmodern and poststructuralist philosophy more generally, a dominant concern was to examine the relationships between language and subjectivity.²³ Deleuze grounds his own differential conceptions of subjectivity and language in Spinoza's thought. What in Spinoza's philosophy does Deleuze find to address these concerns? It is first of all in Spinoza's ontology – and in the triadic structure that Deleuze discerns there at a variety of levels – that he finds a way to conceive of sense outside of representational and egoic models, and secondly it is on the basis of this idea of sense that Deleuze will reinterpret philosophy as *ethos*, a practical and collective model of subjectivity.

Deleuze locates a generative and differential power in Spinoza's metaphysics. Correcting the often distorted notion of Spinoza as a thinker of monist unity, Deleuze reads Spinoza as a key figure in the development of a productive and positive concept of being as difference that develops especially in late-medieval and modern philosophy. As a way of orienting his own concepts of difference and repetition, Deleuze traces a genealogy of difference in univocal conceptions of being stretching from Duns Scotus through Spinoza to Nietzsche.[24] According to this conception as Deleuze understands it, difference no longer serves as a secondary and derivative concept that would presuppose the concept of identity. Instead, difference is conceived as creative and subsists as a positive concept in its own right. An example drawn from biology illustrates the point: the classificatory differences of organic species in Linnaeus are not simply opposed but exploded, reoriented and ultimately explained by the self-differentiating evolution of species in Darwin.

It may seem strange that Spinoza – a profound and committed thinker of unity and the One – would supply Deleuze with grounds for thinking of the philosophical tradition in terms of a differential transformation.[25] How does Spinoza's philosophy and specifically the concept of being expressed in the *Ethics* promote or evoke the kinds of practices Deleuze associates with difference and repetition? Deleuze's most detailed and comprehensive reading of Spinoza is found in *Expressionism in Philosophy: Spinoza* (*Spinoza et le problème de l'expression*).[26] For Deleuze the grounds of Spinoza's contribution to a concept of positive difference are found in the basic threefold structure of substance, attributes and modes in the *Ethics*. Deleuze begins by analysing how Spinoza specifies the unity of substance in terms of the form of distinction by which the attributes are infinitely differentiated. Recall that Spinoza defines *substance* as 'what is in itself and is conceived through itself, that is, that whose concept does not require the concept of another thing, from which it must be formed', and *attribute* as 'what the intellect perceives of a substance, as constituting its essence'.[27] This has led some scholars to view the distinction between substance and attribute as merely a difference relative to the mind which happens to perceive it, that is, in the terminology of Scholastic philosophy, a merely rational distinction, or distinction of reason. For Deleuze, on the contrary, the Spinozist distinction between attributes should be conceived as a real distinction, not merely a rational or formal distinction – again, to speak in terms of medieval Scholastic thought.[28] The attributes would thus be understood as differentiated according to the strongest possible kind of distinction available to Scholasticism. Yet although the differences among attributes are *real*, they are not differentiated in *number* – the real distinctions of attributes do not imply a numerical distinction. In other words, one cannot 'count' the attributes despite the fact that they are really distinct.

Indeed, it is because they are distinct in an absolute and not merely a relative sense that no procedure of comparison or enumeration could place them on a common footing with one another in order to count them.[29] 'Each' attribute (but there is no logical quantifier supple enough to range over them) expresses 'all' of substance (but there is no possible conceptual operation of collecting or totalising this universal domain). There is no competition or parcelling-out among them. There is only the unilateral difference of expression and expressed. The attributes are prior to any common terms, substance itself being not a common term in relation to the attributes but the very element of their expressive differentiation. The substance-attribute relation is so far from being that of two distinct 'levels' like those of genus and species that practically its entire philosophical purpose is exhausted in establishing a form of difference (an immanent yet differential relation) that remains thoroughly indifferent to such hierarchies. In this way the relation between substance and attributes expresses a unique way of framing the classical philosophical theme of the One and the Many. Here, rather than distinguishing and then conceptually reconnecting a transcendent unity to a manifold of worldly diversity, unity is already differentiated/differentiating in itself.

Deleuze views the relation of substance and attributes as Spinoza's unique contribution to the history of the concept of difference. In effect, Spinoza's real but non-numerical distinction between the attributes and their common differentiation in substance signals a new image of difference in the Western philosophical tradition. In this relation Spinozist thought makes of difference no longer a secondary relation between beings that would presuppose their prior, individual identities but instead understands difference as a productivity immanent to the Being of beings: 'Detached from all numerical distinction, real distinction is carried into the absolute, and becomes capable of expressing difference within Being, so bringing about the restructuring of other distinctions.'[30] Spinoza's philosophy conceives substance *as* the infinite differentiation of the attributes, their infinite dispersion and radical incommensurability. Because the attributes are understood to be absolutely different from one another, their difference is not incompatible with their numerical identity as attributes of a single substance. Here, the absolute difference of the attributes is one with their indifference as substance. At the level of the relation between substance and attributes the dyadic opposition of identity and difference is thereby transformed. Thus Deleuze sees the conception of a real, non-numerical distinction as Spinoza's answer to the question, 'What is the character of distinction within infinity? What sort of distinction can one introduce into what is absolute, in the nature of God?'[31]

Yet the form of the distinction between substance and attributes alone remains insufficient. This distinction may be expressive of Being, but it does not express the differences of individuated and relational *beings*. As a mode of philosophical operation, the concept of difference at work here remains formal and is neither incarnate nor situated. The relation of One and Many at the level of the infinite must be expressed with respect to the relation of One and Many at the finite level, and the resultant relation of these finite and infinite relations must itself be conceived as a positive difference. It thus becomes imperative that the finite modes also contribute to the form of difference in Spinoza's ontology; indeed the role of the modes becomes central. In *Difference and Repetition*, appearing the same year as *Expressionism in Philosophy: Spinoza*, Deleuze already specifies a limitation in Spinoza's thinking. 'Spinoza's substance appears independent of the modes, while the modes are dependent on substance, but as though on something other than themselves.'[32] Instead of this, as Deleuze expresses the view: 'Substance must itself be said *of* the modes and only *of* the modes.'[33] In other words, the creative difference expressed in the relation between substance and attributes must be reconceived as the very element of relations and differences among the modes themselves.[34] Negri makes a similar point in *The Savage Anomaly*, and indeed organises his complex reading of the composition-history of the *Ethics* around precisely this issue.

The conceptual relations among substance, attributes and modes together constitute the framework that Deleuze calls *expressive*. In contrast to a conception of ontological difference as a 'twofold' of Being and beings, difference in Spinoza's ontology is structured triadically.³⁵ In the relationships between the three levels Deleuze sees Spinoza's ontology as fundamentally expressive in nature, making this often overlooked term in the *Ethics* the key to conceiving Spinoza's thought as an integrated whole.³⁶ For Deleuze, expression provides a way of thinking in which the one and the many are intimately related through dynamics of explication, involvement and complication (*explicare, involvere, complicatio*).³⁷

Deleuze sees Spinoza's reworking of these concepts as his contribution to a long-standing Neoplatonic tradition for which these terms are interpreted according to a metaphysics of emanation. 'The interplay of these notions, each contained in the other, constitutes expression, and amounts to one of the characteristic figures of Christian and Jewish Neoplatonism as it evolved through the Middle Ages and Renaissance.'³⁸ Yet Deleuze understands Spinoza as transforming the emanative interpretation of expression to the point of making expression thoroughly immanent in nature. In this respect Spinoza represents a transformation of one particular strand of Neoplatonic thought. '[T]he idea of expression explains how Neoplatonism developed to the point where its very nature changed, explains, in particular how emanative causes tended more and more to become immanent ones.'³⁹

The three levels of formal analysis – substance, attribute and mode – set up a triadic structure through which each third term differentiates the other two.

> We everywhere confront the necessity of distinguishing three terms: substance which expresses itself, the attribute which expresses, and the [modal] essence which is expressed. It is through attributes that essence is distinguished from substance, but through essence that substance is itself distinguished from attributes: a triad each of whose terms serves as a middle term relating the two others, in three syllogisms.⁴⁰

By conceiving of the relations between substance, attributes and modes as syllogistic, Deleuze emphasises their relational character. By interpreting the syllogistic relations themselves as mutually enfolded – 'a triad each of whose terms serves as a middle term relating the two others' – Deleuze opens up Spinoza's thought from within. What Deleuze suggests in this passage is that an expressive ontology takes the form of mutually mediating syllogisms rather than oppositional differences. The basic terms of Spinoza's analysis – substance, attributes and modes – are conceived as pure relations, not independent terms. This in turn entails a process of thought that develops through elaboration rather than negation and exclusion. But where does one begin? How does philosophy engage and express these relations concretely?

Deleuze's reading analyses similar relational triads functioning at several levels in the *Ethics*. In addition to the basic framework of substance, attributes and modes, Deleuze identifies a set of three triadic structures at the level of substance itself and a general triad at the level of the causal genesis of the modes as a whole. He also notes a pair of triadic structures that characterise particular modes in their processes of individuation. These various triadic structures are schematised in the table below.[41]

> Substantial triads:
>   attribute – essence – substance
>   perfect – infinite – absolute
>   essence as power – that of which it is the essence – capacity to be affected
>
> Modal triad:
>   attribute – mode – modification
>
> Individual modal triads:
>   essence – characteristic relation – extensive parts
>   essence – capacity to be affected – affections themselves

While it is not necessary for our purposes here to outline all the various relations among these triads as Deleuze conceives them, it is important for us to consider how Deleuze understands what he himself registers as the 'constant triadic character' of his Spinoza interpretation and how he distinguishes it from the 'dyads' comprising the concepts of cause and idea in representational thinking.

Deleuze contrasts the triadic form of expression with dyadic models of cause and effect on the one hand and the dyadic structure of representational ideas on the other. For the general and representational modes of thought Deleuze means to transform from within philosophy, causes are usually understood to correspond to effects and ideas to objects according to dyadic relations. The importance of the concept of expression as the organising principle of Spinoza's thought is then located by Deleuze in the way the nature of expressive triads modifies such dyads and develops or explicates them in new ways. Deleuze summarises:

> This constant triadic character means that the concept of expression cannot be referred either to causality within Being, or to representation in ideas, but goes beyond both, which are seen to be particular cases of expression. For with the dyad of cause and effect, or that of idea and object, there is always associated a third term that transposes one dyad into the other.[42]

How, in Deleuze's view, does the triadic form of Spinoza's ontology provide the grounds for a creative transformation of dyadic modes of thought?

We might follow Deleuze's notion here in terms of the way it both complicates and transposes the idea of causality. A dyadic notion of causality pairs definite causes with definite effects according to a general model: the Earth's gravity causes the stone to fall; marriage (with luck) causes happiness. Such examples in their specificity may lead us to notice complicating and qualifying factors that would call such a general model of causality into question. The structure of causality is not so simple, we reason, and so we examine a wider context and look for singular aspects involved in the case at hand: Why is gravity everywhere? How did marriage become a state institution? This movement into questioning and elaboration would constitute one form of the passage from dyadic thinking to triadic expression. Similar passages from the general to the singular might be elaborated in Deleuze's view through the various practices of thought entailed by Spinoza's philosophy in virtue of its triadic form.[43]

The kinds of transformations such thinking makes possible and enacts in specific contexts, Deleuze collects under the term *sense*. The role of the modes ('what is expressed' in the basic triad of expression) is here essential:

> In short, what is expressed everywhere intervenes as a third term that transforms dualities. Beyond real causality, beyond ideal representation, what is expressed is discovered as a third term that makes distinctions infinitely more real and identity infinitely better thought. What is expressed is *sense*: deeper than the relation of causality, deeper than the relation of representation.[44]

Transposition is transformation. Spinozist expression is understood by Deleuze as a way of thinking through singular modes that transforms general, dyadic ideas of causality and representation by participating in processes that are ideal and material at once, processes that express or enact sense in some determinate context. There is nothing especially mysterious in this – it could be as simple as complaining to the grocer that tomatoes are too expensive this week. Such an act produces sense, more exactly a host of senses – the grocer's potential indignation, for example – which cannot be described simply as physical effects or as general ideas. The strength of Spinoza's triadic ontology, in Deleuze's view, should be understood in terms of how through the formal arrangement of its concepts this newly-conceived region of sense becomes disclosed as operative and thinkable within philosophy itself.

By developing the concept of sense as the differentiating power of the modes, creative transformation is brought into the field of finite practice, particularly the practices of philosophy. Such transformation can only happen *somewhere*, in a determinate context. Deleuze understands Spinoza's *Ethics* as a unique site of interpretation for realising such a concept of difference in the context of philosophy's modern and contemporary history.[45] Within the modern philosophical tradition, Spinoza's thought has a unique place because of the specific concepts it develops and the form in which their relations are established, both of which reorient how the world is perceived and how life is experienced. It is this that Deleuze finds compelling in Spinoza's philosophy. Not only does Spinoza develop in his theoretical apparatus a triadic structure, but through it he enacts an event of sense within the tradition of philosophy itself, both the philosophy of Spinoza's own day and potentially the philosophical context to which Deleuze himself speaks – ours.[46]

Language, Sense and Singularity

Deleuze's *The Logic of Sense* was published in 1969, the year following the joint 1968 appearance of *Expressionism in Philosophy: Spinoza* and *Difference and Repetition*. The term *sense* concludes *Expressionism in Philosophy: Spinoza* and becomes the central focus of *The Logic of Sense*. It is as though with the concept of sense Deleuze finds an implicit element of Spinozist thinking that remains unthematised and indeterminate, and in *The Logic of Sense* Deleuze sets himself the task of clarifying and explicating that concept. In this way the category of sense as it appears especially in *The Logic of Sense* may be understood to mark Deleuze's own creative response to Spinoza and the issues outlined above.

It is *sense* as a third term that breaks open and complicates the relations between cause and effect on the one hand and representational idea and represented thing on the other. The difference introduced into these relations by sense guarantees that Deleuze's philosophical project expresses the desire to preserve and condition the possibility of creation within thought. Sense is related to language but is not identified with it. It is – to return to Merleau-Ponty – the 'variation' introduced, immanently, into 'a field of existence already instituted'. Sense is the two-sided event that makes a semiotic relation of language and bodies possible.

We have seen how the place of language in Spinoza's *Ethics* becomes problematic for both theory and practice. Deleuze's concept of sense resituates the terms that may be presupposed in our ideas about language by linking linguistic meanings to physical events. While not reducible to language, sense for Deleuze has a unique relation to the propositions of language.[47] Deleuze distinguishes sense from three 'distinct relations within the proposition': *denotation* concerning the relation of propositions to individuated states of affairs; *manifestation* relating a proposition to someone who speaks and thereby reveals him or herself as speaker; and *signification* as a matter of the relation between propositions and logical concepts, the implications and deductions that a given proposition makes possible.[48] As Deleuze succinctly puts it, 'The one who begins to speak is the one who manifests; what one talks about is the denotatum; what one says are the significations.'[49] Take the statement or phrase *Pass the salt* – even as an imperative or request (not strictly a proposition), these words still denote the table setting with reference to which they are said, manifest a particular subject (salt-desiring and polite) present at the table, and signify an abstract and potentially translatable meaning: 'I ask you for the salt.'

In contrast to these three dimensions of language, Deleuze understands sense as uniquely 'evanescent', conceivable only from within the specific practices or acts that constitute it.[50] Sense is thus not meaning in terms of a represented content but rather the actual transformative event of meaning in some context. The 'sense' of *pass the salt* is not its denotation, manifestation or signification, but rather the enacted scene itself, the event which *pass the salt* constitutes both as a complex relation in itself and as a shift in relations among the collective components of the given scene: the dispositions of the diners, the flavourless broccoli, the salt shaker.

On Deleuze's understanding, sense is in this way not merely linguistic, but is also physical or quasi-physical. More exactly, sense involves a transformative relation between linguistic and physical modalities of being; it designates a region of pure flux or becoming implicated equally in language and bodies, or rather co-implicating these latter 'regions' themselves. Deleuze conceives of sense as the middle-ground in and through which ideal meanings and bodily events transpose one another.[51] We see the dynamics of sense exhibited clearly, for example, in the significations of ritual, where the transformations in what occurs are not reducible to subjective or egoic intentionality and where the transformations of meaning are communal, as in a theatre.[52] The stage actor *becomes* Othello or Iago or Desdemona in and for a collectively organised context: audience, stage, costumes, generic expectations. In such events of becoming, bodies act as interactive complexes of signs, not as isolated individuals. Such a transformation necessarily takes place in a collective and relational context, although it is not a matter of subjective intentions.

For Deleuze philosophical language and practice in particular must be understood in terms of their sense, that is, on the basis of the transformations they enact and make possible. Such transformations are always relative to the embodied situation and immediate context of actual expressive events. Instead of general meanings in philosophy, then, we have singular events. Indeed, Deleuze develops a unique concept of interactive *singularities* as the basis of a 'hypothesis for the determination of this domain [of sense] and its genetic power'.[53] By singularities Deleuze means the event-character of sense, the actual happening of sense as the point at which ideality and materiality enter into relations of mutual transformation. Such singularities for Deleuze exhibit both linguistic and mathematical aspects. Singularities are thus expressed in language, but they may apply equally to the dynamic and turbulent processes of nature. In a way that draws the thematic of sense into coordination with both Spinozist immanence and contemporary mathematical physics, the non-Euclidean geometries of Gauss and Riemann are understood to allow for the rigorous construction thereby of 'an organization belonging to the many as such, which has no need whatsoever of unity in order to form a system'.[54] Such organisation is intrinsically, that is immanently, relational. Singularities serve as the non-individuated constituents of these organised yet non-unified systems, or multiplicities. The principles of such organisation are the 'recurrent topological features' – the singularities – that draw multiple possible states of a given system into regular or recurrent patterns.[55]

The subtle relation between the verbal and the mathematical conceptions of singularity points to a power operative in thought that is irreducible to subjectivity understood as individual and personal. For Deleuze singularities *are* multiplicities. Deleuze therefore argues that one of the primary failings of representational thought has been that it could never adequately distinguish between individuality and singularity: 'For representation, every individuality must be personal (I) and every singularity individual (Self).'[56] In contrast, Deleuze's non-representational notion of singularity emphasises its 'pre-individual' and 'impersonal' character.[57] Deleuze's notion of singularity thus provides a way to conceive of semiotic or meaningful transformations without having to ground those processes in a subjective, egoic individual. This then has important implications for what philosophy means and how it is done.

What justifies the application of an essentially mathematical idiom (singularity) to the human sphere? Deleuze writes:

> The relation between mathematics and man may thus be conceived in a new way: the question is not that of quantifying or measuring human properties, but rather, on the one hand, that of problematizing human events, and, on the other, that of developing as various human events the conditions of a problem.[58]

Thus Deleuze's examination and reduction of the category of sense from the perspective of pre-personal and pre-individual singularities does not constitute a disavowal of the human sphere. Rather, human, personal and individual dimensions are understood as constituted problematically and quasi-reciprocally through this pre-personal level. Just as human characteristics are mathematised, then, the abstract level of mathematics is itself reinterpreted on the basis of sense. What Deleuze shows is that the problematic and eventful character of singularities as the constituent factors in sense produce within language a variety of effects that are not themselves linguistic, and this expressivity rebounds immanently upon social, political, physical and other concomitant structures. Sense is the membrane through which the ideal and material are exchanged – in nature, in the meanings of human practice, in philosophy.

In this way, the operators and transpositions of sense are eminently diagrammatic, and even mathematically so. In this regard, Deleuze affirms Lewis Carroll's mathematical narratives in *The Dynamics of a Particle* and *Sylvie and Bruno* in which mathematical entities are described in terms of desires and characteristics usually reserved for human characters. In Carroll's work, Deleuze rejects the notion that such a strategy represents 'a simple allegory or a manner of anthropomorphizing mathematics'. Instead, Deleuze asserts that 'one must remember rather that psychological and moral characters are also made of pre-personal singularities, and that their feelings or their pathos are constituted in the vicinity of these singularities: sensitive crisis points, turning points, boiling points, knots, and foyers [. . .]'.[59] We may recall here Spinoza's explicit methodological injunction in investigating human affects such as joy, love, hate, jealousy and compassion to 'consider human actions and appetites just as if it were a question of lines, planes, and bodies'.[60] In the philosophical line from Spinoza to Deleuze, thinking becomes increasingly structural, increasingly diagrammatic.

Diagrammatic subjectivity

When philosophy engages the category of sense in an immanent manner, the philosophical problem of subjectivity is transformed. For Deleuze, philosophy is always inseparable from the problems it addresses. Yet rather than aiming at the decisive coordination of open problems with exhaustive solutions that would come to annihilate them, philosophy should work to understand and repeat the problems themselves and to formulate what exactly is problematic in the distinctive problems it faces so that it can make those problems generative. In a Deleuzian conception philosophical problems always have two sides, one face turned towards the world and its rush of experiential variety, the other directed to the construction of concepts. Against the horizon of the world, events and objects appear and give rise to thought, and it is primarily what is problematic in some practical sense that serves as the index of philosophy's origin, its worldly side. Yet philosophy does not have to do with just any problems, but particularly those that involve a moment of abstraction and a tendency towards conceptualisation. In this way the second face of the problem is turned not to the world but to an element of abstraction that takes the problem as such into view and looks to formulate it in some way.

In the case of subjectivity, Deleuze reintroduces the practical focus and triadic form of Spinoza's thinking in a philosophical context conditioned by the legacies of Descartes, Kant and Husserl. Deleuze himself took this legacy to present a new and determinative problem of philosophical method. For models of philosophy that begin with the subject, reflexive methods predominate. In place of a subjective or reflexive method, Deleuze, however, begins with events, habits and responses that are prior to consciousness and constituted through practical and sensible relations. On this basis Deleuze finds resources to reinterpret the problem of subjectivity in an abstract diagrammatic fashion by supplementing Spinoza's ontology with a Leibnizian turn to convergent and divergent relations between series of singularities, individuals and worlds.

Deleuze turns the subjective tradition of philosophy on its head, so to speak. He maintains the term *transcendental* but radically transforms its sense. In Deleuze's conception, the transcendental is understood as populated by impersonal events without any necessary correlation to the syntheses of egoic experience. Rather than the unifying, synthetic power of a transcendental ego, on Deleuze's terms the transcendental domain becomes structured by the Leibnizian convergences and divergences of series of predicate-events. Where the Kantian transcendental ego implies a set of ontological categories to which all possible objects of knowledge and experience must conform, Deleuze's transcendental field of predicate-events organises convergent and divergent diagrams of becoming.

Deleuze introduces this revised conception of the transcendental by contrasting it not only with Kantian subjectivity but also with the transcendental ego of Husserl's phenomenology. Where Husserl, Deleuze claims, remains bound to an equation of the transcendental sphere with the implicitly representational categories of 'good sense' and 'common sense', Deleuze intends to explore the possibility of a transcendental field of *singularities* that would relate ideas and bodies through events of sense. In contrast to the egoic-based tradition of philosophy stretching from Descartes to Husserl and the phenomenological tradition, Deleuze maintains that the 'bestowal of sense', that is, the creative practice of thought, requires 'an impersonal transcendental field, not having the form of a synthetic personal consciousness or a subjective identity – with the subject, on the contrary, being always constituted'.[61]

In Deleuze's view, because the Husserlian transcendental field resembles in its contours the structures of identity and difference proper to the empirical ego and the general category of the person, it cannot genuinely *produce* the supposedly immanent effects and structures of consciousness to which it bears witness. In a dense but carefully worded passage, Deleuze puts the issue as follows:

> The Husserlian bestowal of sense assumes indeed the adequate appearance of a homogeneous and regressive series degree by degree; it then assumes the appearance of an organization of heterogeneous series, that of noesis and that of noema, traversed by a two-sided instance (*Urdoxa* and object in general). But this is only the rational or rationalized caricature of the true genesis, of the bestowal of sense which must determine this genesis by realizing itself within the series, and of the double nonsense which must preside over this bestowal of sense, acting as its quasi-cause.[62]

In other words, Husserlian philosophical consciousness stands *outside* the actual genetic events of sense as an effect that takes itself to be a transcendental condition, rather than *enacting* sense as an immanent difference or 'quasi-cause'. As Deleuze puts it, 'The foundation can never resemble what it founds.'[63] Husserl, so far as Deleuze is concerned, carries empirically determined characteristics of the self into his description of the transcendental sphere. In contrast, Deleuze means 'to determine an impersonal and pre-individual transcendental field, which does not resemble the corresponding empirical fields, and which nevertheless is not confused with an undifferentiated depth'. Because it would transcend all relations of resemblance to the empirical subject, '[t]his field can not be determined as that of a consciousness'.[64] Instead, this new transcendental field would require a distribution of singularities capable of *tracing* the emergence of subjectivity as a structure not already presupposed in the transcendental itself.[65] In other words, the empirical forms of subjectivity as they appear in history and society must be accounted for in their contingent emergence through expressive causation, rather than on the basis of *a priori* structures or conditions that would resemble them. The histories of human forms of knowing are thus naturalised. Deleuze himself is of course immersed in these histories and saturated by them; his own claim thus appears as an immanent problem *for* these histories. In the case of his precursor Spinoza, a similarly problematic event appears as the assertion within early modern European culture of an idea of nature with human being no longer at its centre. The reality of consciousness and human meaning are not denied by this assertion, but they no longer ground it. Indeed, the very structure of grounding becomes undone and instead the infinite relations among natural events are 'lifted' to an immanent surface. In Deleuze's view only such an unconscious and self-problematising surface taken together with the dynamic singularities that traverse it is capable of constituting a genuine transcendentality. Or as Deleuze has it, 'Only when the world, teeming with anonymous and nomadic, impersonal and pre-individual singularities, opens up, do we tread at last on the field of the transcendental.'[66]

How does Deleuze understand the transcendental if not in the manner of phenomenological consciousness? Rather than in relation to an egoic subject or transcendental subjectivity, Deleuze traces sense to a process that takes place as the individuation of worlds. Here the colligation of series of predicates replaces the predication of subjects as the basic form or grammar of synthesis. Synthesis no longer requires the guarantee of the unity of consciousness. Instead, predicates, or events, link up with one another in series to constitute worlds. Individual entities are understood as the result and consequence of compossible predications, rather than the reverse.

Deleuze conceives this in two steps, distinguishing two levels of 'static genesis' in his account of subjectivity as emergent and constituted within an impersonal field of sense. The first level of actualisation of static genesis concerns the production of individual beings and worlds from the convergence of sets of singularities. The second level of actualisation concerns the emergence of subjectivity, although in a form that is radically heterogeneous to the Cartesian ego as well as to Kantian and Husserlian modes of transcendental subjectivity. At the first level we cannot yet describe any form of consciousness or ego, only individuals (in the sense of individuated beings) and the worlds they inhabit. Here Deleuze reinterprets the Spinozist account of individuation in terms borrowed from Leibniz.[67] As relational series of singular events circulate and gather in the pre-individual transcendental field, individuals are formed; in intra-relations of the convergences of individuals, worlds then arise as forms of logically possible constellations of relatives. A world in this sense is thus no more than the function of convergent series within discrete monadic individuals that are able to coexist (Leibnizian compossibility). 'This convergence defines "compossibility" as the rule of a world synthesis.'[68]

To provide an image of Deleuze's meaning here, we might construct a narrative from which all proper names and grammatical subjects are subtracted or replaced by variables, leaving only a series of distinct predicates. The narrative itself would then be reconfigured diagrammatically as a complex set of relations through which the detached predicates become colligated with one another. Take, for instance, the story of Dante's journey through Hell, Purgatory and Paradise in the *Divine Comedy*. For Deleuze's Leibnizian view

5.1

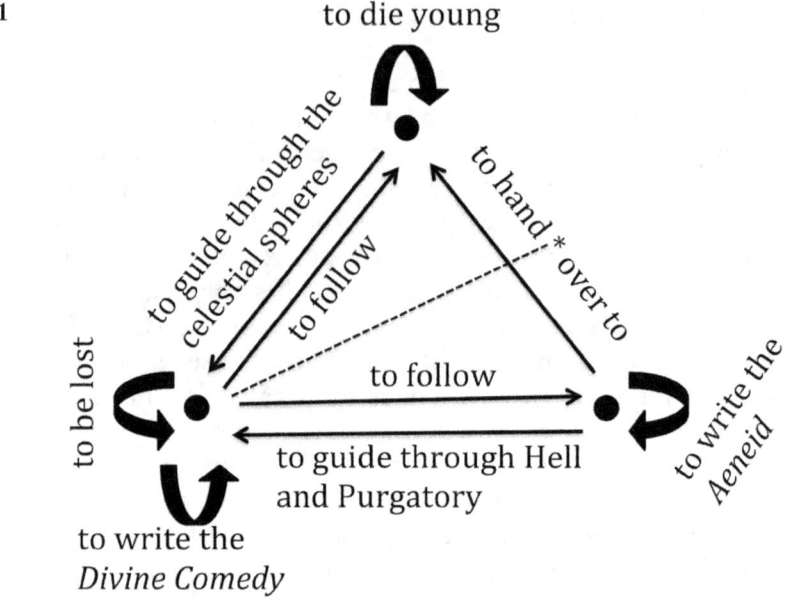

the individual Dante would appear in the narrative not as an egoic subject undergoing certain travels and subjective experiences but as a convergence or bundling of predicates themselves, a series best expressed in and through infinitives: to be lost in the woods, to encounter the ghost of the dead poet, to drink the water of Lethe, and so on. Other individuals in the work would be understood as being constituted similarly through different bundles of separate and interlocking predicates – Virgil, for example, expressed through the series: to write the *Aeneid*, to guide, to explain the levels of Hell and Purgatory, to hand one's charge over to Beatrice. The convergences of these various individual series themselves into further relations and common settings constitutes in turn the individuated *world* which those individuals share – in this case, the allegorical world imagined by Dante the poet.

The most important aspect of this model for Deleuze is that it conceives of logical relation first of all on the basis of convergence and divergence, or compossibility and incompossibility rather than through logical exclusion or negation. Different worlds diverge from one another not because of antagonistic relations of abstract opposition or negation, but rather through the intrinsic qualities of the events, or predicates, themselves. The actualisation of one series does not negate or exclude, but rather *diverges* from the simultaneous actualisation of other possible worlds. Thus, rather than presupposing a total field of pregiven logical possibilities, the individuation of worlds and the individuals inhabiting them constitute real processes or genetic events, not merely abstract possibilities.[69]

What becomes then of subjectivity on such a model? At the first level of actualisation, individuals are constituted not as subjects of experience but as bundles of predicates or events. Just as in Spinoza's account of individuation as examined in Chapter 1 in which the minds, or souls, of bricks, flowers, men and women are conceived as parts of a continuum, not discrete levels, so here too the individuation of persons is not different in principle from the individuation of things (consider the predicate-series constituting the river Lethe in the *Purgatorio*: to flow, to be drunk, to cause to forget).

It is the second level of actualisation that pertains to the genesis of the ego's transcendence from within this space of individuated worlds, the emergence of conscious and subjective experience. At this level Deleuze's concerns initially intersect with those of phenomenology in terms of the question of otherness. In worlds constituted at an initial level by series of convergence, where is the Other? Deleuze writes: '[w]e face again the Husserlian problem of the Fifth Cartesian Meditation: what is it in the Ego that transcends the monad, its appurtenances and predicates?'[70] Yet for Deleuze, '[t]he solution here cannot be the phenomenological one, since the Ego is no less constituted than the individual monad'.[71] In other words, once a pre-individual and non-subjective transcendental field has been established, it becomes impossible to ground otherness in the ego because the ego must itself be grounded in the otherness of nomadic difference.

Deleuze's own strategy is to interpret subjectivity not as synthetic unification and objective constitution on the basis of egoic transcendence but as a singular event of communication across divergent worlds: 'the Ego as a knowing subject appears when something is *identified* inside worlds which are nevertheless incompossible, and across series which are nevertheless divergent'.[72] This point of contact or identification serves as the 'dark precursor' of subjective processes, the spark of what may and under further determining conditions must become manifest as egoic consciousness.[73] As Deleuze writes, 'Only when something is identified between divergent series or between incompossible worlds, an object = x appears transcending individuated worlds [. . .].'[74] Subjectivity is understood here on the basis of divergence and identification, not multiplicity and unity. The 'ego' is here no longer a substantial unity, but an actual relation between divergent worlds. What does this mean, and what kind of relation is it?

To take the step through which an identification is made *across divergent series* requires that we bring about 'an operation according to which two things or two determinations are affirmed *through* their difference, that is to say, that they are the objects of simultaneous affirmation only insofar as their difference is itself affirmed and is itself affirmative'.[75] The identification of incompossibles cannot be a mere identity of contraries (the construction of a contradiction) but must develop and elaborate a real difference. Simultaneous contraries have to manifest the structure of their own difference from within a creative process. Unity becomes a function of difference, rather than the reverse, 'for divergence is no longer a principle of exclusion, and disjunction no longer a means of separation. *Incompossibility is now a means of communication*'.[76]

Communication in this sense does not refer to an exchange of information. The communication across incompossible worlds should be understood rather as the formation of a habit or set of habits oriented to variable possible outcomes. These are habits whose intrinsic modality is that of the possible, or rather the *variable*.[77] It is important to follow the order of Deleuze's explanation here. He does not first presume the thing that is to be explained – in this case, subjectivity or the ego – and then find conditions that would accommodate it. Instead, he creates a hypothetical conceptual narrative of the genesis of difference or divergence and then shows how this narrative produces something that allows us to understand subjectivity as the effect of a logical-metaphysical field of operations: transcendental sense. By introducing impersonal sense and affirmative difference into the heart of subjectivity, Deleuze does not render personality meaningless, but instead shows how its continuity is grounded not in an operation of synthetic unification but rather in one of differentiation and fracture. As Deleuze puts it,

> Instead of a certain number of predicates being excluded from a thing in virtue of the identity of its concept, each 'thing' opens itself up to the infinity of predicates through which it passes, as it loses its center, that is, its identity as concept or as self. The communication of events replaces the exclusion of predicates.[78]

Continuity of the discontinuous event: subjectivity in this sense takes the form of a structural or diagrammatic problem. To the Cartesian *problem of method* that tends to dominate the subjectivist line of philosophy, Deleuze counters with a Spinozist and Leibnizian *method of problems*. This methodology does not presume a common strategy that would solve various philosophical problems in the same way, but rather locates an impetus for diverse experimental practices within philosophical problems themselves. Philosophy needs its own field of diagrammatic operations in order to deploy its constitutive mode of subjectivity.

A problem in Deleuze's sense – like his notion of singularity – is both meaningful and mathematical. Using a mathematical example Deleuze compares the issue at stake with the algebraic-geometrical construction of conic sections (the various sets of points of intersection composed as a plane cuts a cone through a range of angles) as discussed by Leibniz in his mathematical writings. Here Deleuze's model of expressive sense is interpreted in terms of the genetic relation of a problem to its solutions.

> A problem, [Leibniz] said, has conditions which necessarily include 'ambiguous signs', or aleatory points, that is, diverse distributions of singularities to which instances of different solutions correspond. Thus, for example, the equation of conic sections expresses one and the same Event that its ambiguous sign subdivides into diverse events – circle, ellipse, hyperbola, parabola, straight line. These diverse events form so many instances corresponding to the problem and determining the genesis of the solutions.[79]

The '"ambiguous signs", or aleatory points' which relate a problem to the forms of its specific solutions are essentially logical, algebraic or mathematical *variables*. They are diagrammatic dots, lines and planes *at the appropriate level of abstraction*. These discrete Leibnizian regions of indetermination are not mere placeholders for a set of possible values, but serve rather as *ways* or *modalities* through which a problem's multiple conditions can become instantiated in specific solutions. A variable in this sense is more like a virtual operation or affect than a logical symbol.[80] A variable is a real *problem*. The solutions themselves are not specificities corresponding to the problem's generality, but rather concrete forms of the problem in so far as the internal divergences of its conditions express themselves in various ways. Deleuze goes on to relate this example directly to the question of how incompossibilities become identified:

> We must therefore understand that incompossible worlds, despite their incompossibility, have something in common – something objectively in common – which represents the ambiguous sign of

the genetic element in relation to which several worlds appear as instances of solution for one and the same problem (every throw, the result of a single cast).[81]

Subjectivity on this model is neither an empirical determination of individuals nor a fixed, transcendental structure. It has rather the structure of an 'ambiguous sign', a singular problem of the genetic event that is, intrinsically, both relational and differential. In contrast to the philosophies of transcendental subjectivity, the ego and its relations are no longer *the* site or problem of philosophy, but only one among others, always actualised in relation to other simultaneous and diverse problems. The relations among problems themselves constitute signs in Peirce's sense: icons, indices and symbols of various orders, with shades of iconicity providing perhaps the most experimental and generative type. Deleuze's frequent and emphatic rejections of the logics of resemblance and analogy should not mislead us here. What Deleuze rejects is the notion of analogy that would depend on an external recognition of commonality. The diverse solutions to a common problem express that problem precisely by diverging from one another only at the level of what can be externally noted. Their iconic commonality is thus less an actual similarity than a virtual vicinity within an otherwise aleatoric distribution.

Subjectivity is therefore a throw of the dice, which as Ramey has shown functions in Deleuze as both a game of chance and a divinatory practice.[82] What Deleuze calls chance in *Difference and Repetition* (arguably the most obscure element of his systematic ontology) must be understood as the necessary embedding of any actual system of local relations in an indefinite multitude of extensive (lateral) and intensive (higher-order) systems, such that the slightest perturbation of the local system has untold immediate ramifications across the entire coordinated (or at least connected) space. Unlike Spinoza or Maimon, this abstract space of relations need not form an overall synthetic unity, but for any given system it nonetheless extends into infinite ever-increasingly extensive and abstractive domains. On the one hand, this interpretation (or modelisation) of Deleuzian chance clarifies the sense in which chance and necessity are one for Deleuze in his superposition of Nietzschean and Stoic ontology as well as Nietzschean and Stoic ethics. On the other hand, Deleuze's own particular way of reading the dice throw of chance in terms of an ambient Nietzschean logic of Eternal Return now takes on a rigorous sense. The space of abstract relationality is uniquely sensitive to infinitesimal changes resulting in non-local, systemic fluctuations. Experimentation of *any* kind on and within some actual state of affairs cannot help but relaunch an infinite and tangled hierarchy of abstract categories. At the upper reaches of the hierarchy, everything is always in flux. Where Spinoza suggests an approximation to pure stasis as one approaches the Whole ('the whole of nature is one individual, whose parts, that is, all bodies, vary in infinite ways, without any change of the whole individual'), Deleuze affirms a pure becoming or difference, in this respect much like the 'mad God' of Schelling's *Ages of the World* although without the notion of a *unique* discontinuity or original cut in being as characteristic of the late Schelling.

An ethics of signs

What makes itself felt in the discourse of a philosophy that would move beyond Husserl in the direction of an impersonal and pre-human transcendentality can only be 'a free and unbound energy' that cuts across specific and generic differences to express creative activity equally at all levels of the organisation of being. In other words, it is the idea of nature that Deleuze finds first and foremost in Spinoza, an idea in which human being is understood as a part of nature, not primarily in its essential difference from nature:

> As for the subject of this new discourse (except that there is no longer any subject), it is not man or God, and even less man in the place of God. The subject is this free, anonymous, and nomadic singularity which traverses men as well as plants and animals independently of the matter of their individuation and the forms of their personality.[83]

In other words, this conception of philosophy is expressed via a 'discourse' of semiotic processes independent but not exclusive of egoic subjectivity.[84] In this respect, Deleuze invokes a distinction upheld by the Stoics between necessity and destiny. While physical relations are determined by strictly necessary causal structures, the 'incorporeal effects' to which they give rise are related to each other only through relatively loose relations of 'quasi-causality'. Thus, a particular incorporeal surface effect maintains relations of *necessity* with the physical structures that causally undergird it, but only *destined* or non-necessary quasi-causal relations with the

192 *Diagrammatic Immanence*

incorporeal effects with which it interacts on the exterior surface where events of sense occur. There is a kind of rigid, 'vertical' causal structure (or necessary depth) between the movements of physical bodies and the events to which they correspond, but only a sort of dynamic relational flow along the 'horizontal' relations (or destined superficiality) among incorporeal events themselves.[85] Destiny is therefore a matter of sense and functions primarily through the relatively abstract and 'structural' communication of affects. Deleuze maintains that subjectivity itself is in this way not causal in any necessary sense, but rather 'quasi-causal' and intra-effectual; in other words, it functions as an expressive *sign*, rather than an intelligible object or transcendental category.[86] Signs thus inhabit the space opened by Deleuze's immanent yet 'two-sided' metaphysics, represented schematically in the diagram in Figure 5.2 where the upper and lower planes represent the Virtual (arrow = differentiation) and Actual (arrow = differenciation) respectively, with vectors of actualisation (right) and counter-actualisation (left) on either side.

As a result, from personality as substance we turn within philosophy to communicative practices as signifying *ethos*. To live according to this vision is to experience oneself as a sign, to know the events

5.2
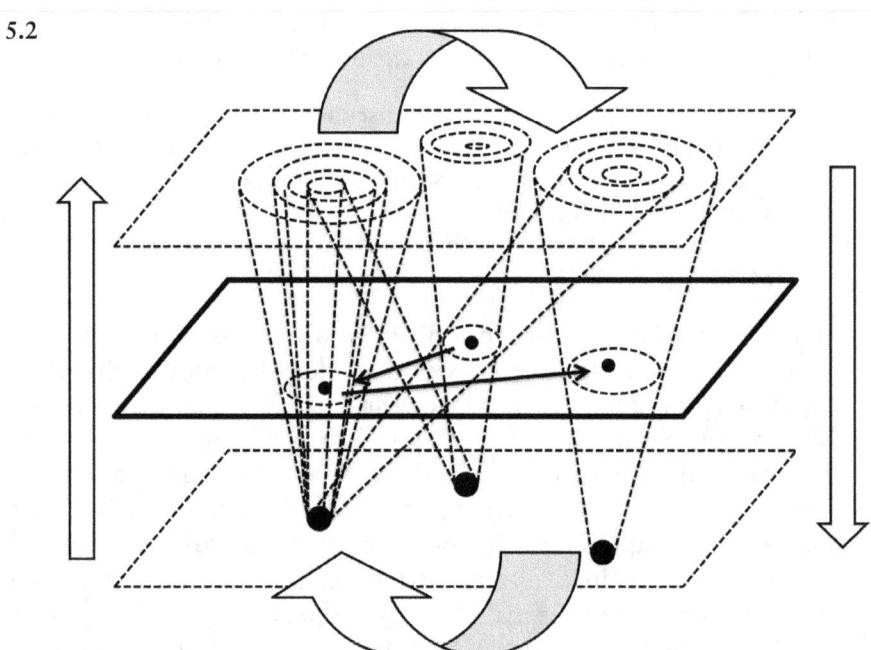

that happen to one as expressive of a sense that passes beyond the individuality and personality of one's own self, to live as a sign bridging incompossible worlds. 'The splendor and the magnificence of the event is sense. The event is not what occurs (an accident), it is rather inside what occurs, the purely expressed. It signals and awaits us.'[87] For Deleuze the predicate of a proposition – '. . . heals' – holds significance (or rather sense) exceeding its possibility and propensity for any colligation to a grammatical subject – she, you, I – or a transitive object – her, you, me. This sense is best demonstrated and expressed in the infinitive form: 'to heal'. To live this way is to act without a script across intersecting stages, signifying always something other than oneself, or even *a* self:

> The role played is never that of a character; it is a theme (the complex theme or sense) constituted by the components of the event, that is, by the communicating singularities effectively liberated from the limits of individuals and persons.[88]

Such an *ethos* is thus no longer attributable to individual subjects but instead only to at least partly anonymous relational complexes such as those that constitute cultural traditions. In this respect Deleuze refers to 'the theater of Leibniz' as against Husserl's 'cumbersome [phenomenological] machinery'.[89] In a theatre, plots are generated through the roles that actors take upon themselves in order to resolve (or simply to explicate) the conflicts such plots give rise to. The 'solutions' that close a play are thus built into the 'problems' that the actors' roles typify, and any plot's resolution is never anything more than one side of the form initiated by the posing of the conflict. Deleuze is quite fond of referring to this 'theatrical' correlation of solutions to the conditions of well-posed problems because it places emphasis on the productive and creative energy of problems considered in themselves. According to this way of thinking, philosophical and practical solutions are not mere answers to pre-given questions, but are rather correlates to the proper construction of some problematic form.[90] Deleuze's strength is to conceive of *ethos* as both above and below the level of the individual or conscious subject. An *ethos* is not predicable of individual subjects but is constituted in the relations between them. These relations are semiotic without necessarily being egoic or conscious. Deleuze's conception of *ethos* thus amplifies its differential and associative character rather than its integral and synthetic function – it is closer to the co-evolution of separate species than to the individuation of a single essence.[91]

The Deleuzian account of transcendental singularities and subjective life places difference – disjunctive synthesis – at the very heart of the individuated subject. Subjectivity is thereby related to creative difference prior to and in lieu of identity, and Spinoza's expressivist ontology becomes transformed into an ethos. In this way Deleuze emphasises the fractures and differences constituting the ego as a life lived in and through affective relations.[92] For Deleuze the otherness of pre-individual singularities 'swarm' as expressive signs in and through egoic subjectivity. The ego is thus already inhabited by otherness through the very event of its constitution.[93]

This is evident, for example, in Deleuze's concept of the 'structure-Other' that appears in both *Difference and Repetition* and Appendix II of *The Logic of Sense*.[94] For Deleuze, the 'structure-Other' serves as the ground of representational thought and reinforces the negative limits of subjectivity. 'Everything happens as though *the Other integrated the individuating factors and pre-individual singularities within the limits of subjects and objects*, which are then offered to representation as perceivers or perceived.'[95] In other words, the Leibnizian multi-level processes of constitution through convergence and divergence of predicate-events prior to and independent of subjectivity are reduced to a dyadic interpretation of the subjective correlation of subject and object. The Other in Deleuze's sense would be the formal structure that effects this reduction. What is the structure-Other? In *Difference and Repetition* Deleuze distinguishes between the I (*Je*) and the Self (*Moi*) as two poles of the 'fundamental psychic correlation' characterising the cogito.[96] The I determines a comprehensive unity for the cogito while the Self represents the reciprocal organisation of its various faculties. The important point for Deleuze is that both of these poles are caught up in the universal structures of representation. Thus, Deleuze contrasts the I-Self correlation with the now-familiar singular and non-representational 'fields of individuation' which interact in a 'demesne which disrupts the matter of the Self as well as the form of the I'.[97] Thus, he distinguishes the process of individuation from the relations between self and other. The structure-Other is then interpreted as a functional component of the 'I-Self system':

> There must none the less [sic] be values of implication in psychic systems in the process of being explicated; in other words, there must be centres of envelopment which testify to the presence of individuating factors. These centres are clearly constituted neither

by the I nor by the Self, but by a completely different structure belonging to the I-Self system. This structure should be designated by the name 'other' [*le nom de « autrui »*].[98]

In a manner that might initially seem similar to that of Levinas, the other (*l'autrui*) is understood to disrupt the reflexive identity of the self.[99] Yet in Deleuze the other is not understood as a concrete other, a singular face, but is rather a general structure, the universal figure of experience as subject to representational categories. For Deleuze the Other – understood as a structure of the 'I-Self system' – both grounds and ultimately guarantees thought as representation.

In his essay on Michel Tournier's novel *Friday* (*Vendredi ou les limbes du Pacifique*), Deleuze develops this notion of the structure-Other not in abstract terms, but through a specific literary context.[100] Tournier's novel is an imaginative reworking of Daniel Defoe's early eighteenth-century novel *Robinson Crusoe*. By retelling Defoe's story of solitary abandonment and encounter on a deserted island with subtle and abrupt shifts in perspective, Tournier brings to light and reinterprets the story's themes of isolation, modernity and otherness from the perspective of a later historical and cultural context. In his explorations of the island and his psychological and physical struggles, Robinson becomes an allegorical figure of European modernity itself. Deleuze reads Tournier's depiction of Robinson's solitude as a kind of experimental hypothesis, a literary thought-experiment. For Deleuze, Tournier's literary investigation of Robinson's experiences under the conditions of an 'island of the absence of Others' thereby provides knowledge of our everyday conditions of experience 'of the presence of Others in our habitual world'.[101] In other words, by imagining and fictionally demonstrating the effects of a world *without* Others we will see in contrast the shape and features of our familiar world *with* Others which are otherwise invisible by virtue of that world's very familiarity.[102] Through foregrounding the familiar against the unfamiliar the familiar thus comes into view in a new way.

In the world devoid of Others, Robinson's solitary experience on his island is reduced, in Deleuze's words, to 'the brutal opposition of the sun and earth, of an unbearable light and an obscure abyss: the "summary law of all or nothing"'. In this world of absolute and unmediated dyads, Robinson confronts a 'harsh and black world, without potentialities or virtualities: the category of the possible has collapsed'.[103] From this we learn how the structure-Other has been functioning all along prior to Robinson's confrontation with solitude: the Other represents the possible. Deleuze's analysis of Tournier means to show that when reduced to or conceived as a general structure, the Other becomes a kind of enforcement of the patterns of representational thought. It is 'the grand leveler'.[104] In fact, Deleuze understands this structure to be always at work in our everyday experience as the phenomenological field of possibilities that makes the world intersubjectively organised and stable.[105]

Deleuze recognises uniquely creative possibilities for thought in those experiences in which the structure-Other is bracketed or disappears, such as Robinson's island. In this world without Others, a new possibility emerges, that of a new form of encounter irreducible to the pre-configured possibilities of representation. Yet this encounter with an otherness more radical than the 'structure-Other' still remains correlated to Robinson's individual isolation. Prepared by his solitude without Others, Robinson discovers the boy Friday who 'alone is able to guide and complete the metamorphosis that Robinson began and to reveal to him its sense and aim'.[106] Encountered outside the frame of the generalised structure-Other, Friday appears under a dual aspect as both less and more than Robinson himself, oscillating between abjection and a kind of transcendence. Robinson thus relates to Friday in two different ways, both of which elide the symmetrical and 'levelling' structure of the Other in Deleuze's sense: 'Sometimes he treats him almost like an object or an animal, sometimes as if Friday were a "beyond" with respect to himself, a "beyond" Friday, his own double or image. Sometimes he treats him as if he were falling short of the Other, sometimes as if he were transcending the Other.'[107] The individual Friday is both more and less than a general structure. He is, in Deleuze's words, 'Not an Other, but something wholly other (*un tout-autre*) than the Other; not a replica, but a Double: one who reveals pure elements and dissolves objects, bodies, and the earth.'[108] This otherness more radical than the structure-Other 'separate[s] desire from its *object*, from its detour through the body, in order to relate it to a pure *cause*: the Elements'.[109] Can – and should – this more radical otherness be brought into the philosophical tradition, and if so, how?

How philosophy learns to become

For Deleuze, Spinozist immanence remains the site of contemporary philosophy's greatest potential. At the individual level, Deleuze writes of the peculiar capacity of Spinoza's work to evoke sudden insights in artists, writers and thinkers with little philosophical training:

> [Spinoza] is a philosopher who commands an extraordinary conceptual apparatus, one that is highly developed, systematic, and scholarly; and yet he is the quintessential object of an immediate, unprepared encounter, such that a nonphilosopher, or even someone without any formal education, can receive a sudden illumination from him, a 'flash.'[110]

Deleuze implies here that Spinoza's philosophy has a unique power. What is it about Spinoza's philosophy that allows it to speak readily to the 'nonphilosopher' in this way? The relation between the 'conceptual apparatus' of Spinoza's system and the illuminative 'flash' of insight that speaks in even a cursory reading of his text serves as the focus of Deleuze's own interpretation.[111] The flash of illumination generated by the *Ethics* corresponds to Peirce's concept of secondness. Yet the secondness of the flash is already the seed of a signification, a thirdness. It already holds the potential for an apprenticeship into the naturally creative aspects of the universe that Deleuze analyses in terms of signifying affects and singularities. To encounter Spinoza's *Ethics* in this way is to experience the direct philosophical sense of a triadic sign.

In particular, Spinoza's combination of geometrical method and thematic emphasis on the affects provides unique communicative possibilities linking philosophy with its neighbouring disciplines, particularly science, art and (though Deleuze barely hints at the possibility) religion. A different model of otherness is developed implicitly here in Deleuze in coordination with his more general conception of problems and the problematic relation of philosophy as a discipline and field of collective practices to *its* others. The concepts of learning and apprenticeship then become key both for understanding Deleuze's own relationship to the philosophical tradition and for charting its potentially Deleuzian transformations. In *The Non-philosophy of Gilles Deleuze*, Gregg Lambert writes:

> For Deleuze, it has never been a question of 'breaking out' of the world that exists, but of creating the right conditions for the expression of other possible worlds to 'break in' in order to introduce new variables into the world that exists, causing the quality of its reality to undergo modification, change and becoming.[112]

Lambert's formulation expresses well the dynamics of a somewhat reconfigured Deleuzian concept of creation. Here it would not be an elemental vision *without* otherness that would provide creative power, but the establishment of new relations that *invite* or *allow* otherness to appear and to take place. To create in this sense would be first and foremost to establish conditions for learning – an apprenticeship.[113] This would be true at the individual level of course, but *a fortiori* at the level of collective practice.

Already when Deleuze reinterprets the Kantian Ideas as transcendental singularities, or sense-events, this implies a reconception of the relationship between learning and knowledge:

> In fact, the Idea is not the element of knowledge but that of an infinite 'learning', which is of a different nature to knowledge. For learning evolves entirely in the comprehension of problems as such, in the apprehension and condensation of singularities and in the composition of ideal events and bodies.[114]

The process of learning thus becomes inseparable from a process of becoming. At the individual level one learns by decomposing oneself along certain axes of organisation or with respect to particular habits of interaction and risking the encounter, the composition with something whose potential relations remain untested and untried:

> Learning to swim or learning a foreign language means composing the singular points of one's own body or one's own language with those of another shape or element, which tears us apart but also propels us into a hitherto unknown and unheard-of world of problems.[115]

Learning is expressed here as a veritable imperative to *become*. Deleuze asks: 'To what are we dedicated if not to those problems which demand the very transformation of our body and our language?'[116] This question becomes especially pertinent at the level of collective tradition and disciplinary practice. If Lambert is right that Deleuze's philosophy is concerned less with 'breaking out' of the world than with exploring ways to allow other possible worlds to 'break in', this would be true first and foremost of the 'world' of philosophy.[117]

In this respect, it is important to note that Deleuze's own work undergoes a major shift subsequent to Deleuze's encounter with Guattari.[118] Especially relevant in the present context is the fact that it was through Guattari that Deleuze was introduced to the diagrammatic semiotics of Peirce, which appears in *A Thousand Plateaus* and also in Deleuze's cinema books. With Guattari the question is posed more directly: What constitutes philosophy's Other as a discipline? How should it be treated? In *What is Philosophy?* Deleuze's final collaborative effort with Guattari, philosophy is contrasted and coordinated with art and science as three ways to 'cast planes over the chaos'.[119] The three disciplines are distinguished above all according to the different types of planes they construct in and across chaos: the 'plane of immanence' in philosophy, the 'plane of composition' in art, and the 'plane of reference or coordination' in science.[120] Deleuze and Guattari then distinguish three ways art, science and philosophy may interfere or communicate with one another.[121] The first form of interference is labelled 'extrinsic': an artwork is analysed according to philosophical concepts and methods, for example, or a form generated scientifically such as a mathematical fractal is appropriated by art for its beauty; the results or products of one discipline are taken into one of the others, but without changing the way that the latter discipline functions. For this form of relation, 'each discipline remains on its own plane and utilizes its own elements'.[122] A second form of interference is considered 'intrinsic': here, the translation is less that of content than of a 'subtle' deformation of one of the disciplines itself in and through another. Deleuze and Guattari provide the examples of Nietzsche's *Thus Spoke Zarathustra* and Mallarmé's *Igitur* as intersections of philosophy and art that produce 'complex planes that are difficult to qualify'.[123] Lastly, there are interferences of each discipline, not by either or both of the other disciplines, but by its own 'negative': 'each distinct discipline is, in its own way, in relation with a negative: even science has a relation with a nonscience that echoes its effects'. Deleuze and Guattari make this last form of interference turn on the question of *teaching* and the condition of teaching in a relation to its other:

> It is not just a question of saying that art must form those of us who are not artists, that it must awaken us and teach us to feel, and that philosophy must teach us to conceive, or that science must teach us to know. Such pedagogies are only possible if each of the disciplines is, on its own behalf, in an essential relationship with the No that concerns it.[124]

It would be wrong to interpret what is translated here as the 'No' of each discipline as a negation or dialectically necessary correlate.

It is rather a 'non-'. The No here is not a negation, but an Other (although not a personal or transcendent Other in Levinas's sense). Deleuze and Guattari specify:

> *Philosophy needs a nonphilosophy that comprehends it; it needs a nonphilosophical comprehension just as art needs nonart and science needs nonscience.* They do not need the No as beginning, or as the end in which they would be called upon to disappear by being realized, but at every moment of their becoming or their development.[125]

In other words, the philosophical goal of absolute self-transparency and self-grounding that one finds for example in Hegel is here dismissed in favour of a constitutive relation with otherness that continues along the entire path of philosophical becoming. What results on such a basis is a philosophical practice that makes of philosophy a process of (distinctively philosophical) learning. To learn – rather than to know – becomes philosophy's primary task and, more particularly, to learn how to learn philosophically in singular and variable contexts. Far from dominating all other academic, scientific or – more generally – knowledge-based disciplines, philosophy on this view must learn to learn from them and be transformed by them in its own way. The imperative mood here, the *must*, arises among other things from a singular history, a modern trajectory of philosophy that has, in subtle and not so subtle ways, led to tragic and intolerable historical effects. It is in response in part to these effects that the discipline of philosophy itself should be transformed, not just particular philosophers.

We can now see why it is so important for Deleuze that Spinoza is capable of generating the 'flashes' of insight that link philosophy to nonphilosophy. For Deleuze, Spinoza's thought manages to straddle the divide between abstract reason and the immediate power of the affects in a unique way and at a unique moment in the history of philosophy. By drawing the singularity of each unique event of encountering the *Ethics* into the very process by which the immanent logic of the *Ethics* sustains itself, Spinoza's thought constitutes an eminently *practical* philosophy for rethinking the modern philosophical tradition. More fundamentally than representing a set of propositional contents to the reader, it effects a transformation in the way that reader thinks, leading him or her from a representational model of thought to a non-representational and active mode of thinking. Yet the *Ethics* does this in the very medium of language, the domain of representation. Spinoza's way of thinking thus leads from representation and reflection to embodied action in which one becomes a *diagram* of thought, no longer a subject. As Deleuze says, 'What is unique about Spinoza is that he, the most philosophic of philosophers [. . .] teaches the philosopher how to become a nonphilosopher.'[126] This would be the case at collective, institutional and disciplinary levels even more so than at that of the individual thinker.

It is in this context that all the Deleuzian talk of creation must be understood. Philosophical creation is not creation *ex nihilo* but creation as learning. Deleuze shows us how learning and creation – far from being opposed – are intimately entwined. To work within a philosophical tradition is to apprentice oneself to an idiom, to accommodate certain habits of language and thought to the conventions of a given genre and its sedimented practices. As read by Deleuze, Spinoza's own philosophical idiom participates in a different modernity, one that does not simply break with the traditions of the past but rereads them both immanently and differently in order to make what lives in them more active, rational and unbound.

To be a Spinozist in a Deleuzian mode entails that one not *stop* at Spinoza or find in his *Ethics* a proof-text or final word. Instead, one must find in Spinoza's own thinking and in his life the signs of other singularities to which one is referred and which entail further creative exploration and expression. Deleuze's own encounter with Spinoza may itself be understood as a semiotic event in which Deleuze's own later philosophy develops. This event would be internal to a specific post-war French philosophical tradition, but also implicitly an encounter thereby with Spinoza's own early modern encounters – with Rabbis Mortera and Mennaseh ben Israel, Francis van den Enden, the Dutch Quakers, Willem van Blyenbergh and Lodewijk Meyer as well as the impersonal forces of Dutch politics, nascent mass-printing technology and the dusty craft of lens-grinding.

Deleuze situates Spinoza in a line of thought divergent in both impulse and development from the dominant Continental stream of the philosophy of consciousness from Descartes to Kant to Husserl. In Deleuze's reading of Spinoza the human ego is displaced from its foundational role as the ground of philosophical inquiry and knowledge in favour of an a-subjective field of singularities and engendered affects. What Deleuze shows is that another way of doing philosophy is not only possible, but is already actual in the modern philosophical tradition as a shadow or double of its major development, present alongside it and engaged with it through its history.

What does Deleuze finally offer us in this regard? The critique of Cartesianism is a touchstone for many strands of contemporary philosophy. By offering the lineaments of a real alternative, Deleuze opens up a different path, not only critical but constructive. This path is not an abstract possibility, but a concrete programme for conceiving the philosophical tradition as it exists in actual and potential relations to the mutually transformative conditions of art, science and other disciplines and traditions. Deleuze's reading is not simply an alternate modernity, but a diagrammatic reading that maps positive potentialities at the same time that it traces a real critique of the dominant tradition. Deleuze's project is thus corrective as well as creative.

It is important to remember the roots of the postmodern criticisms of Cartesianism. It was not primarily epistemological failures or logical inconsistencies that brought the dominant philosophical tradition into question, but concrete social, institutional and political problems that emerged at various scales. Husserl was already motivated philosophically by the sense of social, political and scientific crisis in early twentieth-century Europe, not to mention Nietzsche and the generalised European crises of the previous century. Any deliberate movement in thought towards regions of singularity and transcendental constitution abstracting from concrete history and ordinary experience risks devaluing that experience and the network of real relations that holds it together. It is thus not a matter of opposing diagrammatic immanence to representationalist transcendence but of rereading and revising a broadly Spinozist mode of thinking in light of critical revisions of the dominant philosophical tradition, its development and limitations, and the historical effects to which it has contributed. Reforming the immanentist tradition in contemporary philosophy does not entail siding with one set of philosophical positions or methods as against others so much as producing within a certain mode of thinking new conceptions of how such thought might respond to contemporary concerns.

Notes

1. Jean-Pierre Marquis, *From a Geometrical Point of View*.
2. Bryant, *Difference and Givenness*, p. 203.
3. Ibid.
4. Ibid., p. 217.
5. Ibid., pp. 27–9.

6. This is the general tenor of the readings proposed in Eleanor Kaufman, *The Dark Precursor*.
7. The epigraph is from Merleau-Ponty, *In Praise of Philosophy*, pp. 114–15.
8. See Beth Lord, *Kant and Spinozism*, pp. 134–6.
9. This tendency may be seen, albeit expressed in quite different ways in each case, in the research of D. Smith, Lord, Kerslake, Toscano, MacKenzie and Bryant.
10. Kerslake (interestingly, on both sides), Ramey, Salzano, and in a somewhat different manner Barber.
11. Daniel Barber, *Deleuze and the Naming of God*, p. 154.
12. Ibid., p. 49.
13. Ibid., pp. 163–4.
14. Ibid.
15. Peter Hallward, *Out of this World*.
16. Deleuze, *Difference and Repetition*, p. 1, emphasis added. Hereafter abbreviated DR.
17. The critique of representation is common to a wide variety of thinkers who may be included under the general heading of postmodern philosophy, including for example Rorty, Lyotard, Levinas and Derrida. For representational models of thought the role of thinking is to mirror nature as accurately and objectively as possible; representational thought does not create or enact, but rather reflects. Philosophy on this model tends to become reducible to epistemology since the relation of thought to reality is expressed in exemplary form by reflective knowledge.
18. This is evident especially in his reading of Bergson and in his extensive use of biological and ethological examples in *A Thousand Plateaus*.
19. DR, p. 139. Second emphasis added.
20. Ibid., pp. 139–40.
21. Ibid.
22. It is not necessary to look very hard to recognise the importance of Spinoza's philosophy for Deleuze. The centrality of Spinoza from the early monographs all the way through to the final collaborative work with Guattari is textually explicit. Deleuze's two books devoted to Spinoza demonstrate ample sourcing of Deleuze's own conceptions in his readings of Spinoza's works, particularly the *Ethics*. Spinoza also figures prominently in the central work *Difference and Repetition* as the definitive philosopher of univocity. In addition, there are the later works with Guattari in which Spinoza is celebrated as the 'Prince of philosophers' and again as the 'Christ' of philosophers.
23. Deleuze's own philosophical context at the cultural level was the French post-war philosophical milieu on the one hand dominated by the figure of Sartre, influenced by Kojève's and Hyppolite's readings of

Hegel and the innovations of structuralist linguistics and anthropology; and on the other transformed by the political and cultural shifts leading up to and culminating in spring 1968. Besides the figures already mentioned, we might add in particular Foucault, whose genealogical studies of discourse, power and subjectivity were important points of reference for Deleuze's own thought (see his *Foucault*).
24. See the genealogy in DR, pp. 35–42, which could be expanded to include Nicholas of Cusa and Bergson. Badiou has accused Deleuze of remaining a thinker of the 'One-All' (*Clamor of Being*, *Theoretical Writings*). This reading neglects Deleuze's revised notion of Spinozist unity in terms of positive difference. If the 'One-All' is understood as 'difference-in-itself' (*Difference and Repetition*), the very notion of unity (of the One) is transformed.
25. A number of critics of Deleuze have pointed out this apparent discrepancy. See, for instance, Gillian Howie's reading in *Deleuze and Spinoza* as well as Badiou's critiques in *Deleuze: The Clamor of Being* and Slavoj Žižek's in *Organs without Bodies*.
26. Deleuze's *oeuvre* is often divided – perhaps too neatly – into three periods: the early monographs in the history of philosophy on Hume, Nietzsche, Bergson and Spinoza; the central studies of *Difference and Repetition* and *The Logic of Sense*, together serving as a kind of axis or hinge in Deleuze's creative development; and finally the later collaborations with Guattari and Deleuze's solo work from the same period. In this framework, *Expressionism in Philosophy: Spinoza* plays an important yet ambiguous role – the last of the early monographs, it nevertheless remains thematically and methodologically connected to the central works, *Difference and Repetition* and *The Logic of Sense*.
27. Spinoza, *Ethics* Id3 and Id4.
28. Deleuze, *Expressionism in Philosophy: Spinoza*, pp. 37–9. Hereafter abbreviated EP.
29. In other words, the logic of the differences among attributes cannot be grasped by the logic that is formalised in set theory. By placing this conception of creative difference at the heart of his thought, Deleuze commits himself to a model of philosophy contrary in basic impulse to the path pursued by Badiou in *Being and Event* and *Logics of Worlds*. For first-hand accounts of this important difference see Deleuze and Guattari, *What is Philosophy?*, pp. 151–3, and Badiou, *Theoretical Writings*, ch. 6.
30. EP, p. 39.
31. EP, p. 28.
32. DR, p. 40.
33. Ibid.
34. Deleuze will call this modal field *sense*.

35. Heidegger's concept of ontological difference is structured through the *Zweifalt* of Being and beings. See the reading comparing Heideggerian and Deleuzian ontology in Miguel de Beistegui, *Truth and Genesis*.
36. As Deleuze points out, 'The idea of expression is neither defined nor deduced by Spinoza [. . .].' EP, p. 19. Nonetheless it appears at several key junctures in the text. By making the undefined but functional term *expression* the central axis of his analysis Deleuze takes advantage of a slippage between natural language and formal structure.
37. EP, pp. 15–16.
38. EP, p. 19.
39. Ibid.
40. EP, pp. 27–8.
41. This table and the formulations it uses are adapted from the table in the Appendix to EP, pp. 337–9.
42. EP, p. 334.
43. A similar movement may be traced in the development of the representational dyad of idea and object into a triadic conception of ideas as active processes. This is equally true whether the representational dyad is understood in terms of the difference between signifier and signified or the distinction between meaning and reference.
44. EP, p. 335, emphasis added.
45. Negri's reading of Spinoza in *The Savage Anomaly* expresses this contextualised reading of Spinoza even more strongly than Deleuze. Macherey also emphasises the historical dimension of Spinoza's thought in a similar way, in *Avec Spinoza*.
46. Spinoza's logic is affective, in that it produces sense. As Duffy puts it, Spinoza's philosophy develops a triadic logic of expression such that the affects are themselves 'the affects of the logic of expression, which is not an abstract logic that merely represents the movement of these affects, but the very logic by means of which these affects are expressed'. Simon Duffy, 'The Logic of Expression in Deleuze's *Expressionism in Philosophy: Spinoza:* A Strategy of Engagement', p. 51.
47. In what follows, Deleuze draws frequently upon Stoic thought and the Stoic conception of *semeia*. For background see the work of Emile Brehier – Deleuze's own source – and the discussion of Stoic sources in Deely, *Four Ages of Understanding*. The most detailed discussion of Deleuze's philosophy of language is found in Jean-Jacques Lecercle, *Deleuze and Language*.
48. Deleuze, *The Logic of Sense*, pp. 12–14. Hereafter abbreviated LS.
49. LS, p. 181.
50. As Deleuze puts it: 'It is not that we must construct an a posteriori model corresponding to previous dimensions, but rather the model

itself must have the aptitude to function a priori from within, were it forced to introduce a supplementary dimension which, because of its evanescence, could not have been recognized in experience from outside. It is thus a question *de jure*, and not simply a question of fact.' LS, p. 17. In other words, Deleuze's idea of sense – like the aspect of semiotic singularity in Peirce examined in Chapter 3 – should not be understood as an objective correlate of a representational intention. It is rather an impersonal event occurring at the level of intra-worldly affects among bodies.

51. In *The Logic of Sense* Deleuze points to the 'double causality' that links 'incorporeal sense' to physical causation on the one hand and incorporeal 'quasi-causes' on the other. See the 'Fourteenth Series of Double Causality', LS, pp. 94–9. In the later work with Guattari, this notion is developed more fully through the idea of *incorporeal transformation*, the dynamic aspect of sense: 'The incorporeal transformation is recognizable by its instantaneousness, its immediacy, by the simultaneity of the statement expressing the transformation and the effect the transformation produces.' Deleuze and Guattari, *A Thousand Plateaus*, p. 81.
52. See Gil, *Metamorphoses of the Body*.
53. LS, p. 99.
54. DR, p. 182, quoted in DeLanda, *Intensive Science and Virtual Philosophy*, p. 13.
55. DeLanda, *Intensive Science and Virtual Philosophy*, p. 15.
56. DR, p. 276.
57. DR, p. 277.
58. LS, p. 55.
59. Ibid.
60. E III preface.
61. LS, pp. 98–9. Deleuze refers in this regard to Sartre's article from 1937, 'The Transcendence of the Ego', the thesis of which Sartre summarises in the claim, 'transcendental consciousness is an impersonal spontaneity'. See Jean-Paul Sartre, *The Transcendence of the Ego: An Existentialist Theory of Consciousness*, p. 98.
62. LS, p. 98
63. LS, p. 99.
64. LS, p. 102.
65. In Deleuze's own words, the singularities must eventuate 'on an unconscious surface and possess a mobile, immanent principle of auto-unification through a *nomadic distribution*, radically distinct from fixed and sedentary distributions as conditions of the syntheses of consciousness'. LS, p. 102.
66. LS, p. 103.
67. In this respect, Deleuze's reading of Spinoza in *Expressionism in*

Philosophy should be interpreted in light of his later readings of Leibniz in *The Logic of Sense* and *The Fold*.
68. LS, p. 111.
69. In this way, Deleuze's reading of Leibnizian compossibility and individuation relates structurally to Peirce's account of discreteness in terms of the potentialisation of mathematical continua. As Putnam interprets Peirce on this issue: 'The metaphysical intuition that is behind all this is that we live in a world [...] in which there are an enormous number of possibilities: *compatible* possibilities. [...] The Peircean picture is that the multitude of possibilities is so great that as soon as we have a possible world in which some of these possibilities are realized [...] then we immediately see that there is a possible world in which still *more* divisions can be made, and hence there is no possible world in which all these *non-exclusive* possibilities are *all* actualized. We might summarize this by saying that the metaphysical picture is that possibility intrinsically outruns actuality, not just because of the finiteness of human powers, or the limitations imposed by physical laws.' 'Peirce's Continuum', in Ketner, ed., *Peirce and Contemporary Thought*, p. 19.
70. LS, p. 113.
71. Ibid.
72. Ibid.
73. See DR, pp. 119–21. See also the studies collected in Kaufman, *The Dark Precursor*.
74. LS, p. 113.
75. LS, p. 172.
76. LS, p. 174, emphasis added.
77. This is precisely Peirce's notion of thirdness. For a comparison of Deleuze and Peirce in the context of educational theory, see the work of Inna Semetsky.
78. LS, p. 174.
79. LS, p. 114.
80. For an attempt to show how Deleuze's concept of the virtual depends on the mathematical conception of Albert Lautman, with potential links to category theory, see Rocco Gangle, 'Mathematics, Structure, Metaphysics: Gilles Deleuze and Category Theory'.
81. LS, p. 114.
82. See Joshua Ramey, *The Hermetic Deleuze*.
83. LS, p. 107.
84. Habermas notes a tendency in Peirce's thought along similar lines, which Habermas calls 'the anonymization of the interpretative process'. Habermas is concerned especially with the social and ethical implications of a philosophy based in signs in which 'the fundamental semeiotic structure can be completely defined without

recourse to forms of intersubjectivity, however elementary'. 'Peirce and Communication', in *Peirce and Contemporary Thought*, pp. 245, 246.
85. LS, p. 169.
86. 'What brings destiny about at the level of events, what brings an event to repeat another in spite of all its difference, what makes it possible that a life is composed of one and the same Event, despite the variety of what might happen, that it be traversed by a single and same fissure, that it play one and the same air over all possible tunes and all possible words – all these are not due to relations between cause and effect; it is rather an aggregate of noncausal correspondences which form a system of echoes, of resumptions and resonances, a system of signs – in short, an expressive quasi-causality, and not at all a necessitating causality.' LS, p. 170.
87. LS, p. 149.
88. LS, p. 150.
89. LS, p. 113.
90. See also DR, p. 159: 'problems must be considered not as "givens" (data) but as ideal "objectivities" possessing their own sufficiency and implying acts of constitution and investment in their respective symbolic fields. Far from being concerned with solutions, truth and falsehood primarily affect problems.'
91. This notion is developed in DeLanda, *Intensive Science and Virtual Philosophy*.
92. In addition to the account drawn above from the body of *The Logic of Sense*, we should also indicate Deleuze's analyses of time in *Kant's Critical Philosophy* ('For Kant, it is a question of the form of time in general, which distinguishes between the act of the I, and the ego to which this act is attributed: an infinite modulation, no longer a mould. Thus time moves into the subject, in order to distinguish the Ego from the I in it.' Preface, p. ix) and his reading of the 'crack' in Emile Zola's *Human Comedy*, 'Zola and the Crack-up', in Appendix II to *The Logic of Sense* ('It is as if the crack runs through and alienates thought in order to be also the possibility of thought, in other words, that from the vantage point of which thought is developed and recovered. It is the obstacle to thought, but also the abode and power of thought – its field and agent.' LS, pp. 332–3).
93. This is the meaning of the 'third synthesis' of time discussed in *Difference and Repetition* which both creates and extends a future and at the same time punctures the self-enclosed and self-coherent subject 'as though the bearer of the new world were carried away and dispersed by the shock of the multiplicity to which it gives birth: what the self has become equal to is the unequal in itself'. DR, pp. 89–90.

94. Compare also the analysis of 'faciality' in *A Thousand Plateaus*, pp. 167–91.
95. DR, pp. 281–2.
96. DR, p. 257.
97. Ibid.
98. DR, pp. 259–60/333–4.
99. The most important works of Levinas are the twin pillars of *Totality and Infinity* and *Otherwise than Being*. The latter is probably most relevant to thinking through the still largely unexplored connections between Levinas and Deleuze.
100. Appendix II in LS, pp. 301–21.
101. LS, pp. 304–5.
102. In the later terms of Deleuze and Guattari's *What is Philosophy?* Robinson here plays the role of a *conceptual persona*.
103. LS, p. 306.
104. LS, p. 312.
105. Deleuze writes: 'The Other presides over the organization of the world into objects and over the transitive relations of these objects. These objects exist only through the possibilities with which Others filled up the world; each one was closed onto itself, or opened onto other objects, only in relation to possible worlds expressed by Others. In short, it is the Other who has imprisoned the elements within the limits of bodies and, further still, within the limits of the earth.' LS, p. 312.
106. LS, pp. 315–16.
107. LS, p. 316.
108. LS, p. 317.
109. Ibid.
110. Deleuze, *Spinoza: Practical Philosophy*, p. 129. Deleuze writes similarly of a 'double reading of Spinoza', on the one hand 'systematic' and on the other 'affective' (ibid.). Zourabichvili's 'strategy of the chimera' as interpreted here corresponds to the complex unity of this 'double reading', in a certain sense its dialectic.
111. In *A Thousand Plateaus*, Deleuze and Guattari consider a pragmatic semiotic that is 'defined by a decisive external occurrence, by a relation with the outside that is expressed more as an emotion than an idea, and more as effort or action than imagination [. . .]; by a limited constellation operating in a single sector; by a "postulate" or "concise formula" serving as the point of departure for a linear series or proceeding that runs its course, at which point a new proceeding begins. In short, it operates *by the linear and temporal succession of finite proceedings, rather than by the simultaneity of circles in unlimited expansion*' (p. 120).
112. Lambert, *The Non-philosophy of Gilles Deleuze*, p. 37.

113. Deleuze's own use of the term *apprenticeship* begins in *Difference and Repetition* and continues in *Proust and Signs* and throughout his work. Michael Hardt's helpful study of Deleuze as a reader of Bergson, Nietzsche and Spinoza is entitled *Gilles Deleuze: An Apprenticeship in Philosophy* and develops the notion of Deleuze's own apprenticeship to the thinkers he reads.
114. DR, p. 192.
115. Ibid.
116. Ibid.
117. Lambert, *The Non-philosophy of Gilles Deleuze*.
118. See Deleuze's own brief account of how Guattari changed his approach to philosophy in the preface to the Italian edition of *The Logic of Sense*, translated into French in *Deux régimes de fous*.
119. Deleuze and Guattari, *What is Philosophy?*, p. 202. Hereafter abbreviated WIP.
120. WIP, p. 216.
121. WIP, pp. 216–18.
122. WIP, p. 217.
123. WIP, p. 217.
124. WIP, p. 218.
125. WIP, p. 218. It is in this light that Badiou's criticism of Deleuze as a thinker of the 'One-All' shows itself to be mistaken. As Deleuze himself argues, his conception requires 'at least two multiplicities'. What this entails in practice is that a global ontology of the sort Badiou proposes is not feasible. Because philosophy occurs only *in relation* to a determinate experience and encounter with nonphilosophy, philosophical practice is irreducibly situated and relational. Set-theoretic ontology must give way to a pragmatic interpretation of category theory.
126. Deleuze, *Spinoza: Practical Philosophy*, p. 130. Deleuze continues, alluding to the importance of the third kind of knowledge, 'And it is in Part V – not at all the most difficult, but the quickest, having an infinite velocity – that the two are brought together, the philosopher and the non-philosopher, as one and the same being.' Ibid.

CHAPTER 6

Diagrams of Difference: Adjunctions and Topoi

Category theory intersects with philosophy at various levels. But perhaps nowhere is the direct utility of category theory for philosophy more evident than in the area of logic. This chapter examines two important constructions in category theory with particular relevance for logic: adjoint functors (adjunctions) and topoi. These are mathematically precise and quite technical notions, and their generality is astonishing. More so than in previous chapters it will be necessary at points for the sake of an introductory presentation to omit certain formal details that while essential for higher-level mathematical work would only obscure the matter at a first or even fifth encounter. The mathematical and philosophical ramifications of these two concepts are immense, and it will be impossible to survey them all here. The reader is encouraged to pursue these concepts further, especially by considering them in light of recent philosophical proposals such as those of Williamson, Zalamea and Badiou that encourage a strong linkage between formal methods (either logical or mathematical) and metaphysics. Such proposals lend themselves readily in a categorical framework to formulation in terms of diagrammatic immanence.

Logic studies extremely general relations, relations so general that they are meant to structure necessarily anything that may be coherently thought. When logic and metaphysics are brought into alignment, which is quite natural, the general relation between sameness and difference becomes especially salient. Typically, logicians and metaphysicians privilege unity and sameness over multiplicity and difference for reasons that are perhaps endemic to representational models of thought, but it is also possible to work philosophically from the standpoint of the priority or privilege of difference and multiplicity. We saw in the previous chapter how Deleuze shares some of the core philosophical commitments of Spinoza and Peirce – in particular their respective commitments to different types of philosophical immanence – and yet develops on this basis a philosophy of creative difference that makes divergence primary with respect to identity and treats subjectivity as the purely differential spark of communication across incompossible worlds. Most importantly, for Deleuze this differential communication structures philosophy itself 'in an essential relationship with the No that concerns it' (like each of the disciplines of art and science, too, in their own distinctive ways).[1] The two categorical structures explored in the present chapter are uniquely poised to help develop the formal tools necessary to diagram and experiment with such differential relations.

Diagrams exploit the fact that relations exist *for* beings who are able to perceive and manipulate them externally all the while that these beings are themselves partly determined by their own relationships to these relations and are themselves modified, even if only in infinitesimal ways, by their very own acts of perception and manipulation. To perceive a relationship, for instance that of a similarity of shape between the hole in the puzzle and the piece in one's hand, is after all to stand in a certain relationship to that relationship itself, that of perceiver to perceived first of all and, in this example, that of solver to solution. In any actual context of perception and action, the 'frame' of ambient relations that determines the context extends through roughly concentric zones of proximity. Yet sometimes the most relevant relations in any particular case are not the most proximate or the most visible. Adjunctions and topoi represent very general relational structures that in application help to gauge the real relevance of what may not be immediately apparent.

Adjunctions

An adjunction is a special relationship between a pair of functors. The basic diagrammatic shape of the relationship is pictured in Figure 6.1 below, where the two dots represent two categories and the 'down-and-up' functors labelled G and F between those two categories constitute the adjunction itself. More precisely, the adjunction is the ordered relation between G and F that is notated by the left-pointing turnstile at the centre of the diagram. The directionality of this turnstile is essential to the adjunction's sense. In the diagram shown, G is *right adjoint* to F and (equivalently) F is *left adjoint* to G. For any adjunction between two functors, it is insufficient merely to state that the two functors stand in the adjoint relation; the relative 'places' of left and right adjoint must be specified as well.

Much of the mathematical utility and philosophical interest of adjunctions stems from their unusual combination of complex inner machinery on the one hand and highly abstract and relatively 'simple' conceptuality on the other. This latter aspect, the conceptual simplicity of adjunctions, is manifest especially in their surprising ubiquity. It was with good reason that one of the founders of category theory, Saunders Mac Lane, proposed the mathematical slogan 'adjoint functors arise everywhere', and indeed it seems that not only in mathematics but in practically any domain involving relationships between the particular and the universal or between tokens and types there are more subtle adjunctive relations lurking somewhere in the structural depths.

The philosophical question to which adjunctions provide the mathematical answer is the question of the essence of relatively universal or 'systematic' structural relation itself. Certainly there are many different kinds of relations. Yet there is also the purely immanent or conceptual-real relationship between all these different types of relations on the one hand and the universal concept or field of relationality as such on the other. This is not the brutally external dichotomy of genus and species; this is the richly fundamental philosophical problem of ideality itself. With respect to this problem it is not a matter of classifying objects but of treating a unique type of asymmetrical yet partly reciprocal condition that appears to ground the possibility of any sort of systematic thinking whatsoever. What *kind* of relationship, for instance, does Deleuze ask us to think between the virtual and the actual? It is much like the relationship between substance and attributes in Spinoza: a real yet non-numerical difference. It is in any case not something simple or straightforward, given ordinary habits of human thinking. It seems to necessitate a kind of rigorous finesse even to pose it as an evident problem. To pose the problem well directly manifests the kind of relationship at stake, one that exposes an intrinsic dialectic of difference and identity at the heart of any manifestation at all. The relationship is in that sense both immediately conceptual and immediately real. An adjunction is the mathematical formalisation within category theory of relationships of this sort. From a philosophical point of view, it may even be the paradigm of such relationships.

The most important thing to be clear on about adjunctions is that they are essentially meta-relational. They are pairs of functors going back and forth between two categories in such a way that the relationship itself between those functors (a relationship that is *oriented* or arrow-like) provides information about how the images of the two categories that the functors select are related to one another as well as how the source and target categories are internally structured in themselves. From a simply external and informal point of view, an adjunction is just a certain kind of relationship between two functors going in opposite directions between a given pair of categories. It is a sort of oriented quasi-inverse relationship between the functors themselves. Since functors are structure-preserving mappings from one category into another, adjunctions are – like natural transformations in this respect – relations between relations between systems of relations. Yet even though they are thus not only intrinsically meta-relational but indeed meta-meta-relational, this in no way implies that they are less rigorously determined or somehow less meaningful. If anything, the lesson of adjunctions is that of category theory more generally: as one moves from relations to meta-relations between those relations and so forth, one tends to *gain* rather than lose insight into the most interesting and relevant structural features in play.

What defines an adjunction between two functors as represented in Figure 6.1 is a correspondence between the categorical 'position' of the image of the lower category in the upper as carried by F on the one hand and the 'position' of the image of the upper category in the

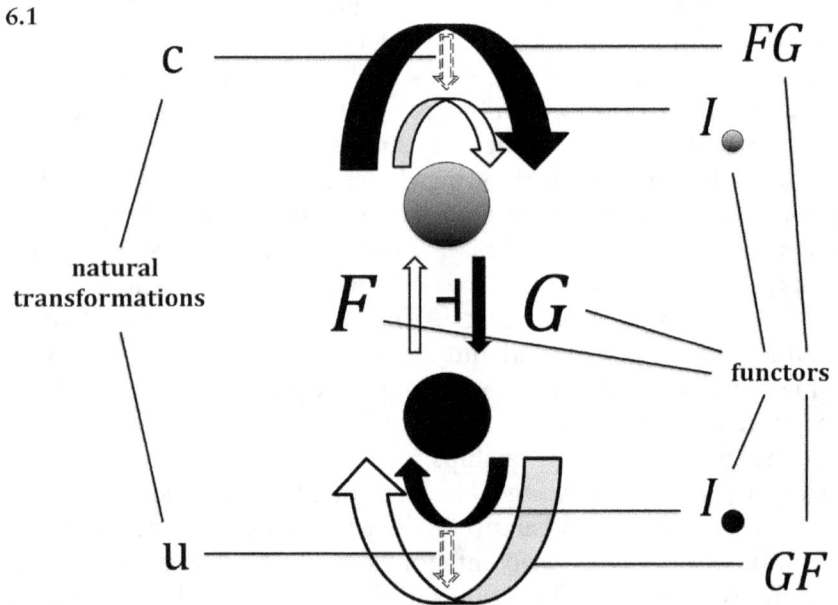

6.1

lower as carried by G on the other. This informal language of 'position' may be made precise in the following way:

1. For every arrow f in the upper category that has as its source the image F(A) of some object A in the lower category as mapped by the functor F, there is an arrow in the lower category from A into the image mapped by the functor G of the target of f (call it B), and vice versa. In other words, there is a one-to-one correspondence between arrows F(A)→B in the upper category, and arrows A→G(B) in the lower category, for all A and B. The thing to notice here is that while the object A 'lives' in the lower category and the object B 'lives' in the upper category, the one-to-one relationship between arrows is defined between arrows that are each 'half'-determined by B or A on the one hand and 'half'-determined on the other hand by the *images* of A or B as selected in the 'opposite' category by the functors F and G respectively. So the overall correlation F(A)→B::A→G(B) between arrows in the two categories is, in a sense, 'half'-determined by the inner structure of the categories themselves and 'half'-determined by the two functors F and G that pass between them.

2. In order to constitute an adjunction, the one-to-one relationship just described between arrows in two categories as structured by two functors must be 'natural' in both of the categories. This is what is indicated in the diagram by the dashed arrows representing natural transformations labelled 'c' and 'u'. Given the two identity-functors on each category (labelled I in the diagram with iconic subscripts) and a one-to-one relationship between internal categorical arrows as described above that are determined by the two functors F and G, in order to form an adjunction the functor-compositions FG and GF must be mapable by corresponding natural transformations either into or out of the relevant identity functor as indicated in the diagram.[2] That's it.

No doubt the formal definition is somewhat difficult to follow, and a more conceptual explanation would be helpful. Conceptually, an adjunction may be thought of as a generalised or relaxed version of isomorphism of categories. Consider two isomorphic categories. Being isomorphic, there necessarily exists a pair of functors that go back and forth between them such that the composition of these functors is the same as the identity arrows on each of the categories. The commutative diagram on the right side of Figure 2.10 back in Chapter 2 shows the essential relationships. It shows this with the identity arrows on each dot labelled 'i' and indexed with iconic subscripts. In that diagram, which applies in any category to determine an isomorphism, the two arrows that go back and forth between the two dots are unlabelled. In **Categories** a commutative diagram with this shape represents an isomorphism between categories (the dots are categories and the arrows are functors). Note that this diagram may be embedded directly into Figure 6.1. The unlabelled arrows in Figure 2.10 become in Figure 6.1 the two functors labelled F and G.

If the two categories indicated by the dots *are* in fact isomorphic and F and G are inverses of one another, then the composition FG (*F following G* – remember the function-like order inversion!) will be the same as the identity functor on the upper category and the composition GF (*G following F*) will be the identity on the lower category. Conceptually speaking, such inverse functors guarantee a structural identity between the two categories, and G and F would provide a way to pass from one category to the other and back again without 'shifting position' in the original category. The two dots would for all practical purposes (that is, with respect to all possible categorical relations) represent the same category. Yet notice that in Figure 6.1 the identity functors on the two categories *are not the same* as the compositions FG and GF. They are only *structurally correlated* by the natural transformations that both separate and connect them. The difference or slippage represented by the natural transformations is what constitutes the difference between the strictly inverse relation of functors that defines isomorphism and the more relaxed relation that comprises functorial adjunction.

What happens if we now relax the isomorphism, allowing the two categories to vary somewhat in their internal structure with respect to one another and letting the functors back and forth between them alter accordingly? Thus the back-and-forth movements of FG and GF will no longer necessarily bring every dot and arrow back to their original 'position' in the original category after 'passing through' the opposite. Instead, the identity functors that *conceived as compositions FG and GF* would determine F and G to be inverses are allowed to 'slip' or 'differentiate' so that there is now a difference between remaining inert on the one hand (the identity functor on each category) and circulating on the other through the opposed category via F and G in whichever appropriate order (the composition functors FG and GF). Nonetheless, a compositionally secure transformation between these two functors might still be definable within each category. If so, this will constitute the natural transformation called either unit or counit. In Figure 6.1 these are, again, the natural transformations labelled 'u' and 'c' respectively (in the mathematical literature they are often designated with the Greek letters 'eta' and 'epsilon').

From this enlarged perspective, identity functors and inverses appear as merely special cases of more general relational variabilities, namely natural transformations and adjoints. These more differential relations appear as conceptually prior and determine more precisely the basic 'grammar' in which identity itself may be expressed. Isomorphism was already a loosening of the notion of strict identity that reduced it to the structural and hence possibly compositional relations determining it in some categorical context. Adjoint functors represent an even more differentiated relation than isomorphism, but this is not simply a more extreme loosening but rather the induction of a new kind of relational/meta-relational orientation.

EXAMPLES OF ADJUNCTIONS

Like partial orders, but in a quite different way and at a more abstract level, adjunctions seem to pop up nearly everywhere there is structure, which is to say everywhere. Probably the best way to begin to understand adjunctions is not to attempt to sort out the purely formal relations between functors and natural transformations as described above, but rather to see how these relations actually apply to a variety of cases. Like diagrams in general, how adjunctions work is really what they are.

1. In some cases, adjunctions generalise in a striking way the kinds of universal mapping properties that arise frequently in partial orders and other categories. UMPs such as initial and terminal objects, pullbacks, products and more generally limits of all sorts may be represented by adjoint relations between canonical functors. In this way the existence of an adjunction can provide information about the internal structure of a category, particularly with respect to the distribution of limits within it. For instance, every category **C** may be cross-indexed with itself to generate what is called the *product category* **CxC**.[3] As objects (dots) it has all ordered pairs of objects (dots) of **C**. For any two objects C_1 and C_2 in **C**, there is a single object (C_1, C_2) in **CxC**. An arrow in **CxC** from one such ordered pair to another is then a pair of arrows $(C_1 \to C_3, C_2 \to C_4)$ for any such pair that exists in **C**. Then, just as a square table coordinating rows and columns labelled by the same series of indices (like chessboard squares labelled A to H in both directions from one corner) possesses a natural 'sameness line' along its diagonal (the squares labelled AA, BB,...HH), there is a natural functor $D: \mathbf{C} \to \mathbf{CxC}$ (the 'diagonal functor') that takes each object X of **C** to the object (X,X) and each

arrow *f* of **C** to the arrow pair (*f,f*). If this functor has a right adjoint, then the category **C** has products (that is, limits for 'two dot only' diagrams) for any given pair of dots.[4] More strongly, the product of any two objects of **C** is given by the image in **C** coming from the corresponding object in **CxC** according to the right adjoint functor itself. The adjunction 'encodes' the product information for all the category's pairs of objects. The important point is that the diagonal functor **C**→**CxC** is well-defined for *any* category. There is therefore an externally determined property (whether or not a functor right adjoint to the diagonal functor exists) that provides information about a category's internal distribution of a universal property (the existence of products for any two dots in the category). The existence of such an adjunction is the 'external', thoroughly relational mark of the global distribution of a universal mapping property *within* the category. In a very loose analogy, the syntactic fact that any two sentences in a language may be conjoined with the particular word 'and' may be read off that language's semantics combined with the 'external' syntax-semantics mapping itself. Worlds where 'P' and 'Q' are both true are always worlds where 'P-and-Q' is true as well. Yet this relation that defines, in a sense, the very essence of 'and' is not a mere similarity of structure: a world where two statements happen to be true in no way 'looks like' their conjunctive syntax.

In the example shown in Figure 6.2, the category **2** shown below the line 'lifts' to the product category **2x2** and the diagonal functor *D* maps the one non-identity arrow *h* in **2** to the pair (*h,h*) and the initial and terminal objects in **2** to the corresponding objects in **2x2** (the assignments of *D* are shown by the 'upward' dashed arrows in the diagram). When this functor *D* is plugged into the role of the functor labelled *F* in the general adjunction diagram above (Figure 6.1), the right adjoint to *D* (the functor from **2x2** into **2** that then plays the role of *G*) takes each pair of dots, that is, each particular object in **2x2** to the *product* of that pair of dots in the category **2**. For this very simple category, the result is more or less trivial, although logically interesting (if the two objects in **2** are taken to be the values 'true' and 'false' with the one non-identity arrow going from 'false' to 'true', then the products of the pairs in **2x2** mapped by the right adjoint to the diagonal functor correspond precisely to the logical operation of conjunction: only 'true and true' = 'true'). Exactly the same functorial relation holds for *any* category in which products exist for any pair of objects, which means that the range of 'models' for the adjunction diagram as restricted to the specific type of adjunction described here

6.2

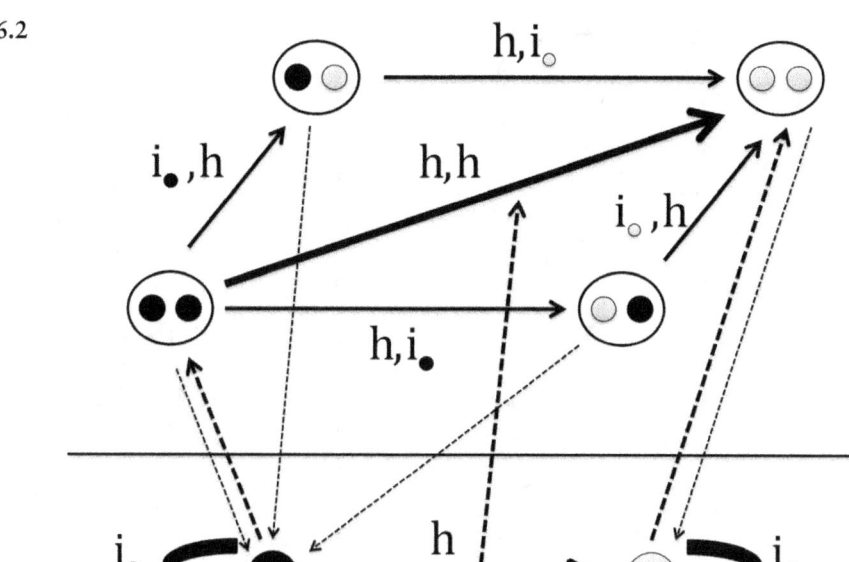

may be understood to provide theoretical and experimental access to the class of all categories with universal products.

2. Adjunctions often represent solutions to optimisation problems. This is one way to understand how they encode information concerning limits within a category, where these exist (as in the previous example of products). Limits are locally 'optimal' solutions to certain diagrammatic structures within a category, as the discussion of limits in Chapter 2 showed. An especially intuitive class of related examples is given by how adjunctions emerge naturally from pixilations of a space.[5] For simplicity, consider the Euclidean plane. A partial order (and hence a category) is first defined on all closed figures that may be inscribed in the plane as follows: given two figures F_1 and F_2, an arrow $F_1 \to F_2$ exists from F_1 to F_2 if and only if F_1 is entirely included in F_2, that is, if it nowhere extends outside the boundary of F_2. The diagram on the left in Figure 6.3 illustrates the basic idea. Let us call this category **Figures**. It is easy to check that the definition given indeed defines a category. This category **Figures** will then substitute for *both* the dots (upper and lower) in the general adjunction diagram above (Figure 6.1) and the two functors F and G will each be constructed as functors **Figures**→**Figures** with this single category as both source and target. To define the pair of functors, it will first be necessary to impose a 'pixilation' on the plane. Most simply, we

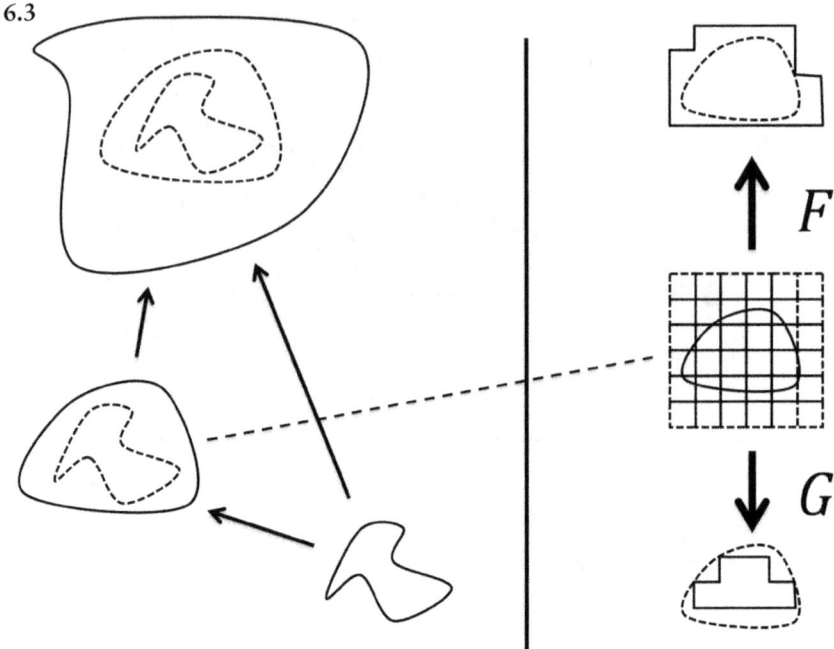

6.3

may consider a grid of squares of some chosen size that carves up the plane into equal granular subregions. Each figure X in **Figures** (each object in the category) then naturally determines a pair of 'pixilated' figures, one defined maximally by the squares that have *any* part of X in them, and one defined minimally by the squares that are *entirely* included within X. See the right side of Figure 6.3 to understand how these two constructions work.

The mapping that takes all the figures of **Figures** to their *maximal* pixilation in fact preserves the partial order structure of **Figures** and thus constitutes a functor (the reader should check this). Call this functor F. Similarly, the mapping that takes all the figures of **Figures** to their *minimal* pixilation preserves the partial order structure of **Figures** in a different way and thus constitutes a different functor (the reader should check this too). Call this functor G. There is then an adjoint relation between the two functors F and G exactly as presented in the diagram in Figure 6.1. F is left adjoint to G and G is right adjoint to F. Indeed, this type of adjoint relation holds for any pixilation of the Euclidean plane and may be generalised to higher-dimensional spaces. The effects of this adjunction on the presheaves that may be built up over such spaces offer a very interesting field for further diagrammatic investigation.

Diagrams of Difference: Adjunctions and Topoi 221

3. Another type of categorical optimisation is the adjoint relation between 'free' and 'forgetful' functors of various kinds. For example, illustrated in Figure 6.4 is an internal fragment of such a pair of functors passing back and forth between the category of **Graphs** and the category of **Categories**. We have been working with the mathematical structure of directed graphs since the beginning of Chapter 2. As suggested in that chapter, graphs in fact form a category **Graphs** in their own right, with maps between graphs that conserve sources and targets of graph-arrows as the category's arrows. It is possible to define a functor F called the 'free' functor from the category **Graphs** to the category **Categories**. This functor, intuitively, 'lifts' any given graph into the unique category that 'glues in' all identity arrows and composition arrows, thus turning the graph into a category that preserves all the graph structure and simply supplements that structure with all the additional structure needed to turn the graph into a category. It is 'free' in the sense that it 'makes no choices' (adds no determinations) other than what is strictly necessary in terms of the axioms C1–C3 of categories. In the other direction, it is possible to define a 'forgetful' functor G from **Categories** into **Graphs** that takes each category to the graph that 'looks just like it', that is, has all the same dots and arrows, but because it is a graph has no defined relations of identity or composition. The functor 'forgets' this categorical structure. It is a good exercise to try to demonstrate why and how these two mappings do indeed determine functors (remember that functors preserve categorical mappings between objects in the appropriate way and are not just functions of objects to objects). In any case, what is interesting for present purposes is that these two functors constitute an adjunction. F and G are left and right adjoint to one another, just as in Figure 6.1.[6]

Figure 6.4 illustrates the basic idea. **Graphs** is represented below the line and **Categories** is represented above the line. The one-to-one correspondence of arrows $F(A) \to B :: A \to G(B)$ is diagrammed by a single case: the thick arrows at the top and bottom that are elaborated 'internally' by the dashed arrows 'behind' them. Notice that the composite functor GF is a functor *inside* the category **Graphs**. 'Factoring through' the category of categories as a natural 'completion' of any given graph into a category followed by a direct mapping back into graphs with the new structure 'glued in' is thus naturally conceived as a functor from **Graphs** into itself. The natural transformation that takes the identity functor on **Graphs** into this functor GF is the 'unit' of the adjunction ('u' in Figure 6.1).

6.4

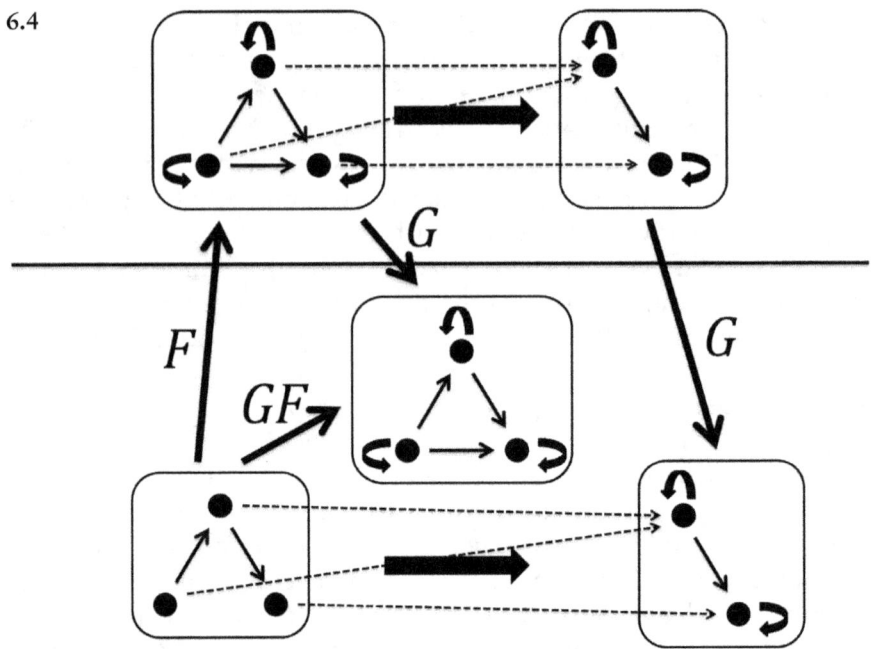

There are many similar cases of free/forgetful adjunctions. For instance, there is a functor from **Sets** to the category of mathematical groups **Groups** that takes each set to the free group defined on that set (with corresponding 'lifting' of set functions to group homomorphisms). And there is a functor from **Groups** to **Sets** that takes each group to its underlying set. The former is 'free' and the latter is 'forgetful'. They are left and right adjoint to one another in exactly the same way as above.

Many other examples of different types of adjunctions could be given. Practically all interesting logical constructions and operators may be defined in terms of appropriate kinds of adjoint pairs of functors. They are capable of representing universal and existential quantification, for instance, and can be used to pick out structurally interesting relations between axiom-systems and the possible models of those systems. They have also been shown to exhibit a deep connection to the process of abductive inference (roughly, hypothesis-formation) over sets of raw data according to different sorts of theoretical criteria.[7]

All of these examples demonstrate how the right kind of relationship between functors, which are themselves relations between categories, may carry a compact 'synopsis' of interesting global or systematic features of those categories themselves that may not necessarily be immediately evident. In other words, by scaling up from relations to meta-relations and beyond, categorical investigation does not simply become more abstract and more general. It can also bring to light new kinds of information with sometimes surprising and important consequences for levels 'lower down'. This feature is an important clue as to the philosophical relevance of these strange 'oriented inverses'. The conceptual relations expressed by adjoint functors cut across the usual hierarchies of the abstract and the concrete. From a philosophical and especially immanentist perspective, they provide a good model perhaps for thinking the relations between ideality and materiality in a non-representational and non-reductive manner. In the context of the proposal of diagrammatic immanence, this provides an indication of how higher-order diagrams may be constructed from abstract and ideal relations themselves in ways that nonetheless become useful for investigating more concrete phenomena and for determining knowledge of their structural and affective properties. Sometimes the right kind of idealisation is the quickest path to materialisation.

Topoi

We turn from adjunctions to an even more general and powerful construction within category theory, topoi. A *topos* is a category rich enough in its supply of dots and arrows and their structural interplay that the basic operations out of which ordinary mathematics may be built may be modelled in a rigorous way within it. It is commonly known that set theory has the resources to model nearly all mathematics, and it is this property that has led many to speak of 'the' universe of sets as a foundation for mathematics in general. But there is in fact no single universe of sets, only variable modelisations of different axiomatisations of set theory. A more relational and experimental approach to foundational issues in mathematics is thus already implicit in the emergence of model theory out of set theory, which became necessary in the wake of the Lowenheim-Skolem theorems showing that infinitely varied, non-isomorphic models of the axioms of set theory are possible.

It is of course not necessary in any way to reject set theory, only to circumscribe its pretension to serve in a unique foundational role for mathematics and perhaps to question the very (modern) project of foundationalism. This project is probably best understood from the perspective of topoi. Indeed, the category of sets and functions is a topos and plays a certain canonical role in this regard, if only because of the contingent historical development of mathematics over the past century and a half. But the category **Sets** of sets and functions is finally only one topos among very many, and the presumptive status of a unique 'foundation' is little more than a historically conditioned myopia. Instead, as Zalamea has emphasised, some of the most innovative research programmes in contemporary mathematics treat the relationship between axiomatisations and modelisations of various mathematical domains as a controlled parameter. It is much more in the spirit of diagrammatic immanence to consider mathematical structures as the result of experimentation on variable *kinds* of axiomatic foundations, rather than presuming some Platonic realm of mathematical structure that would be correctly or incorrectly represented by a more or less language-like model of logical syntax.

There are a number of different definitions of topoi, all of which are logically equivalent. One of the simplest characterisations is as follows.[8] An elementary *topos* is a category **T** that satisfies three criteria (axioms T1–T3) in addition to those expressed by the categorical axioms C1–C3:

(T1) (Universal finite limits) For any finite diagram D that may be selected in **T**, the limit L of D exists in **T**. This implies in particular that **T** must have all products and a terminal object (the limit of the 'empty diagram'). Conceptually, this means roughly that every topos is rich enough in its relational structure to single out a unique-up-to-isomorphism object that 'encapsulates' in a categorical way the relational information expressed by any finite selection of its dots and arrows. The relations immanent to a topos thus always include the minimal 'conceptual' or 'representational' relational power of universal limits.

(T2) (Exponential objects) For every pair of objects A and B in **T**, there is an object in **T** determined up to isomorphism called the *exponential object* that effectively tracks and distinguishes by way of 'evaluation maps' all the arrows in **T** that go from A to B. This object is conventionally notated B^A. For instance, in **Sets** the object B^A is essentially the set of all functions from the set A to the set B (this set has exactly as many elements as there are arrows from A to B in the category). In **Categories** the object B^A is similarly the category of all functors from the category A to the category B. The precise technical characterisation of such exponential objects and evaluations in their full generality may be given in terms of the specification of adjunctions to particular functors defined on **T**.⁹

(T3) (Subobject classifier) There is in **T** an object Ω called the subobject classifier and an arrow called 'true' from **T**'s terminal object (which must exist because of T1) into Ω, such that every monic or inclusion arrow in **T** may be represented by an arrow from the target of that arrow into Ω. The composition of this latter arrow following the inclusion must be the same arrow as the composition of the unique arrow from the source of the monic into the terminal object followed by the arrow 'true'. In addition, the commutative square thus formed must be universal for its type (it forms a kind of limit that is called a 'pullback'). A clarification of this admittedly obscure definition is provided below and the conceptual meaning of this axiom is addressed there in greater detail.

Taken together, axioms T1–T3 specify a type of category that contains within itself – immanently – sufficient representational resources to indicate and distinguish various fundamental mathematical relations using arrows only. Thus a topos serves as an abstract 'locus' or 'milieu' (hence the name 'topos') where basic formal operations including the standard operations of logic may be performed and tracked in an intrinsically categorical way. The mere existence in a category of limits for all finite diagrams, of an exponential object for any given pair of objects and of a 'classifying object' Ω entails an enormous class of possible formal constructions, self-modelling structures and representational powers within that category. It guarantees, roughly, that all basic mathematical and logical operations may be performed inside the category itself.

A rough analogy might be made with types of languages. Take the class of all conceivable languages (quite an interesting conceptual object!) and consider the varying degrees of expressive power this class involves. Some languages can distinguish housecats from ocelots, for instance, while others cannot. Especially intriguing to self-reflective beings such as philosophers might well be languages possessing sufficient expressive resources to analyse and evaluate those language's own workings. So it might prove useful to examine the subclass of all languages, for example, that possess terms that are relevantly equivalent to the English words 'language', 'expression', 'term' and 'truth'. One could investigate, for instance, if any concomitant notions always follow from the conjunction of these (perhaps they always together imply the existence of a term equivalent to 'false expression').[10]

Analogously, topoi represent a very general class of categories that are capable of expressing certain mathematical objects and operations by way of distinguishing their own internal relations in a structurally immanent fashion (using only their own arrows). If it is known only that some given category satisfies axioms T1–T3 above, the theorems of topos theory guarantee that much additional information and expressive power is necessarily carried by that category as well.

The most philosophically interesting component of a topos in this regard is perhaps the subobject classifier Ω. In the previous discussions we have made extensive use of inclusion maps, both within and between categories. The subobject classifier functions in a topos as a kind of measurement apparatus or translation device for what are called monic arrows, of which the inclusion maps we have examined up to this point are instances. It is called a subobject classifier because it classifies monic maps, which are reliable representations within a category of the discernable 'parts' (the subobjects) of any given object.

The subobject classifier essentially translates every monic map into any object X of a category into a map from the object X into Ω, and vice versa. Thus if one knows everything there is to know about the maps from an object X into Ω, one knows everything there is to know about the monic maps into X, or equivalently, the subobjects or 'parts' of X. The key point is that the object Ω is *unique* (up to isomorphism) for the entire category (topos). It stands as a *single* object within the category (modulo isomorphism) that serves to differentiate and classify *all* the subobjects of *any* of the category's objects. It thus functions as a sort of universal critical apparatus immanent to the category of which it is a mere component part. Arrows into the subobject classifier 'are' (in the sense of isomorphically represent) the internal parts of the object at their source.

In order to understand the subobject classifier, it is first necessary to provide a thoroughly categorical characterisation of what we have considered so far as inclusion or 'selection' maps. In other words, it is necessary to conceive inclusions – or what we have previously called selections – from an 'external' categorical perspective that takes into account only the arrows and compositions within a category, irrespective of the inner structure of the objects represented by the category's dots.[11] This passage from internal to external perspectives – which we have already encountered multiple times in various contexts – is the mathematical analogue, realised within category

Diagrams of Difference: Adjunctions and Topoi

6.5

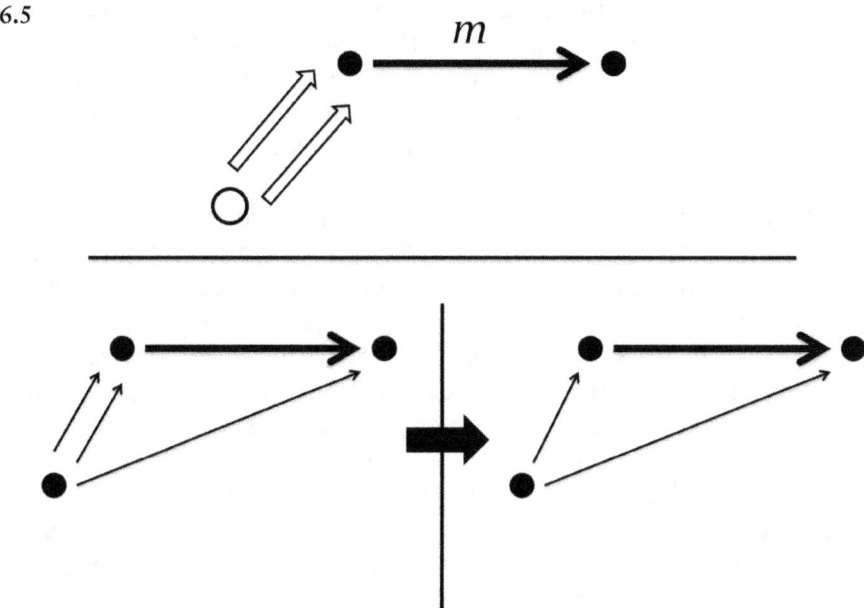

theory, of the conceptual shift, realised within the philosophies of immanence, from an object-oriented to a relational ontology. In a way that is adequate to our intuitive understandings of parthood in directed graphs, partial orders and sets and that in fact may be generalised to all categories, an arrow m is called a *monic arrow* if for any pair of arrows from the same dot with the source of m as the target of both, the identity of the resulting compositions implies the identity of the initial pair. In other words, m is monic if no distinct arrows into m's source-dot collapse into identical arrows when 'extended' to m's target (that is, when composed with m itself). In Figure 6.5 the diagram at the top suggests the conditions for an arrow being monic. The hollow dot and two hollow arrows represent any object in the ambient category and any two arrows from that object into the source of m. The arrow m is monic if, given any two such arrows and a diagram like that at the lower left that commutes (the two compositions with m result in the same arrow), the two arrows chosen must in fact be one and the same arrow. This is represented informally by the thick arrow from the left to the right, which should be read as a sort of inferential animation where the two arrows collapse into one. Formally, m is monic if for any object X and any two arrows f and g with X as source and the source of m as target, $mf=mg$ implies $f=g$. Intuitively, since sameness and difference in a category are ultimately measured by distinctions and identities of arrows, a monic arrow should be understood as an arrow that 'preserves differences' in the sense that nothing collapses 'inside' its mapping such that two *different* arrows into its source could ever collapse into the *same* arrow into its target (and thus lose information) when composed with the monic arrow itself.

The categorical characterisation of monic arrows provides a way to speak in a completely general and rigorous mathematical manner about the 'subobjects' of any given object in any category. When a category is a topos, its subobject classifier Ω contains 'just enough' structure to distinguish the *kinds* of parts (subobjects) that that category tolerates, or equivalently to distinguish the 'degrees of truth' expressible within the category by way of maps alone.

Formally, a *subobject classifier* in a category **C** with a terminal object 1 is an object Ω of **C** equipped with an arrow called 'true' from 1 into Ω (true: $1 \to \Omega$) such that for any monic arrow m in **C** there is an arrow C_m from the target of m into Ω, the 'characteristic map' for m, that satisfies two criteria:

(1) The 'square diagram' as pictured in Figure 6.6 involving the arrow from the source of m into 1 (by the definition of terminal objects, there is exactly one of these) composed with the arrow 'true' on the one hand and C_m following m on the other, commutes. That is, both two-arrow paths compose to the same arrow from the source of m into Ω (the diagonal arrow in the diagram).

6.6

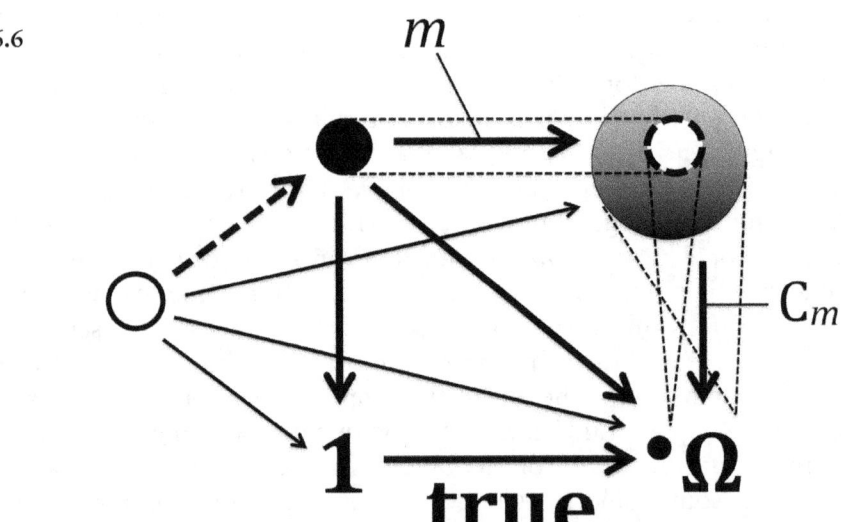

Diagrams of Difference: Adjunctions and Topoi 229

(2) The square diagram in (1) is universal for its type. That is, for any object in **C** and any arrow from that object into the target of m that also squarely commutes with the arrow 'true', there is exactly one arrow from that object into the source of m such that the resulting composed diagram commutes. This is shown in Figure 6.6 by the hollow dot to the left (representing 'for any object' in **C**) and the dashed arrow into the source of m (representing 'there exists exactly one such arrow').

In Figure 6.6 the bare arrows-only categorical diagram expressing the nature of the subobject classifier is overlain with a more iconic representation that may help the reader to understand the inner dynamics of the diagram.

A very simple example of a subobject classifier – indeed the simplest non-degenerate example – is provided by Ω in the category **Sets**. In **Sets** any two-element set may play the role of the subobject classifier Ω. The 'two-valued' status of internal components of any set (its elements) corresponds to the simple binary logic that governs the universe of set theory. A selected 'dot' is either an element of a given subset or not. No intermediate degree of belonging is possible. Expressed otherwise, the internal diagrams of sets are effectively 'dots only'. Unlike the objects of many other categories and topoi, there is no internal richness of structure found within the objects of **Sets**. See below in Figure 6.7 on the left-hand side a diagrammatic representation of the subobject classifier in **Sets** at work. Compare that diagram to the more general framework shown above in Figure 6.6. The function represented (internally) by the three arrows at the top of the diagram in Figure 6.7 (an obvious monic inclusion) is itself fully characterised by the function on the right side of the 'square'. The three 'selected' dots are all mapped to the dot in Ω selected by the arrow 'true', and the one dot that is not selected by the function at the top is mapped to the only other dot in Ω (which may be thought of as signifying 'false' or 'not').

In general, the internal complexity of the subobject classifier serves as a measure of the richness of internal structure for the objects of a given topos. In this sense, **Sets** reveals itself to be a deeply impoverished universe of discourse for representing anything other than purely abstract congeries of abstract individuals. To be sure, more or less arbitrary complexity and richness may be built up 'externally' with such objects via iterated nestings and mappings between sets, but the fact remains that sets as such are singularly 'unstructured' objects. Practically nothing in ordinary experience

6.7

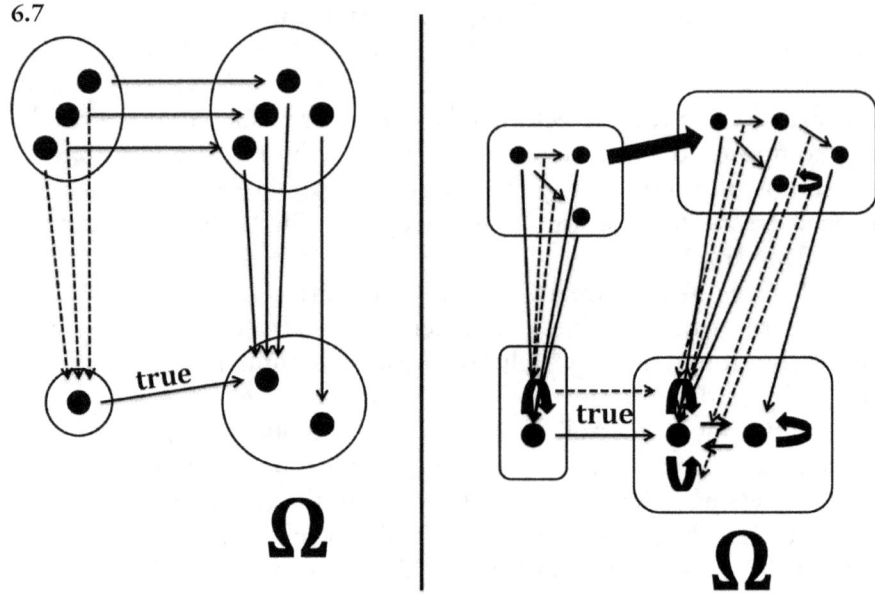

or in the world investigated by the various sciences ever appears as radically severed from all internal relational composition in this way. But this type of non-relational diagrammatic selection certainly has its uses.

As an example of a topos with objects composed of somewhat more structure than that of **Sets**, the category of directed graphs and graph homomorphisms, **Graphs**, suggests itself as a useful contrast. In **Graphs** the subobject classifier takes the form of a graph as shown in Figure 6.7 on the right-hand side at the bottom right corner. Again, compare the 'square' of relations in that diagram with the general Ω framework pictured in Figure 6.6, and note the differences with the **Sets** diagram immediately to the left.

First of all, the contrast with the subobject classifier for **Sets** is evident. The extra complexity of the subobject classifier in **Graphs** corresponds to the greater internal structure of graph-objects as compared with set-objects. The constituent dots of any given graph are, considered independently of the graph's arrows, essentially as 'atomic' and unstructured as any set. In fact, they determine a unique set in every case, precisely the set of the graph's dots. Corresponding to this fact is the 'two-dot' structure of the subobject classifier, which essentially reproduces the 'two-element' structure of the subobject classifier for **Sets**. The arrows of graphs, however, carry more information than mere existence. Each arrow indexes a source-dot and a target-dot that are, from the point of view of the graph's internal structure, intrinsic 'parts' of the arrow itself. For this reason, arrows require a more variable range of 'truth-values' than the simple binary of belonging/non-belonging. A particular arrow may be positively included in some selected part of a graph in a variety of ways or in different degrees: it may be *fully* included; its *source-dot* or its *target-dot only* may be included; or *both* its source and target (but not the arrow itself). In order to express these different degrees of belonging, the arrow-components of the subobject classifier must be fivefold, corresponding to the four positive possibilities just mentioned plus the single entirely negative result of not being included to any degree whatsoever.

From both a mathematical and a philosophical perspective, what are most interesting about topoi are the deductive consequences that follow from axioms T1–T3. Such necessary consequences – the theorems of topos theory – are effectively as vast in extent as the virtual universe of mathematics itself. For the purposes of conceptualising diagrammatic immanence, it is worth singling out three important theorems:

1. Epi-monic factorisation: every arrow in a topos may be broken down in a unique way into the composition of an epi arrow followed by a monic arrow, where a monic arrow is understood as explained above and an epi arrow is simply the 'dual' description of a monic (precisely the same characterisation but with all the arrows in the definition reversed). From the present point of view, this may be interpreted in a roughly 'semiotic' way: every simply dyadic relation (each arrow) is equivalent to a canonical triadic composition in any topos. This seems to suggest that a theory of triadic relations in the spirit of Peirce might be built up formally within the mathematical theory of topoi. If so, this would provide an interesting arena for investigating some of the more delicate structures of Peirce's EG and their connections to his theory of signs.

2. Every slice category of a topos is a topos. In general, a *slice category* is simply a category that may be induced from the choice of any category **C** and the selection within **C** of some particular object A. The slice category over A (usually notated **C**/A) is then defined as *the category of arrows in **C** with A as their target*. These arrows into A are the dots, or objects of **C**/A. An arrow from one such dot to another in the slice category is *any arrow in **C** from source to source of these objects* (arrows into A) *such that the resulting triangle in **C** commutes*. Essentially, then, a slice category may be thought of as a given category 'as restricted to' or 'focused on' some particular object

A within that category. The interpretation here is in terms of immanence: every topos is rich enough to support all of its essential characteristics even in restriction to the collection of relations concerning only its smallest components. If a topos consists of a multiplicity of relational perspectives on itself, this theorem shows that although internally differentiated and therefore not homogeneous, the 'topical nature' of any topos is pervasive and equally present everywhere within it.

3. For any topos **T** and any category **C**, the category of all functors **C**→**T** and natural transformations between them is a topos.[12] In particular, all presheaf categories are topoi, since **Sets** is a topos. But this appears now as just one special case of a much more general result. In accordance with the now familiar categorical principle that moving from a given level of relations to that of meta-relations among those relations counts not as an inevitable loss but at least potentially as an epistemic gain, the fact that given any topos on the one hand and any category whatsoever on the other, the system of functorial relations and natural transformations from the latter into the former *also* forms a topos, seems to suggest that not only can we conceive of a metaphysics that is 'relations all the way down', but there is good mathematical sense to the notion that once a certain degree of consistent, representationally operative structure is in place, we possess rich, interesting and reliable meta-structure 'all the way up'. And in general we have seen that examining the right meta-relations in a system tends to correspond to selecting its deeper structures that may not be immediately evident but which are ultimately most relevant for the purposes of understanding that system.

The categorical model of general diagrams based on Peirce's triadic semiotics that was presented in Chapter 4 relied heavily on the use of presheaves. These were seen to be especially useful constructions because they carry the sort of information that tracks variable strata in some domain (in the model category) as correlated with ordered relations among parts of some other structural framework (the base category). Different possible 'contents' or 'values' ranging over larger and smaller parts of a given topological space are one important type of this presheaf relation. Another type is given by a semantic field (for example, sets of possible worlds) represented in the model category ranging over statements in some logical syntax (whether linear, diagrammatic or what have you) forming the order-structure in the base. Despite the enormous variety of possible presheaves and their many diverse types of application, one limitation in the standard definition as given in Chapter 4 is that the model category (the target of the presheaf functor) is always **Sets** or some subcategory of **Sets**. Now we can see that in fact this was a more or less arbitrary restriction. In very many cases, a topos other than **Sets** will also serve as the target of a presheaf functor, and since topoi in general support objects with much richer internal structure than mere sets it is often convenient to use a non-**Sets** topos as the model category for a presheaf when the 'values' or the 'semantics' of the intended correlation are themselves structured in some common although variable way.

Boolean and Heyting Algebras

Among the most fascinating aspects of topoi are the deep structural relations they share with formal logic. Although they are defined axiomatically simply as mathematical categories with certain intrinsic limit, closure and representational properties among their dots and arrows, the structures upon which standard logic depends, such as negation, conjunction and disjunction, existential and universal quantification and so on, emerge naturally from within these strictly categorical relations as just some of their many immanent consequences. In particular, by way of well-defined operations on the subobject classifier Ω every topos comes equipped with an internal subsystem of objects and arrows that mimic basic logical operations, much as the set-theoretical operators of intersection, union and complementation may be used to 'diagram' the logical operations of conjunction, disjunction and negation in classical logic. In general, the logic that is naturally embedded in a topos takes the structure of what is called a Heyting algebra, which is the algebra of logical operations that characterises intuitionistic logic and includes classical logic as a special case. The fact that this very general logical structure emerges from within an essentially geometrical and topological mathematics of relation points to a profound affinity between logic on the one hand – which first developed, after all, as the philosophical science of linguistic statements, meaningful concepts and reasonable inferences – and the mathematical continuities, symmetries and related structures that derive ultimately from the human experiences of space and time on the other. It is this rich structural correlation between concepts and spaces (logic and topology) that ultimately underwrites the possibility of diagrammatic immanence.

We have already had occasion to examine Peirce's EG-alpha graphs, the topologically diagrammatic logical notation that inscribes on a 'sheet of assertion' certain characters and cuts to mirror logical relations among propositions and the conjunctions and negations of propositions. We may now use this system of diagrammatic logic to build up a single complex object whose internal relations will model in an exhaustive fashion the logical relations of classical propositional logic. This object will be, perhaps unsurprisingly, a category.

We begin by taking the collection of all possible alpha graphs. We will then make use of a simple but very powerful technique, passing from a preorder to a corresponding partial order. The first category we construct we will call **EG**$_a$. The objects of **EG**$_a$ are all well-formed EG-alpha graphs.[13] An arrow will exist with graph G_1 as source and graph G_2 as target if and only if G_2 may be derived from G_1 by repeated application of Peirce's alpha transformation rules, which are sound and complete with respect to classical propositional logic. This means that as one 'follows arrows' in **EG**$_a$, one passes from diagrams representing particular logical assertions to other diagrams representing other logical assertions that may be logically derived from the former. The resulting category, a preorder, serves as a faithful representation of the standard theoretical objects and operations of propositional logic.

It is then possible to reduce this easily defined but infinitely complex object to its categorical skeleton by treating all logically equivalent assertions as an equivalence class, and thus, roughly, as a single object. This may sound somewhat complicated, but from a categorical standpoint the mapping involved is very simply expressed. We just define a functor from **EG**$_a$ to a new category **Skel-EG**$_a$ that collapses all isomorphic objects in **EG**$_a$ into a single dot in **Skel-EG**$_a$, the categorical skeleton of **EG**$_a$. What we have, then, is a well-defined partial order category with a rich internal structure intimately connected to Boolean algebras. See Figure 6.8 and note the 'flow' of arrows from bottom to top. At the very 'bottom' of the partial order is a single EG-alpha graph (an object in **Skel-EG**$_a$) for which an arrow exists from it to every other object in the category, that is, it is the initial object in the category. This is the EG-alpha graph consisting of nothing but an empty cut – a negation, but not a negation of anything in particular. Just 'pure' negation. It represents the truth-value 'false'. From it anything and everything follows (*ex falso quodlibet*). Similarly, there is a single object at the 'top' of the order, the terminal object in the category, representing the corresponding 'pure' truth-value 'true'. It is the empty sheet of assertion. Anything and everything implies it. Between the two are a variety of sheets with

6.8

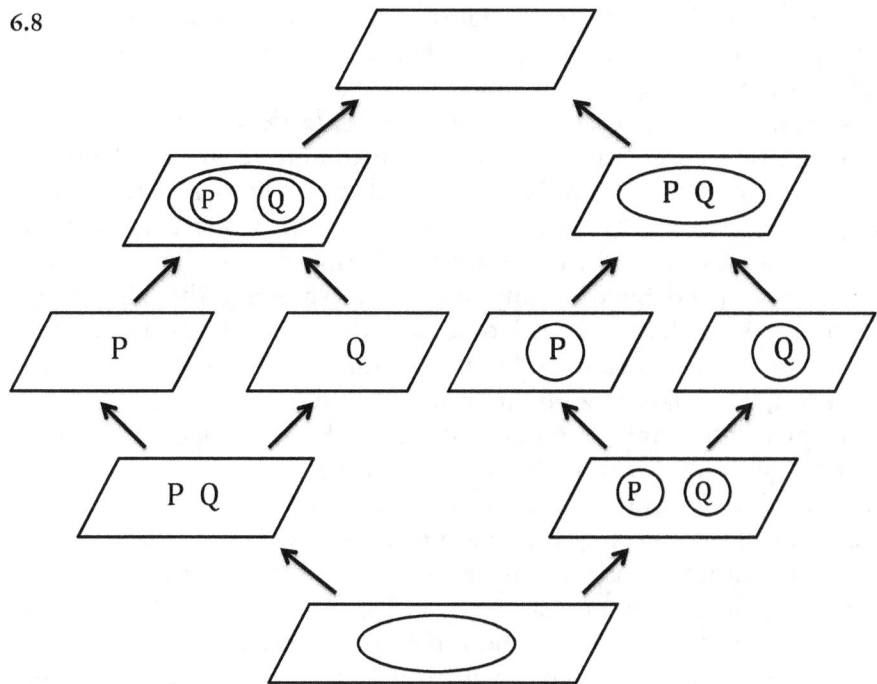

diagrams inscribed on them. As one moves 'upwards', following the flow of arrows, the diagrams carry less and less determinate information. On the left side, the diagram representing the conjunction of P and Q 'says more' than either of the diagrams that 'say' only P or only Q, although each of the latter is implied logically by the former. In turn, both P alone and Q alone each imply the disjunction P or Q near the top, but to know the disjunction P or Q is to know less than to know P or to know Q. On the right side, exactly the same diagrams appear, but they are each encircled by a cut of negation (note that a 'double cut' – a double negation – effectively erases itself). The result, logically, is that their flow is reversed. This simple mirror-and-reversal illustration is just a small fragment of the category **Skel-EG**$_a$, but in an informal diagrammatic fashion – conjoined with the right kind of interpretive experimentation and evaluation – it represents much of the logical structure that the category as a whole carries. In a general way, this kind of structure is called a Boolean algebra. This notion will be clarified below.

More general than Boolean algebras are Heyting algebras. Every Boolean algebra is Heyting, but not every Heyting algebra is Boolean. It is convenient, then, to define Heyting algebras and then treat Boolean algebras as a special case. We will be interested in their difference, and the easiest way to characterise the contrast between the two types of logical algebra is to begin with what they have in common. Both may be conceived as types of *lattices*, a kind of order-structure that we encountered already in Chapter 2. Recall from the discussion of partial orders understood as categories that lattices may be expressed as categorical partial orders for which every pair of dots has a product (called the meet) and coproduct (called the join). These are limits defined for any two dots as shown in the diagram in Figure 2.14 in Chapter 2. A lattice is further specified as a *bounded lattice* if it has a 'bottom' and a 'top' element. Expressed in categorical terms, it is a lattice with an initial and a terminal object.

To guarantee that a bounded lattice is a Heyting algebra requires only a single step. It must be possible to define an operation on all pairs of dots X and Y that picks out a unique dot designated Y^X such that given any dot Z, if there is an arrow $Z \rightarrow Y^X$ from Z into Y^X in the lattice, then there is an arrow from the meet of X and Z (which has to exist in any lattice) into Y, and vice versa. This in fact defines an adjunction (think about the one-to-one correspondence of arrows). Logical negation of an element X may then be defined as the dot 0^X, where 0 represents the initial object in the lattice/category. For Boolean algebras it is always the case that the negation of the negation is the object itself. In fact, this property is sufficient to *define* Boolean algebras as a subclass of Heyting algebras. But for Heyting algebras that are not Boolean the negation of the negation is not always the object itself. The 'law' of double negation fails. The logic of Heyting algebras is generally not classical, but intuitionistic.

The strictly structural difference between Boolean and Heyting algebras, because of the difference between the kinds of logic – classical and intuitionistic, respectively – that they represent, carries philosophical significance. For instance, understanding the distinction between Boolean and Heyting algebras is essential to understanding the break and the bridge between Badiou's *Being and Event* and *Logics of Worlds*. In *Being and Event* Badiou uses set-theoretical forcing to model the immanent logic of truth-procedures with respect to the transcendence of generic truths. The former are local and finite 'inquiries' that extend themselves sporadically and taken in their aggregate approximate to the latter. In *Logics of Worlds* the phenomenology of worlds depends primarily upon the selection of a transcendental T for each world S and a function from the set SxS into T and an order-preserving functor from T into the powerset of S.

Diagrams of Difference: Adjunctions and Topoi 237

For present purposes, the important thing is that the transcendental takes the form of a complete Heyting algebra. 'Collapsing' functors that take T into the Boolean algebra (0,1) – corresponding to the subobject classifier in **Sets** – are then closely connected to what Badiou calls 'points' and which ground his 'materialism'. Badiou's ultimate privileging of Boolean over Heyting algebras (the former are truly 'ontological' whereas the latter are merely 'phenomenological') corresponds to an unreconstructed preference for set theory over category theory in his overall system, a preference that from the standpoint of diagrammatic immanence remains quite puzzling.

In a general way, Boolean algebras are strongly associated with sets and powersets, while Heyting algebras are strongly associated with topologies and topoi. More precisely, the lattice ordered by inclusion of the powerset of any given set satisfies the conditions of a Boolean algebra. Conversely, any Boolean algebra may be represented by a lattice of sets ordered by inclusion (this result was proven by Stone). Similarly, the lattice of open sets in any topology forms a Heyting algebra. Since every powerset of a given set defines a topology – called the discrete topology on that set – every Boolean algebra is necessarily Heyting, but in general the open sets that define a topology do not satisfy all the conditions of a Boolean algebra. This is because the open sets that define a topology on some set S are in general *selected* from among the nodes of the lattice of the powerset of S. By effectively abstracting away from some of its constituent subsets, a topology typically induces *greater structure* on those it selects. This greater topological structure is reflected in less logical symmetry. Even more structure may be imposed by abstracting from sets altogether and defining topologies entirely algebraically (as described in Chapter 4). Although it is *not* the case in general that every Heyting algebra may be represented by a lattice of sets, every Heyting algebra *can* be represented by a topology in this more abstract sense.[14]

These concepts may seem unwieldy – even unworldly – at a first approach. It may be helpful to try to capture the difference between Boolean and Heyting algebras in the simplest possible diagrammatic fashion. The partial order on the left below in Figure 6.9 is a simple example of a Boolean algebra, in fact the simplest non-degenerate example. It is the category **2** as discussed above in the section on adjunctions. The product relation that we defined there in terms of the right adjoint to the diagonal functor **2x2** corresponds, as was mentioned, to logical conjunction. An easy way to see this (and to use the diagram diagrammatically) is to put two fingers on two dots

6.9

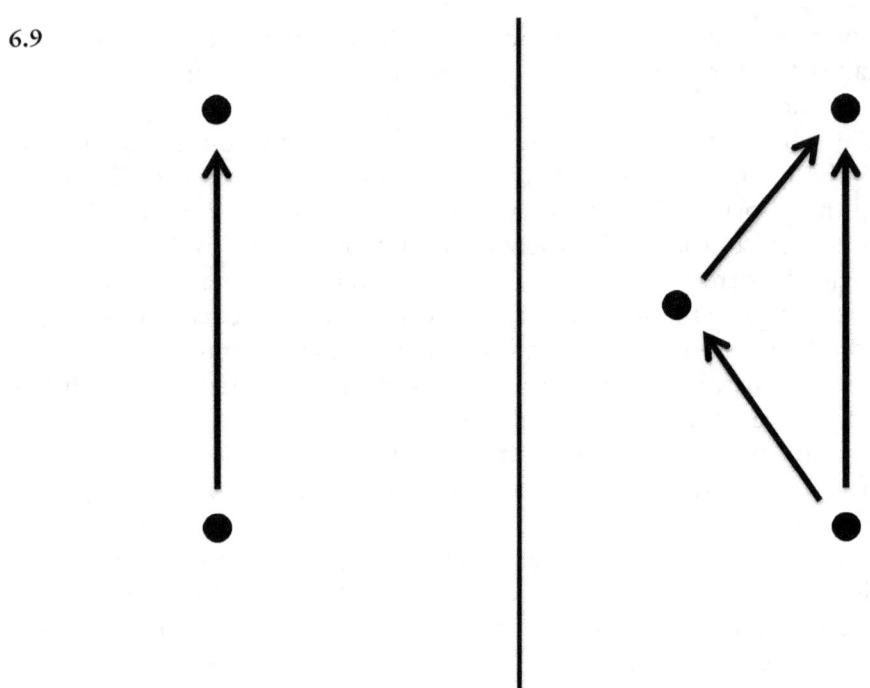

on the diagram, thus selecting them (they may be the same dot), and then ask what is the greatest element of the order as a whole that is less than or equal to both selected dots. It should be clear that the only time the answer will be the upper dot is if both selections are in fact of the upper dot. A consideration of the similar although reversed situation of asking about the least element of the order that is greater than or equal to both selected dots should provoke a recognition of logical disjunction, the operator 'or'. Negation is simply a matter of exchanging upper for lower or lower for upper, as the case may be. To put it otherwise, if we label the lower dot '0' and the upper dot '1', then $0^0=1$ and $0^1=0$ and these two operations relate to one another such that the law of double negation holds.

The partial order on the right in Figure 6.9 is the simplest example of a Heyting algebra that is non-Boolean. If we label the three dots from bottom to top as '0', 'X', and '1', then the negation operation is defined as $0^0=1$, $0^X=0$, and $0^1=0$. It follows that the negation of the negation of X is not X but 1. The 'intermediate' truth-value in this lattice – its greater structure as compared with the diagram on the left – disrupts the logical symmetry of negation as it appears in the

Boolean algebra. Considered as a category, the diagram on the right can be mapped into the diagram on the left in two different ways (two different functors) that nonetheless both conserve the 'absolute' values of 0 and 1 in the image. In the other direction, however, there is only one functor from the left category into the right that preserves the initial and terminal objects in this way. The relation itself between the two diagrams is asymmetrically structured.

It should be clear that the immanent and relational metaphysics outlined via Spinoza, Peirce and Deleuze and especially the interpretations of their respective ontologies in terms of diagrams are essentially topological in structure, privileging continuity over discontinuity, relationship over objecthood, and intensive singularities over extensional collectives. They are intensive or conceptual spaces – structures in a uniquely philosophical sense – like those described by Deleuze in his article 'How to Recognize Structuralism':

> Space is what is structural, but an unextended, preextensive space, pure *spatium* constituted bit by bit as an order of proximity, in which the notion of proximity first of all has precisely an ordinal sense and not a signification in extension.[15]

Deleuze's conceptual distinction here between 'ordinal sense' and 'signification in extension' maps quite neatly onto the mathematical difference between category-theoretic and set-theoretic approaches to topology. This difference is itself a diagrammatic sign of a much more general contrast in philosophy. The logical differences between Boolean algebras and Heyting algebras express the core of this contrast in a purely formal way that opens immediately onto the basic difference in mathematical approach between set theory and category theory. It is perhaps the logical and mathematical expression of what the previous argument consistently distinguished as dyadic and triadic relational structures. Even so, the triadic approach advocated here is not *opposed* to extensity, objects and discontinuity any more than clouds are opposed to raindrops.

Conceptual and diagrammatic elaborations based on Boolean algebras on the one hand and Heyting algebras on the other represent among other things two different philosophical 'points of view' on *negation*. In a playful but suggestive passage, Peirce illustrates the difference at stake by distinguishing what he calls 'logical languages' from those he calls 'quantitative languages':

> In mathematics, the negative of quantity is *zero*; but instead of being set over against quantity as its eternal foe, it is regarded as

merely the limit of quantity, and in a sense as itself a special grade of quantity. This is no violation of the principle of contradiction: it is merely regarding the negative from another point of view. There are some languages in which two negatives make an affirmative. Those are the logical languages. The people who speak them ought, for consistency, to be hard, moral natures. In other languages, probably the majority, a double negative remains a negative, just as 0 x 0 = 0, none of none is none. These are quantitative languages. We should expect the people who speak them to be more humane and more highly philosophical.[16]

Indeed.

Notes

1. WIP, p. 218.
2. See Mac Lane, *Categories for the Working Mathematician*, pp. 79–86. This presentation follows, a bit roughly, Mac Lane's Theorem 2, parts iii and iv, p. 83.
3. More generally, product categories **CxD** may be defined on any pair of categories **C** and **D**. See ibid., pp. 36–7.
4. If the same functor has a *left* adjoint, then the category **C** has coproducts for all pairs of objects. A coproduct is a limit with the same diagram as a product, only with arrows reversed. Products and coproducts are 'dual' UMPs, like initial and terminal objects.
5. This example of adjunction is adapted from François Magnan and Gonzalo E. Reyes, 'Category Theory as a Conceptual Tool in the Study of Cognition', pp. 85–6.
6. For technical details, see Mac Lane, *Categories for the Working Mathematician*, pp. 49–51.
7. Fernando Tohmé, Gianluca Caterina and Rocco Gangle, 'Abduction: A Categorical Characterization'.
8. Robert Goldblatt, *Topoi*, is recommended as a mathematical introduction to topoi that uses set theory as a constant point of reference. A comprehensive reference is Mac Lane and Moerdijk, *Sheaves in Geometry and Logic*.
9. For details see Mac Lane, *Categories for the Working Mathematician*, pp. 97–8.
10. Inversely, one might wish to investigate the minimal expressive resources needed to guarantee that some type of statement – future counterfactuals, say – is always capable of being expressed in a language.
11. In fact, the intuitive notion of an 'inclusion' map is actually best characterised by what is called a *monomorphism*. In some categories, like **Sets**, monic arrows and monomorphisms coincide, but this is by no

means always the case. For present purposes, it is convenient to treat monic arrows as the appropriate generalisation of our informal notion of 'selections'.
12. See Mac Lane, *Mathematics: Form and Function*, p. 405.
13. These may be built up recursively by first defining the empty sheet and all individual propositional variables as graphs then applying the operations of juxtaposing and 'gluing together' already-constructed graphs and enclosing already-constructed graphs in a cut. For details, see Gangle and Caterina, 'The Sheet of Indication'.
14. Such constructions are called *locales*. Their study constitutes the somewhat unfortunately named field of *pointless topology*.
15. Deleuze, 'How Do We Recognize Structuralism?', cited in Bryant, *Difference and Givenness*, p. 170.
16. *The Essential Peirce*, vol. 2, p. 390.

Conclusion

We have followed two largely independent lines of thought, one philosophical and one mathematical. The overall proposal of diagrammatic immanence is meant to chart their possible long-term convergence. Immanent metaphysics has been characterised as intrinsically relational (Spinoza), semiotic (Peirce) and differential (Deleuze). Because diagrams – understood in a sufficiently broad sense – investigate relations by way of expressing relations and experimenting semiotically with differences, diagrams suggest themselves as a very general philosophical method conforming to the requirements of immanence. In elaborating the basic concepts of category theory we have uncovered a highly developed and extremely general field of mathematics that both uses its own type of diagrams as a formal notation and is also particularly adept at tracking how diagrams in general work. The schema of diagrammatic signification expressed in terms of the triad selection-experimentation-evaluation has served as a common locus, an overlap, of the philosophical and mathematical territories explored. As a schema expressible both in terms of Peirce's triadic theory of signs and as a category theoretical construction based in presheaves, it strongly suggests that further coordination along similar lines is possible. No doubt the formal constructions of adjunctions and topoi will be useful in testing this hypothesis. In any case, the pragmatic criterion remains crucial. As an entwined philosophical and mathematical approach to thinking in diagrams, what can diagrammatic immanence potentially do?

First of all, by shifting philosophical terrain both substantively and methodologically from language and textuality to diagrammatic relations and practices, an opening is made for enabling new constructive relations within philosophy itself and between philosophy and a variety of other fields. Obviously, the present proposal sets up multiple ways for metaphysics, formal logic and contemporary mathematics to communicate. In this respect, the present proposal may be broadly aligned with recent work by Badiou, Williamson,

Zalamea and others, opening such work to productive dialogue with the Spinozist, Peircean and Deleuzian traditions in particular. But category theory is of course not just a tool for philosophers. It applies in its own distinctive manner to virtually any system of relations. Working diagrammatically from within the framework of category theory thus potentially enables new types of systematic translations of philosophical concepts into domains of thought and practice of nearly unlimited extent without the ineluctable need for linguistic mediation and without the communicative constraints of any particular language, like English: from computer science and the natural and social sciences, to aesthetic domains of choreography and musical notation, to political and economic programmes.

Secondly, because category theory works within the conceptually liminal space between hierarchically distinct levels of relation on the one hand and flatly generic structures cutting across the relation/meta-relation difference on the other, it appears well-situated for helping to address contemporary philosophical concerns with singularity and relational difference while remaining within the metaphysical and pragmatic framework of immanence. In the present work, we have developed ideas of relation and singularity in the context of a diagrammatic ontology, interpreting *relation* as a form of practice rather than a representation and *singularity* as a differential event and semiotic process rather than a substance. These interpretations took shape by reading relationally, with concern to transform the practices and ways of thinking endemic to current philosophy. Among other things, the diagrammatic and pragmatic interpretation of Spinoza, Peirce and Deleuze has provided a means for conceiving of meaning and event as operative in philosophy not only outside of language but also outside of the structures of egoic consciousness. Understood in this way, philosophy itself becomes capable of being immanently transformed as it learns through its ongoing encounters with the diverse objects of mathematics, art, science and other traditions and disciplines.

It is clear that category theory offers philosophy some very powerful and versatile logical tools. But it also seems to harbour a deeper conceptual and possibly even metaphysical character. Its efficacy in so many different arenas suggests that it is more than a formal game that some mathematicians happen to play. The intuition shared by Albert Lautman and Jean Cavaillès of a conceptual and at the same time real dialectic intrinsic to mathematical development itself has, arguably, been borne out by the extraordinary growth and evident power of category theory. In any case, it is equally clear that philosophy should not simply submit to uncritical mathematical or logical determination. The rigour of mathematics and logic turns quickly to philosophical *rigor mortis* if the singular grain of real human experience (phenomenological, ethical, aesthetic, political) is not respected and conserved for its own sake. This is at least part of what philosophy ultimately is for. The onus, finally, is on philosophy to grasp the relevance of category theory for philosophical thought and practice and to appropriate and amend it for its own needs. Mathematicians and logicians working in category theory have little reason to alter their respective disciplines in order to make them more accessible and flexible in accordance with the vagaries of a reality that is, in essence, neither mathematical nor logical. It is the present task of philosophy to bring the best methods of thinking available from whatever source to bear on the relevant concerns of our pluriform and planetary epoch. The use of diagrammatic methods and, just as importantly, sustained philosophical reflection on how and why diagrams work is one way that philosophy may prepare itself for its own transformation by the potentialities of contemporary mathematics among other engines of theory and practice. At the same time, philosophies of immanence may help to guide mathematical and mathematico-scientific itineraries as they increasingly extend into traditionally philosophical territories. If category theory and its many fields of application are to become truly philosophical, perhaps philosophy must first learn to become diagrammatic.

Bibliography

Althusser, Louis, 'The Only Materialist Tradition, Part I: Spinoza', in Warren Montag and Ted Stolze, eds, *The New Spinoza*. Minneapolis: University of Minnesota, 1998, 3–19.
Aristotle, *The Basic Works of Aristotle*, trans. and ed. Richard McKeon. New York: Random House, 1941.
Atlan, Henri, *The Sparks of Randomness*, 2 vols, trans. Lenn J. Schramm. Stanford: Stanford University Press, 2011–2013 [1999–2003].
Auyang, Sunny Y., *Foundations of Complex-System Theories in Economics, Evolutionary Biology, and Statistical Physics*. Cambridge: Cambridge University Press, 1998.
Auyang, Sunny Y., *How is Quantum Field Theory Possible?* Oxford and New York: Oxford University Press, 1995.
Awodey, Steve, *Category Theory*, 2nd edn. Oxford and New York: Oxford University Press, 2010.
Badiou, Alain, *Being and Event*, trans. Oliver Feltham. New York and London: Continuum, 2006 [1988].
Badiou, Alain, *Deleuze: The Clamor of Being*, trans. Louise Burchill. Minneapolis: University of Minnesota Press, 2000.
Badiou, Alain, *Logics of Worlds*, trans. Alberto Toscano. London and New York: Continuum, 2009 [2006].
Badiou, Alain, *Mathematics of the Transcendental*, ed. and trans. A. J. Bartlett and Alex King. London and New York: Bloomsbury, 2014.
Badiou, Alain, *Theoretical Writings*, ed. and trans. Ray Brassier and Alberto Toscano. London and New York: Continuum, 2004.
Barber, Daniel, *Deleuze and the Naming of God: Post-Secularism and the Future of Immanence*. Edinburgh: Edinburgh University Press, 2014.
Barber, Kenneth F. and Jorge J. E. Gracia, eds, *Individuation and Identity in Early Modern Philosophy*. Albany, NY: SUNY Press, 1994.
Barwise, Jon and Lawrence Moss, *Vicious Circles: On the Mathematics of Non-Wellfounded Phenomena*. Stanford: CSLI Publications, 1996.
Beaulieu, Edward Kazarian and Julia Sushytska, eds, *Gilles Deleuze and Metaphysics*. Lanham, MD and London: Lexington Books, 2014.
Bennett, Jonathan, *A Study of Spinoza's Ethics*. Indianapolis: Hackett, 1984.

Bolaño, Roberto, *Distant Star*, trans. Chris Andrews. New York: New Directions, 2004 [1996].

Bourdieu, Pierre, *Language and Symbolic Power*, trans. Gino Raymond and Matthew Adamson. Cambridge, MA: Harvard University Press, 1991.

Bourdieu, Pierre, *Outline of a Theory of Practice*, trans. Richard Nice. Cambridge: Cambridge University Press, 1977.

Brandom, Robert B., *Between Saying and Doing: Towards an Analytic Pragmatism*. Oxford and New York: Oxford University Press, 2008.

Brandom, Robert B., *Tales of the Mighty Dead: Historical Essays in the Metaphysics of Intentionality*. Cambridge, MA and London: Harvard University Press, 2002.

Bryant, Levi R., *Difference and Givenness: Deleuze's Transcendental Empiricism and the Ontology of Immanence*. Evanston: Northwestern University Press, 2008.

Buchler, Justus, *Metaphysics of Natural Complexes*, 2nd edn. Albany, NY: SUNY Press, 1990 [1966].

Cavaillès, Jean, 'On Logic and the Theory of Science', trans. Theodore J. Kisiel in Joseph J. Kockelmans and Theodore J. Kisiel, eds, *Phenomenology and the Natural Sciences: Essays and Translations*. Evanston: Northwestern University Press, 1970 [1960], 353–409.

Châtelet, Gilles, *Figuring Space: Philosophy, Mathematics and Physics*, trans. Robert Shore and Muriel Zagha. Dordrecht: Kluwer, 2000 [1993].

Châtelet, Gilles, 'Interlacing the Singularity, the Diagram and the Metaphor', in Simon Duffy, ed., *Virtual Mathematics: The Logic of Difference*. Manchester: Clinamen, 2006.

Cooper, Ellis D., *Mathematical Mechanics: From Particle to Muscle*. Singapore: World Scientific, 2011.

Curley, Edwin, *Behind the Geometrical Method: A Reading of Spinoza's Ethics*. Princeton: Princeton University Press, 1988.

De Beistegui, Miguel, *Truth and Genesis: Philosophy as Differential Ontology*. Bloomington and Indianapolis: Indiana University Press, 2004.

Deely, John, *Four Ages of Understanding: The First Postmodern Survey of Philosophy From Ancient Times to the Turn of the Twenty-first Century*. Toronto: University of Toronto Press, 2001.

Deely, John, *New Beginnings: Early Modern Philosophy and Postmodern Thought*. Toronto: University of Toronto Press, 1994.

DeLanda, Manuel, *Intensive Science and Virtual Philosophy*. London and New York: Continuum, 2002.

Deleuze, Gilles, *Deux régimes de fous*, ed. David Lapoujade. Paris: Les éditions de Minuit, 2003.

Deleuze, Gilles, *Difference and Repetition*, trans. Paul Patton. New York: Columbia University Press, 1994.

Deleuze, Gilles, *Expressionism in Philosophy: Spinoza*, trans. Martin Joughin. New York: Zone, 1992.

Deleuze, Gilles, *Foucault*, trans. Sean Hand. Minneapolis: University of Minnesota Press, 1988.
Deleuze, Gilles, *Kant's Critical Philosophy*, trans. Hugh Tomlinson and Barbara Habberjam. Minneapolis: University of Minnesota Press, 1984.
Deleuze, Gilles, *L'île Déserte et Autre Textes*. Paris: Editions de Minuit, 2002.
Deleuze, Gilles, *Proust and Signs: The Complete Text*, trans. Richard Howard. Minneapolis: University of Minnesota Press, 2000.
Deleuze, Gilles, *Spinoza: Practical Philosophy*, trans. Robert Hurley. San Francisco: City Lights, 1988.
Deleuze, Gilles, 'Spinoza and the Three "Ethics"', in Warren Montag and Ted Stolze, eds, *The New Spinoza*. Minneapolis: University of Minnesota Press, 1998, 21–34.
Deleuze, Gilles, *The Logic of Sense*, trans. Mark Lester and Charles Stivale, ed. Constantin V. Boundas. New York: Columbia University Press, 1990.
Deleuze, Gilles and Félix Guattari, *A Thousand Plateaus*, trans. Brian Massumi. Minneapolis: University of Minnesota Press, 1987.
Deleuze, Gilles and Félix Guattari, *What is Philosophy?* trans. Hugh Tomlinson and Graham Burchell. New York: Columbia University Press, 1994.
Della Rocca, Michael, *Representation and the Mind-Body Problem in Spinoza*. Oxford and New York: Oxford University Press, 1996.
Della Rocca, Michael, *Spinoza*. New York: Routledge, 2008.
Della Rocca, Michael, 'The Power of an Idea: Spinoza's Critique of Pure Will', *Nous* 37:2 (2003), 200–31.
Derrida, Jacques, introduction to Edmund Husserl's *Origin of Geometry*, trans. John P. Leavey, Jr. Lincoln and London: University of Nebraska Press, 1978.
Derrida, Jacques, *Speech and Phenomena and Other Essays on Husserl's Theory of Signs*, trans. David B. Allison. Evanston: Northwestern University Press, 1973.
Derrida, Jacques, *Writing and Difference*, trans. Alan Bass. Chicago: University of Chicago Press, 1978.
De Saussure, Ferdinand, *Course in General Linguistics*, trans. Wade Baskin, eds Charles Bally and Albert Sechehaye. New York: McGraw-Hill, 1966.
Descartes, René, *The Geometry of René Descartes*, trans. David Eugene Smith and Marcia L. Latham. New York: Dover, 1954 [1637].
Duffy, Simon, *Deleuze and the History of Mathematics: In Defense of the 'New'*. London and New York: Bloomsbury, 2013.
Duffy, Simon, 'The Logic of Expression in Deleuze's *Expressionism in Philosophy: Spinoza*: A Strategy of Engagement', *International Journal of Philosophical Studies* 12:1 (2004), 47–60.
Duffy, Simon, ed., *Virtual Mathematics: The Logic of Difference*. Manchester: Clinamen, 2006.

Eilenberg, Samuel and Saunders Mac Lane, 'General Theory of Natural Equivalences' *Transactions of the American Mathematical Society*, 58:2 (1945), 231–94.
Ellerman, David P., 'Category Theory and Concrete Universals', *Erkenntnis* 28:3 (1988), 409–29.
Epperson, Michael and Elias Zafiris, *Foundations of Relational Realism: A Topological Approach to Quantum Mechanics and the Philosophy of Nature*. Lanham, MD: Lexington Books, 2013.
Euclid, *Elements*, trans. Thomas L. Heath, ed. Dana Densmore. Santa Fe: Green Lion Press, 2003.
French, Steven, *The Structure of the World: Metaphysics and Representation*. Oxford and New York: Oxford University Press, 2014.
Freyd, Peter J. and Andrej Scedrov, *Categories, Allegories*. Amsterdam: Elsevier, 1990.
Gangle, Rocco, 'Mathematics, Structure, Metaphysics: Deleuze and Category Theory', in Alain Beaulieu, Edward Kazarian and Julia Sushytska, eds, *Gilles Deleuze and Metaphysics*. Lanham, MD and London: Lexington Books, 2014, 45–62.
Gangle, Rocco, 'Theology of the Chimera: Spinoza, Immanence, Practice', in Anthony Paul Smith and Daniel Whistler, eds, *After the Postsecular and the Postmodern: New Essays in Continental Philosophy of Religion*. Newcastle upon Tyne: Cambridge Scholars Publishing, 2010, 26–43.
Gangle, Rocco and Gianluca Caterina, 'The Sheet of Indication: A Diagrammatic Semantics for Peirce's EG-alpha', *Synthese* 192:4 (2015), 923–40.
Garrett, Aaron V., *Meaning in Spinoza's Method*. Cambridge: Cambridge University Press, 2003.
Garrett, Don, 'Spinoza's Theory of Metaphysical Individuation', in Kenneth F. Barber and Jorge J. E. Gracia, eds, *Individuation and Identity in Early Modern Philosophy*. Albany, NY: SUNY Press, 1994, 73–101.
Garrett, Don, ed., *The Cambridge Companion to Spinoza*. Cambridge and New York: Cambridge University Press, 1996.
Gil, Jose, *Metamorphoses of the Body*, trans. Stephen Muecke. Minneapolis: University of Minnesota Press, 1998.
Goldblatt, Robert, *Topoi: The Categorical Analysis of Logic*, rev. 2nd edn. Mineola, NY: Dover, 2006 [1984].
Gueroult, Martial, *Spinoza*, 2 vols. New York: Verlag Hildesheim, 1974.
Habermas, Jürgen, 'Peirce and Communication', in Kenneth Laine Ketner, ed., *Peirce and Contemporary Thought: Philosophical Inquiries*. New York: Fordham University Press, 1995, 243–66.
Habermas, Jürgen, *The Structural Transformation of the Public Sphere: An Inquiry into a Category of Bourgeois Society*, trans. Thomas Burger and Frederick Lawrence. Cambridge, MA: MIT Press, 1991.

Hadot, Pierre, *Philosophy as a Way of Life*, trans. Michael Chase, ed. Arnold I. Davidson. Oxford: Blackwell, 1995.
Hallward, Peter, *Out of this World: Deleuze and the Philosophy of Creation*. London and New York: Verso, 2006.
Hampshire, Stuart, *Spinoza and Spinozism*. Oxford and New York: Oxford University Press, 2005.
Hardt, Michael, *Gilles Deleuze: An Apprenticeship in Philosophy*. Minneapolis: University of Minnesota Press, 1993.
Hegel, Georg W.F., *Lectures on the History of Philosophy*, 3 vols, trans. E. S. Haldane and Frances H. Simson. Lincoln, NE and London: University of Nebraska Press, 1995 [1840].
Heidegger, Martin, *Being and Time*, trans. John Macquarrie and Edward Robinson. San Francisco: Harper and Row, 1962 [1927].
Hookway, Christopher, *Peirce*. London and New York: Routledge, 1985.
Howie, Gillian, *Deleuze and Spinoza: Aura of Expressionism*. New York: Palgrave, 2002.
Husserl, Edmund, *Experience and Judgment*, trans. James S. Churchill and Karl Amerike, ed. Ludwig Landgrebe. Evanston: Northwestern University Press, 1973.
Israel, Jonathan I., *Radical Enlightenment: Philosophy and the Making of Modernity 1650–1750*. Oxford and New York: Oxford University Press, 2001.
Jedrzejewski, Franck, *Ontologie des Catégories*. Paris: Harmattan, 2011.
Kaufman, Eleanor, *The Dark Precursor: Dialectic Structure Being*. Baltimore: Johns Hopkins University Press, 2012.
Kerslake, Christian, *Immanence and the Vertigo of Philosophy: From Kant to Deleuze*. Edinburgh: Edinburgh University Press, 2009.
Ketner, Kenneth Laine, ed., *Peirce and Contemporary Thought: Philosophical Inquiries*. New York: Fordham University Press, 1995.
Kockelmans, Joseph J. and Theodore J. Kisiel, eds, *Phenomenology and the Natural Sciences: Essays and Translations*. Evanston: Northwestern University Press, 1970.
Kramer, Edna E., *The Nature and Growth of Modern Mathematics*. Princeton: Princeton University Press, 1982.
Lambek, J. and P. J. Scott, *Introduction to Higher Order Categorical Logic*. Cambridge: Cambridge University Press, 1986.
Lambert, Gregg, *The Non-philosophy of Gilles Deleuze*. New York and London: Continuum, 2002.
Laruelle, François, *Au-delà du principe de pouvoir*. Paris: Payot, 1978.
Laruelle, François, *Machines textuelles: Déconstruction et libido d'écriture*. Paris: Seuil, 1976.
Lautman, Albert, *Mathematics, Ideas, and the Physical Real*, trans. Simon Duffy. London and New York: Continuum, 2011 [2006].

Lawvere, F. William and Stephen H. Schanuel, *Conceptual Mathematics: A First Introduction to Categories*. Cambridge and New York: Cambridge University Press, 1997.

Lecercle, Jean-Jacques, *Deleuze and Language*. New York: Palgrave Macmillan, 2002.

Lennon, Thomas M., 'The Problem of Individuation among the Cartesians', in Kenneth F. Barber and Jorge J. E. Gracia, eds, *Individuation and Identity in Early Modern Philosophy*. Albany, NY: SUNY Press, 1994, 13–39.

Levinas, Emmanuel, *Otherwise than Being, or Beyond Essence*, trans. Alphonso Lingis. Pittsburgh: Duquesne University Press, 1981.

Levinas, Emmanuel, *Totality and Infinity: An Essay on Exteriority*, trans. Alphonso Lingis. Pittsburgh: Duquesne University Press, 1969.

Levy, Ze'ev, *Baruch or Benedict: On Some Jewish Aspects of Spinoza's Philosophy*. New York, Bern, Frankfurt am Main, Paris: Peter Lang, 1989.

Lord, Beth, *Kant and Spinozism: Transcendental Idealism and Immanence from Jacobi to Deleuze*. Houndmills, Basingstoke and New York: Palgrave-Macmillan, 2011.

Luhmann, Niklas, *Social Systems*, trans. John Bednarz, Jr. and Dirk Baecker. Stanford: Stanford University Press, 1995 [1984].

Macherey, Pierre, *Avec Spinoza: Etudes sur la doctrine et l'histoire du spinozisme*. Paris: PUF, 1992.

Macherey, Pierre, 'The Problem of the Attributes', trans. Ted Stolze, in Warren Montag and Ted Stolze, eds, *The New Spinoza*. Minneapolis: University of Minnesota Press, 1998, 65–95.

MacKenzie, Iain, *The Idea of Pure Critique*. London and New York: Continuum, 2004.

Mac Lane, Saunders, *Categories for the Working Mathematician*, 2nd edn. New York: Springer-Verlag, 1998.

Mac Lane, Saunders, *Mathematics: Form and Function*. New York: Springer-Verlag, 1986.

Mac Lane, Saunders, and Ieke Moerdijk, *Sheaves in Geometry and Logic: A First Introduction to Topos Theory*. New York: Spring-Verlag, 1992.

Macnamara, John and Gonzalo E. Reyes, eds, *The Logical Foundations of Cognition*. Oxford and New York: Oxford University Press, 1994.

Magnan, François and Gonzalo E. Reyes, 'Category Theory as a Conceptual Tool in the Study of Cognition', in John Macnamara and Gonzalo E. Reyes, eds, *The Logical Foundations of Cognition*. Oxford and New York: Oxford University Press, 1994, 57–90.

Maimonides, Moses, *The Guide for the Perplexed*, trans. M. Friedlander. New York: Dover, 1956.

Maldiney, Henri, *Regard Parole Espace*. Lausanne: Editions L'âge d'homme, 1973.

Marquis, Jean-Pierre, *From a Geometrical Point of View: A Study of the History and Philosophy of Category Theory*. Dordrecht: Springer, 2009.

Matheron, Alexandre, *Individu et communauté chez Spinoza*, 2nd edn. Paris: Minuit, 1988.

Mauss, *The Gift: The Form and Reason for Exchange in Archaic Societies*, trans. W. D. Halls. New York and London: Norton, 1990.

Merleau-Ponty, Maurice, *In Praise of Philosophy and Other Essays*, trans. John Wild, James Edie and John O'Neill. Evanston: Northwestern University Press, 1988 [1953, 1968].

Montag, Warren and Ted Stolze, eds, *The New Spinoza*. Minneapolis: University of Minnesota Press, 1998.

Moreau, Pierre-François, 'Spinoza's Reception and Influence', trans. Roger Ariew, in Don Garrett, ed., *The Cambridge Companion to Spinoza*. Cambridge and New York: Cambridge University Press, 1996, 408–33.

Mullarkey, John, *Post-Continental Philosophy: An Outline*. London and New York: Continuum, 2006.

Nadler, Steven, *Spinoza: A Life*. Cambridge and New York: Cambridge University Press, 1999.

Negri, Antonio, *The Savage Anomaly: The Power of Spinoza's Metaphysics and Politics*, trans. Michael Hardt. Minneapolis: University of Minnesota Press, 1991.

Netz, Reviel, *The Shaping of Deduction in Greek Mathematics: A Study in Cognitive History*. Cambridge: Cambridge University Press, 1999.

Nielsen, K. Hvidtfelt, *Interpreting Spinoza's Arguments – Toward a Formal Theory of Consistent Language Scepticism Imitating* Ethica. Lewiston, Queenston, Lampeter: Edwin Mellen, 2003.

Norman, Jesse, *After Euclid: Visual Reasoning and the Epistemology of Diagrams*. Stanford: CSLI Publications, 2006.

Ochs, Peter, *Peirce, Pragmatism and the Logic of Scripture*. Cambridge: Cambridge University Press, 1998.

Oderberg, David S., 'No Potency Without Actuality: The Case of Graph Theory', in Tuomas E. Tahko, *Contemporary Aristotelian Metaphysics*. Cambridge: Cambridge University Press, 2012, 207–28.

Pautrat, Bernard, preface to Benedictus de Spinoza, *Ethique*, trans. Bernard Pautrat. Paris: Seuil, 1999.

Peirce, Charles S., *Collected Papers*, 6 vols, ed. Charles Hartshorne and Paul Weiss. Cambridge, MA: Harvard University Press, 1931–35.

Peirce, Charles S., *Peirce on Signs*, ed. James Hoopes. Chapel Hill: University of North Carolina Press, 1991.

Peirce, Charles S., *Philosophical Writings of Peirce*, ed. Justus Buchler. New York: Dover, 1955.

Peirce, Charles S., *Selected Writings: Values in a Universe of Chance*, ed. Philip P. Wiener. New York: Dover, 1958.

Peirce, Charles S., *The Essential Peirce*, 2 vols, ed. Nathan Houser and Christian J. W. Kloesel. Bloomington and Indianapolis: Indiana University Press, 1998.

Pietarinen, Ahti-Veikko, 'Existential Graphs: What a Diagrammatic Logic of Cognition Might Look Like', *History and Philosophy of Logic* 32:3 (2011), 265–81.

Plato, *Republic*, trans. Allan Bloom, 2nd edn. New York: Basic Books, 1991.

Priest, Graham, *Beyond the Limits of Thought*, 2nd edn. Oxford and New York: Oxford University Press, 2002.

Putnam, Hilary, 'Peirce's Continuum', in Kenneth Laine Ketner, ed., *Peirce and Contemporary Thought: Philosophical Inquiries*. New York: Fordham University Press, 1995, 1–22.

Ramey, Joshua, *The Hermetic Deleuze: Philosophy and Spiritual Ordeal*. Durham, NC and London: Duke University Press, 2012.

Rescher, Nicholas, *Peirce's Philosophy of Science: Critical Studies in His Theory of Induction and Scientific Method*. Notre Dame and London: University of Notre Dame Press, 1978.

Reyes, Marie La Palme, Gonzalo E. Reyes and Houman Zolfaghari, *Generic Figures and Their Glueings: A Constructive Approach to Functor Categories*. Milan: Polimetrica, 2004.

Roberts, Don D., *The Existential Graphs of Charles S. Peirce*. The Hague and Paris: Mouton, 1973.

Rorty, Richard, *Philosophy and the Mirror of Nature*. Princeton: Princeton University Press, 1979.

Rotman, Brian, *Signifying Nothing: The Semiotics of Zero*. Stanford: Stanford University Press, 1987.

Russell, Bertrand, *Introduction to Mathematical Philosophy*. London: George Allen and Unwin, 1919.

Sartre, Jean-Paul, *The Transcendence of the Ego: An Existentialist Theory of Consciousness*, trans. Forrest Williams and Robert Kirkpatrick. New York: Farrar, Straus and Giroux, no publication year given [1936–7].

Semetsky, Inna, 'The Role of Intuition in Thinking and Learning: Deleuze and the Pragmatic Legacy', *Educational Philosophy and Theory* 36:4 (2004).

Shapiro, Stewart, *Philosophy of Mathematics: Structure and Ontology*. Oxford and New York: Oxford University Press, 1997.

Sheriff, John K., *The Fate of Meaning: Charles Peirce, Structuralism, and Literature*. Princeton: Princeton University Press, 1989.

Shin, Sun-Joo, *The Iconic Logic of Peirce's Graphs*. Cambridge, MA and London: MIT Press, 2002.

Short, T. L., *Peirce's Theory of Signs*. Cambridge and New York: Cambridge University Press, 2007.

Sider, Theodore, *Writing the Book of the World*. Oxford and New York: Oxford University Press, 2014.
Simondon, Gilbert, *L'individuation à la lumière des notions de forme et d'information*. Grenoble: Éditions Jérôme Millon, 2005 [1964, 1989].
Smith, Anthony Paul and Daniel Whistler, eds, *After the Postsecular and the Postmodern: New Essays in Continental Philosophy of Religion*. Newcastle upon Tyne: Cambridge Scholars Publishing, 2010.
Smith, Stephen B., *Spinoza's Book of Life: Freedom and Redemption in the* Ethics. New Haven and London: Yale University Press, 2003.
Smyth, Richard A., *Reading Peirce Reading*. Lanham, MD and Oxford: Rowman and Littlefield, 1997.
Spencer Brown, G., *Laws of Form*. New York: Bantam, 1973 [1969].
Spinoza, Benedict [Baruch], *Complete Works*, trans. Samuel Shirley, ed. Michael L. Morgan. Indianapolis and Cambridge: Hackett, 2002.
Spinoza, Benedict [Baruch], *Ethique*, trans. (French) Bernard Pautrat. Paris: Seuil, 1999.
Spinoza, Benedict [Baruch], *The* Ethics *and Other Works*, ed. and trans. Edwin Curley. Princeton: Princeton University Press, 1994.
Spivak, David I., *Category Theory for the Sciences*. Cambridge, MA: MIT Press, 2014.
Steinberg, Diane, 'Method and the Structure of Knowledge in Spinoza', *Pacific Philosophical Quarterly* 79 (1998), 152–69.
Stjernfelt, Frederik, *Diagrammatology: An Investigation on the Borderlines of Phenomenology, Ontology and Semiotics*. Dordrecht: Springer, 2007.
Stjernfelt, Frederik, *Natural Propositions: The Actuality of Peirce's Doctrine of Dicisigns*. Boston: Docent Press, 2014.
Tahko, Tuomas E., ed., *Contemporary Aristotelian Metaphysics*. Cambridge: Cambridge University Press, 2012.
Thalos, Mariam, *Without Hierarchy: The Scale Freedom of the Universe*. Oxford and New York: Oxford University Press, 2013.
Thomas-Fogiel, Isabelle, *The Death of Philosophy: Reference and Self-Reference in Contemporary Thought*, trans. Richard A. Lynch. New York: Columbia University Press, 2011 [2005].
Tohmé, Fernando, Gianluca Caterina and Rocco Gangle, 'Abduction: A Categorical Characterization', *Journal of Applied Logic* 13:1 (2015), 78–90.
Toscano, Alberto, *The Theatre of Production: Philosophy and Individuation Between Kant and Deleuze*. Houndmills, Basingstoke and New York: Palgrave-Macmillan, 2006.
Tournier, Michel, *Friday*, trans. Norman Denny. New York: Pantheon Books, 1985.
Viljanen, Valtteri, *Spinoza's Geometry of Power*. Cambridge: Cambridge University Press, 2014.

Vinciguerra, Lorenzo, *Spinoza et le Signe: La Genèse de l'Imagination*. Paris: Vrin, 2005.
Williamson, Timothy, *Modal Logic as Metaphysics*. Oxford: Oxford University Press, 2013.
Wilson, Margaret D., 'Spinoza's Theory of Knowledge', in Don Garrett, ed., *The Cambridge Companion to Spinoza*. Cambridge and New York: Cambridge University Press, 1996, 89–141.
Wittgenstein, Ludwig, *Philosophical Investigations*, 3rd edn, trans. G. E. M. Anscombe. Oxford: Basil Blackwell, 1967 [1953].
Wittgenstein, Ludwig, *Tractatus Logico-Philosophicus*, trans. C. K. Ogden. London and New York: Routledge, 1922.
Wolfson, Harry Austryn, *The Philosophy of Spinoza: Unfolding the Latent Processes of His Reasoning*, 2 vols. Cambridge, MA and London: Harvard University Press, 1983 [1934].
Yates, Frances, *The Art of Memory*. Chicago: University of Chicago Press, 1966.
Yovel, Yirmiyahu, *Spinoza and Other Heretics*, 2 vols. Princeton: Princeton University Press, 1989.
Zalamea, Fernando, *Peirce's Logic of Continuity*. Boston: Docent Press, 2012.
Zalamea, Fernando, *Synthetic Philosophy of Contemporary Mathematics*, trans. Zachary Luke Fraser. London and New York: Urbanomic/Sequence, 2012 [2009].
Zeman, Jay, 'Peirce on Abstraction', *Monist* 65 (1982), 211–29.
Žižek, Slavoj, *Organs without Bodies: On Deleuze and Consequences*. New York and London: Routledge, 2004.
Zourabichvili, François, *Spinoza: une physique de la pensée*. Paris: PUF, 2002.

Index

abduction (abductive inference), 222
adjunctions (adjoint functors), 212–17
  examples of, 217–23
algebras, logical, 233–40
Althusser, Louis, 34
Aristotle, 33, 54, 122

Badiou, Alain, 13, 211, 236–7, 242
Barber, Daniel, 167
Bolaño, Roberto, 167–8
Boolean algebras *see* algebras, logical
Bryant, Levi, 163–4

category theory, 10–12, 88–102, 162–5
  axioms of, 89–90
  category of categories, 100–2
  examples of categories, 99–102
  as extension of Erlangen Program, 162, 165
  historical development of, 11
Curley, Edwin, 33–4

Dante, *Divine Comedy*, 185–7
Deely, John, 128–30
Deleuze, Gilles
  expressive interpretation of Spinoza, 169–78, 196–201
  and phenomenology, 163–4, 171, 183–5
  structure-Other, 187, 194–6
  subjectivity, 171–2, 181, 182–94
  see also sense
Descartes, Rene, 20–2, 28–30, 33, 36, 38
  Deleuze's critique of, 171, 182–5, 188–9, 201–2
  Peirce's critique of, 104–6, 109, 128, 130
  Spinoza's critique of, 21–2, 26

diagrammatic sign, 121–7
  categorical theory of, 154–6
diagrams, 6–10
  in a category, 90
  commutative, 90
  limits of, 93
  notational ethics of, 131–2

Erlangen Program *see* Klein, Felix
Euclid, 30–2, 162–3
exponential objects, 224–5, 236

functions, 83–8, 99
  complete graphs of, 86
  graphs of, 85
  regular graphs of, 86
functors, 94–8, 101, 141–7
  adjoint *see* adjunctions
  categories of, 142–7, 165
  contravariant, 147; *see also* presheaves
  free/forgetful, 221–2

Garrett, Don, 58–9
giving/gifts, 115–16, 118–20, 170
graphs, 71–3
  category of, 221, 230
  of functions, 85
  as presheaves, 151–2
  subobject classifier of, 230–1
gratitude, 25, 119
Grothendieck, Alexander, 11, 165
Guattari, Felix, 166, 198–200
Gueroult, Martial, 33–4

Heyting algebras *see* algebras, logical
Husserl, Edmund, 127–8
  Deleuze's critique of, 171, 182–5, 191
hypostatic abstraction, 107

immanence, 3–4, 23, 70–1, 118, 139, 142, 155, 166–7, 171, 173, 175, 180, 182, 184, 196, 202, 211, 223, 225–7, 232
inclusion, 72; see also monic arrow
initial object, 92, 101
isomorphism, 91–2, 215–17

join, 99, 236

Klein, Felix, 162–5

lattices, 99, 149, 236
Leibniz, Gottfried Wilhelm, 20, 183, 185–7, 189, 193
Levinas, Emmanuel, 195, 200
limits, 93–4, 217, 224
linear orders see total orders
Locke, John, 20, 129
logical algebras see algebras, logical

Maimon, Salomon, 164–5
Marquis, Jean-Pierre, 162
meet, 99, 236
Merleau-Ponty, Maurice, 164, 179
monic arrow, 227–8

natural transformations, 144–7
Negri, Antonio, 34, 174
Nielsen, K. Hvidtfelt, 48–53
Nietzsche, Friedrich, 166–7, 172, 190

orders see lattices; partial orders; preorders; total orders

partial orders, 73–83
 axioms of, 76
 category of, 99
 sets conceived as, 80–3
Peirce, Charles S.
 and continuity, 164
 doctrine of categories (firstness, secondness, thirdness), 116–17
 ethics of terminology, 131–2
 and negation, 239–40
 philosophy of science, 121–2
 pragmatism (pragmaticism), 121–2, 127, 132–3, 155
Plato, 4, 93, 163, 165, 224
powersets, 83

preorders, 99–100
presheaves, 147–54
 categories of, 153–4, 232–3
 over topological spaces, 149–51

Saussure, Ferdinand de, 109–10
Schelling, F. W. J., 191
selection, 6–8, 41, 71–3, 80, 82, 88, 95, 96, 122–3, 142, 153, 155, 237
sense, 177–80, 193
set theory, 10, 76, 88, 98, 223, 229, 237, 239
sets, 80–3
 category of, 99
signs, 8, 140–1, 170–1, 176–7, 180, 189–90, 191–3, 201
 dyadic models of, 41, 176–7, 231
 triadic models of, 41, 197, 231
 see also sense
skeleton, 92
slice category, 231–2
Spinoza, Benedict, 4, 5
 and adequate ideas, 20, 42, 53
 geometrical order of the *Ethics*, 22, 30–7, 48–53, 58–9, 129, 197
 and immanent metaphysics, 23, 25, 29, 43
 and signs/signification, 22, 27–8, 41–8, 54, 57–8
 theory of modal individuation, 37–41
 third kind of knowledge, 53–9
subobject classifier, 225, 226–31
subsets, 82–3

terminal object, 80, 92, 101, 132
topoi, 223–33
topologies/topological spaces, 148–9, 237
total orders, 76, 99
Tournier, Michel, 195–6

universal mapping properties (UMPs), 92–4, 217–19

Williamson, Timothy, 13, 211, 242
Wolfson, Harry Austryn, 33–4

Yoneda's lemma, 153–4

Zalamea, Fernando, 13, 211, 224, 243